Bot train
p.193

Learn at Home
THE
SESAME STREET
WAY

by Sara Bonnett Stein

in Cooperation with
CHILDREN'S TELEVISION WORKSHOP

SIMON AND SCHUSTER
New York

PUBLISHED BY SIMON & SCHUSTER
A DIVISION OF GULF & WESTERN CORPORATION,
    IN CONJUNCTION WITH CHILDREN'S TELEVISION WORKSHOP
SIMON & SCHUSTER BUILDING
ROCKEFELLER CENTER
1230 AVENUE OF THE AMERICAS
NEW YORK, NEW YORK 10020
SIMON AND SCHUSTER AND COLOPHON ARE
TRADEMARKS OF SIMON & SCHUSTER
SESAME STREET® AND THE SESAME STREET SIGN ARE TRADEMARKS
    AND SERVICE MARKS OF CHILDREN'S TELEVISION WORKSHOP.
    WORKSHOP REVENUES FROM THIS PRODUCT WILL BE USED TO
    HELP SUPPORT CTW EDUCATIONAL PROJECTS.

DESIGNED BY ELIZABETH WOLL
MANUFACTURED IN THE UNITED STATES OF AMERICA

    2 3 4 5 6 7 8 9 10

LIBRARY OF CONGRESS CATALOGING IN PUBLICATION DATA
STEIN, SARA BONNETT.
    LEARN AT HOME THE SESAME STREET WAY.

    INCLUDES INDEX.
    1. DOMESTIC EDUCATION—HANDBOOKS, MANUALS, ETC.
2. CHILDREN—MANAGEMENT—HANDBOOKS, MANUALS, ETC.
3. FAMILY LIFE EDUCATION—HANDBOOKS, MANUALS, ETC.
4. SESAME STREET. 5. TELEVISION IN PRESCHOOL EDUCA-
TION—HANDBOOKS, MANUALS, ETC. I. CHILDREN'S TELEVI-
SION WORKSHOP. II. TITLE.
LC37.S73   372.1'3   79-1343

ISBN 0-671-22482-4

Illustration Credits

All activity illustrations are by Tom Cooke.

P. 11 CTW Photo

P. 13 Art by Michael Smollin, *The Amazing Mumford and His Subtracting Trick*, Western Publishing Company, Inc.; CTW Photo

P. 14 Art by Tom Cooke, *Sesame Gulch*, Western Publishing Company, Inc.

P. 20 CTW Photo

P. 22 Art by Carroll Spinney, *How to Be a Grouch*, Western Publishing Company, Inc.; CTW Photo

P. 23 Jacket, Photos by Richard Hutchings

P. 24 Ernie and Bert, CTW Photo

P. 24 Photos by Neil Selkirk, *Sesame Street Magazine*

P. 26 Photo by Richard Hutchings

P. 27 CTW Photo

P. 28 Photos by Richard Hutchings

P. 29 Art by Joe Mathieu, *Sesame Street Magazine*

P. 30 Photo by Bill Pierce

P. 31 CTW Photos

P. 35 Photo by Richard Goldman

P. 36 Photo by Robert Fuhring

P. 37 CTW Photo

P. 38 Art by Irra Duga, *Ernie's Telephone Call*, Western Publishing Company, Inc.; CTW Photo

P. 42 Photo by Richard Hutchings

P. 44 Photo by Richard Hutchings

P. 45 CTW Photo

P. 46 Photos by Richard Hutchings

P. 47 Art by Joe Mathieu, *Sesame Street Magazine*

P. 48 Ernie, CTW Photo; Mr. Hooper and child, Photo by Emily Kingsley

P. 49 *Sesame Street* film clip

P. 50 Art by Joe Mathieu, *Sesame Street Magazine*

P. 51 CTW Photos

PP. 52-53 Art by Joe Mathieu, *Sesame Street Magazine*

P. 54 CTW Photo; Art by Joe Mathieu, *What Ernie and Bert Did on Their Summer Vacation*, Western Publishing Company, Inc.

P. 55 CTW Photo

P. 57 CTW Photo

P. 59 Ernie and Bert, Art by Joe Mathieu, *Sesame Street Magazine*; Oscar, Art by Sal Murdocca, *Oscar's Alphabet of Trash*, Western Publishing Company, Inc.

P. 61 Photos by Richard Hutchings

P. 62 Art by Mel Crawford, *The Sesame Street 1,2,3 Storybook*, Random House, Inc.

P. 63 Art by Toni Delaney, *Big Bird's Busy Book*, Random House, Inc.

P. 65 Art by Tom Cooke, *Ernie Takes a Bath*, Western Publishing Company, Inc.

P. 66 Photo by Richard Hutchings

P. 69 Art by Robert Dennis, *The Sesame Street Cookbook*, Platt & Munk Publishers, A Division of Grosset & Dunlap

P. 70 CTW Photo

P. 71 CTW Photo

P. 72 Art by Robert Dennis, *The Sesame Street Cookbook*, Platt & Munk Publishers, A Division of Grosset & Dunlap

P. 73 Art by Joe Mathieu, *The Exciting Adventures of Super Grover*, Western Publishing Company, Inc.

P. 74 Photo by Richard Hutchings

P. 79 CTW Photo

P. 81 CTW Photo

P. 82 Art by Joe Mathieu, *I Am A Monster*, Western Publishing Company, Inc.

P. 84 CTW Photos

P. 86 CTW Photo

P. 87 Photo by Judy Ross

P. 88 CTW Photo

P. 90 CTW Photo

P. 92 Art by Michael Smollin, *The Day the Count Stopped Counting*, Western Publishing Company, Inc.

P. 93 CTW Photo

P. 94 Maria and Grover, CTW Photo; Oscar, Photo by Emily Kingsley

P. 95 CTW Photo

P. 96 CTW Photo

P. 99 The Count, Photo by Bill Pierce; Don Music, CTW Photo

P. 100 Bert and Ernie, Photo by Bill Pierce; Grover and Herbert Birdsfoot, CTW Photo

P. 101 Butterfly, Fred Crippen Animation; Whispering, Photo by Richard Hutchings

P. 102 Photo by Richard Hutchings

P. 103 CTW Photos

P. 105 CTW Photo

P. 106 Photos by Richard Hutchings

P. 108 *Sesame Street Magazine*

P. 110 *Sesame Street Magazine*

P. 112 Drawing by Joe Mathieu; Photo by Richard Hutchings

P. 113 Photo by Richard Hutchings

P. 114 Art by Carol Nicklaus, *The Sesame Street Coloring Book*, Western Publishing Company, Inc.

P. 120 Art by Michael Smollin, *Sesame Street Magazine*

Contents

Learn At Home
The Sesame Street Way

Foreword

SESAME STREET began as an experiment, and continues to be an experiment even as we approach our tenth year of broadcast production.

We set out to discover if, through television—a medium irresistible to children and available to almost all families—we could teach cognitive skills that would be useful to children when they entered school.

To carry out our experiment it was necessary to assemble a unique team. We were fortunate to enlist the finest professionals in television production, education, research, and community organization to create a program as entertaining as it was educational and to make the show known and available to a wide audience.*

The next step was to develop a curriculum of preschool skills that we thought could be taught on television and that would help children when they entered school. The curriculum had to be carefully designed, translated into production ideas, and tested to make sure that the resulting show would be both entertaining and educational. Talented performers and advanced production techniques were necessary to hold the attention of the child already sophisticated in television viewing. During the year of research conducted before the show was aired, pilots were made and shown to children. These were tested to determine what appeals to children or fails to attract them, what children comprehend or fail to understand, and how they put to use what they have seen in their subsequent play activities. These observations of children's reactions were then fed back to Sesame Street's producers and writers so that they could improve the program from day to day.

The Sesame Street experiment worked. In the fall of 1969, Sesame Street was aired nationally on Public Broadcast System stations. After Sesame Street had been on the air one year, the Educational Testing Service, an independent organization in Princeton, New Jersey, undertook to determine whether children who viewed Sesame Street made significant learning gains.

---

* Gerald S. Lesser has chronicled this in his definitive book on the development of Sesame Street, *Children and Television: Lessons from Sesame Street*, © 1974. Random House.

9

Groups of children who viewed the show regularly were compared with children who viewed infrequently or not at all. The ETS results showed that children who watched the program made significantly greater learning gains than children who did not; and that children who watched the most gained the most.

Not only did children learn, but our combination of entertainment and education attracted them to watch in great numbers. Today, after Sesame Street has been on the air ten years, eight million children view it regularly.

Sesame Street was also designed to appeal to the adult viewer in order to encourage interaction between parents and their children. This, we felt, would increase the amount of learning—both during the viewing and after the show. Research has shown clearly that parents' participation in their children's viewing does indeed facilitate learning greatly.

The lessons of Sesame Street don't stop when the day's program is over. It was one of our earliest premises that parental involvement would stimulate postviewing activities to reinforce the goals of the show.

Sesame Street was never intended to replace any other learning facilities available to young children in day-care centers, nursery schools, or *the home*. It was meant, at its inception and now, as a supplement to those resources.

Television is only one teaching tool. Your home is a wealth of educational equipment—from the box you buy your eggs in to the paper bag you dispose of your garbage in. A family's routine provides countless learning opportunities daily—in making a purchase, making repairs, or making a cake. Whatever your life-style, your home is an environment richly conducive to learning. This book shows you how.

We offer this Sesame Street handbook of activities in the hope that our experience in developing Sesame Street will be as valuable to you, in the context of your home and neighborhood, as it has been to us in producing an effective educational TV series for young children.

We at Children's Television Workshop believe that Sesame Street begins at home, and that the activities suggested in this book will enrich the shared experiences of parents and their young children.

JOAN GANZ COONEY
President,
Children's Television Workshop

1 Open Sesame

PRETEND FOR a minute. You are baking a cake. Flour has spilled on the counter. Idly, your three-year-old pulls a finger through the flour and and makes a line. "A stick," your child says. You move your finger through the flour, too. "A wiggle," you say. That is learning.

Why are a "stick" and a "wiggle" in spilled flour learning, and what is important about it? Why did it happen? Where will it lead? What was your role, and what was your child's role?

This episode, which probably took your child thirty seconds and you three seconds, is learning because a phenomenon has been discovered—flour can be drawn in; and because a comparison has been made—"stick" is different from "wiggle"; and because a relationship has been noticed—different finger movements create different shapes of line.

It is an important bit of learning because these skills precede writing; letters of the alphabet are made up of "sticks" and "wiggles." It happened because you provided, although incidentally, a learning environment when you spilled flour while your child was present. Your child's role was free exploration of an interesting substance and an imaginative attempt to name the outcome of his effort.

11

Your role was twofold; you did not interfere with that exploration, and you participated in the child's learning by adding new elements—a different line and the word to describe it—to the result he had already noticed and brought to your attention.

This kind of learning—casual, brief, homey and convenient—is what this book is about. The learning environment is your home and your immediate neighborhood. The learning tools are whatever you happen to have in your home. The occasions for learning are the routines of daily life, the games of children, and many accidental opportunities that may arise at any moment. The subjects are a whole range of preschool skills that may be familiar to you and your child from Sesame Street, such as recognizing "numbers," "letters" and "people in your neighborhood," and others that could not be explored through the medium of television, such as colors and manual dexterity.

Following is a brief description of these preschool goals and some examples of how they are presented on the show. This may help you to understand better how Sesame Street teaches young children, and how the same goals can guide you in helping children learn.

SESAME STREET LEARNING GOALS

The Sesame Street curriculum was created to provide the child with many of the skills he will need for a more successful learning experience in school. Also, it was designed to help the child develop a positive attitude about himself and his ability to interact with his environment.

The educational goals originally chosen for Sesame Street, and those that have been added since, can be divided into three categories: cognitive, affective and physical goals.

Cognitive goals are largely those any parent would associate with preparation for school, such as learning to count, the letters of the alphabet, and the names of shapes.

Cognitive goals also include building the child's vocabulary to enable him to talk about the man-made and natural environment, and relational concepts such as "up" and "down."

Other goals that fall into the cognitive area are discrimination skills—recognizing when two objects are the same or different from each other; comparison skills—being able to compare two objects by characteristics such as length or texture; classification skills—sorting objects by their characteristics and naming the group to which they belong; and problem-solving skills—the ability to figure things out or develop strategies to find things out.

These concepts are presented on Sesame Street in many different ways. When The Amazing Mumford, with the aid of his not-so-helpful assistant, Grover, makes pineapples disappear, he is teaching both number recognition and simple subtraction.

When Susan sings "One of these things is not like the others," the children who sing along are practicing classification skills.

When Cookie Monster takes a big bite out of a cookie and says that what's left looks like the letter C, it reinforces both letter recognition and initial consonant sounds.

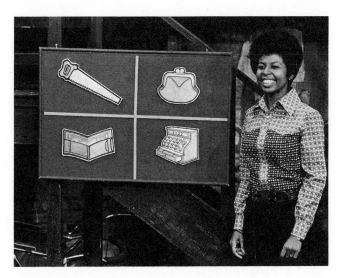

Affective goals are those that have to do with one's feelings and relationships with other people. They include social goals, such as cooperation, recognizing how others feel, and knowing of different ways people live and work. Affective goals also include more personal concepts such as self-image—how one feels about oneself.

The Sesame Street film about the day in the life of a native American Indian child illustrates differences and similarities in life-styles.

When Ernie shares his bread with Bert, and Bert shares his peanut butter with Ernie so that both can have a peanut butter sandwich, they are illustrating the benefits of cooperation.

And when Big Bird sings "Everyone makes mistakes, so why can't you?" he helps children feel good about themselves—even when they're not perfect.

Physical goals are those that have to do with health and physical fitness. They include nutritional goals, hygiene goals such as bathing and brushing teeth, and fitness goals such as good balance, posture and coordination.

When David sings "It's a very simple dance," and children play along, they are practicing coordination and balance while they are having fun. The Count encourages children not only to count their teeth, but to brush them. And even Cookie Monster acknowledges that cookies may taste good, but children need a well-balanced diet to grow up healthy and strong.

Go back to the flour spilled on the counter. The small-muscle coordination your child is practicing is a physical skill. The result of his physical movement is lines in the flour, and as your child learns to describe those lines, he is exercising a cognitive skill. Yet verbal interchange, the sociability of the two of you working side by side, is affective learning.

More important, although on paper these three categories—cognitive, affective and physical—are separated from one another, in practice they may occur simultaneously. And all three influence one another at all times. Imagine eliminating the finger movements, verbal descriptions or sociability from this learning episode. You would lose much of the learning, too.

As you approve of your child drawing lines in flour, you are attending to your child in a reciprocal way: he draws a line, you draw a line, he draws another line. Reciprocity is the basis of "taking turns."

Your child is experiencing the soft texture of flour, the smooth texture of the counter—experiences that are necessary for his ultimate understanding of the words "soft" and "smooth." The flour he is drawing in is being used to make a cake, too. One basis of creativity is multiple uses of the same substance or object.

As your child draws, he keeps his fingers within the confines of the floury area; he is already noting the delimitations of space that he will later take into account when working on paper. And as your child draws that first line and names it "stick," he has abstracted the quality of straightness in a stick and generalized the word to mean a straight line as well.

Our pretended spilled-flour-on-the-counter episode need not have ended here. Noticing the mental association the child was making between "straight" and "stick," an adult might have gone one step further:

"My!" you might have added, "that line *is* as straight as a stick!" This opportunistic support that lends just the right *zing!* of confirmation to a learning experience is the "Open Sesame" we hope this book will give you.

Although Sesame Street is broken up into short segments, each making a specific educational point, your child's life is a continuous stream of educational experiences. This book, therefore, is divided into the more natural segments of everyday life.

The next chapter, "All Through the Day," suggests learning opportunities that are likely to arise during the daily routines of home life: getting up, getting dressed, cleaning the house, doing errands, visiting with friends, cooking, eating, bathing, and going to bed.

All the other chapters characterize a specific type of activity. "Quiet Times" contains quiet, peaceful and relatively inactive things to do, such as guessing games and pencil-and-paper games. It is a particularly useful resource for filling in those times when you have to wait for an appointment or take a long bus ride.

"Creative Materials" presents many types of media, from sand and dough to tempera paints and trash. Its practical information will help you to make better use of incidental opportunities such as a day at the beach, or to create new opportunities for your child.

"Dramatic Play" is a chapter about role-playing, dress-up, playing house, and puppet play. It includes many suggestions for providing props to extend your child's imaginative play.

The last chapter, "Special Times," suggests activities that mark the seasons, celebrate holidays, or take note in an intimate way of your family's heritage and the members' affection for one another.

In general, you will find that "All Through the Day" contains the least time-consuming, most spontaneous activities. "Quiet Times" requires the least physical equipment. "Creative Materials" and "Dramatic Play" both require more of your time and attention, and certainly more supplies. "Special Times" suggests periods of generosity—times when you feel like throwing yourself into the promise of spring or the delight of a birthday.

HOW TO USE THIS BOOK

Use *Learn at Home the Sesame Street Way* as a handbook or resource book. It is not necessary to sit down and read these chapters through from beginning to end. Thumb through them whenever you have the time, and let your eye catch what it will.

For many activities, we suggest both simpler and more complicated versions so that you can adapt them to your own child's progress. If any activity seems cumbersome or risky, drop it in a hurry and choose one more suited to your child's abilities.

For those times when you wish to find a specific entry you recall, or plan for a particular occasion, or wonder what you can do with that box of miscellaneous buttons, the index in this book was made to help you. You can look under the name of a skill—*counting*, for instance—for all the activities and items of information in the book that are based on that goal. You may also look up entries under the type of material needed, such as *boxes* or *blankets*. There are headings that describe the character of an activity, such as *helping*, or *experiments*. You can even look under *Cooking* or *Travel* to find entries that fit in with adult pursuits, or under locations, such as *Outdoors* or *Kitchen*.

With few exceptions, the equipment you need probably consists of things you already have. We have recommended not only commonly available items (ice cube trays and old *mittens* and *plastic bottles*), but also commonly discarded items (magazines and boxes). If an entry calls for something you don't have, such as a *tape recorder* or a *sandbox*, use the index to find another activity concerning the same skill or reflecting a similar interest.

WHO ARE "YOU"?

The word "you" is as liberally sprinkled through this book as the words "your child." "You" are a mother or a father, and maybe you are living with your spouse or maybe you aren't. "You" are any relative, grown-up or less than grown-up, who spends time caring for children aged two-to-six. "You" may be a babysitter. "You" are anyone who can use what this book offers.

"Your child" is any child in your care, permanently or temporarily, whether you gave birth to him or fathered him or not. For those who have more than one, "your child" should sometimes be read as "your children," since it isn't often you are treated to them one at a time.

We would also like to mention that we refer to the child as "he" and "him" in this book for grammatical reasons only. We would prefer to acknowledge throughout that he's and she's are about equally abundant, and certainly equally important, but this becomes extremely awkward to express in every paragraph.

MORE THAN YOU NEED

For the working parent also responsible for running a household, time with the children is more limited. This book can be valuable in helping those parents make the most of that cherished time.

But even the parent who spends all day with children shouldn't expect to engage the child in all the activities described. The amount of material in this book is probably far more than anyone would ever use.

If you look over the entries for a while, you will find that most are considerate of the adult's time and energy. While you are sorting the laundry, for example, it will neither intrude deeply into your concentration nor lengthen your task to ask your child to search for pairs of socks. The game may even make things easier. You could even sing the Sesame Street sorting song (see p. 40).

The intimate, supportive, and responsive atmosphere of the family can create the perfect emotional climate for the sort of learning that occurs in early childhood.

As you guide your child through these activities, you need not be critical or judgmental. At all stages of life, people learn most easily when they are emotionally comfortable. If a new boss makes you feel nervous or harassed, it's hard to *hear* his instructions, much less follow them. Support ("I know you can do it"), encouragement ("You're doing fine"), and patience ("Take your time") help people learn. But if what is communicated instead is doubt that you have the ability to accomplish the task, learning comes to a screeching halt.

Throughout this book you will find suggested ways to compliment a child, to simplify a game that is too difficult, and to avoid situations that might strike a child as a "test."

Speak Sesame Street "language" with your child. Be familiar enough with the show so that, at opportune moments, you can make references that will strike a responsive chord with him. One instance would be to quote The Count when there are things to count. Another would be to talk about the characteristics of things you and your child are putting away together. If you remember this sketch from the show, remind him how Ernie does it—by putting away only the red things and only the things with wheels (one firetruck).

FOLLOW THE LEADER

Children's learning is largely self-motivated. Your child does not know that he is learning to count because it will help him in school, which will help him do his taxes or get a job. Like a flight of stairs to a toddler, he will climb to the next step because it is there. More important, each new step successfully climbed makes the next step more intriguing.

Your child must feel that he can make things happen. It doesn't matter much what he wishes to accomplish—biting his toast into the shape of a truck or counting to a hundred. All curiosity, all interests, all pursuits are equally valid. Nor does it matter that many imagined accomplishments will be frustrated. Perhaps the toast will look more like a blob than a truck. And as he gets to twenty-eleven, the child may discover that counting to one hundred is more confusing than he had thought. The important thing is that his curiosity and his effort be aroused, even if the results are sometimes unsatisfactory.

Parents are in a position to regulate somewhat the success and frustration of their child's pursuits. That's a delicate job. When you understand what a child has in mind, you can often help him achieve it. When you don't, avoid interfering. Wait until you see what the child has in mind before stepping in with aid or advice. A child racing his toy cars across the floor is not about to stop and "choose all the blue ones." Perhaps he is intuitively grasping at a relationship between speed and distance, or between weight and momentum. He will not stop for blue. No doubt color will be the object of his interest some other day, and he will welcome your suggestion on the subject then.

As far as you are concerned, early learning is a game of follow-the-leader. The child leads, you follow, then maybe you lead a little, then it's the child's turn to lead again.

LEARNING BEGINS AT HOME

Learning, of course, occurs in the context of a physical environment. Home happens to be a terrific one. Typically, a home is loaded with things you may not have thought of as educational equipment: plants on the windowsill, pots in the cupboard, socks, boxes, garlic, pencils, magazines, snapshots, sheets, screwdrivers, pets, potatoes, string.

Although you have not bought these items in order to educate your child, they are probably more than any classroom would have. The uses to which you put these objects number in the thousands—a lesson in itself, and one that fascinates children.

What is more, this rich environment is relatively free for a child to explore.

Often without a suggestion from you, a child may put old socks on his hands as "monster paws." He may work a sock like a puppet, use it as a doll's hat, or fill it with small toys as a container. His freedom to imagine, to invent, to pursue his interests at home is wonderfully vigorous.

Some of our suggestions tell how to use your environment in ways you may not have thought of, or to enhance it even more. But *how much* freedom you can allow is always up to you.

This book reinforces and extends the goals of Sesame Street. We hope you find pleasure in sharing with your children things you might not have thought of doing, things that turn out to be great fun—and just happen to be learning experiences as well.

2 All Through the Day

UNTIL A CHILD ENTERS SCHOOL, learning is seldom something that happens at special times of the day. It happens all through the day. Learning occurs when a child matches pants to shirt, when he recognizes the brand name on his breakfast cereal, or when he can tell by a particular TV show that it is nearly time for bed.

His learning is aided by his environment: by what objects are available for him to explore, by what uses they are put to in his home, by how those objects are organized in his family. He is aided by daily routines that teach him what is to be done, what can be expected to happen next, and how time is planned.

He also learns from the people around him. It is the people with whom a child shares his life who help him to observe, who give him the words to say what he has noticed, who offer new alternatives for manipulating his environment and who, by example, show him many ways in which our social and physical world works.

This sounds like a tall order for busy parents. But a great deal of parents' role as teacher occurs in a side-by-side relationship with their child—as they go about their own work, their own errands, their own socializing. "All Through the Day" is a sequence of side-by-side learning episodes from morning, when the family arises, through the day's chores and outings, to night and bedtime. Most of the activities are quite casual, calling for momentary attention rather than long periods of your concentration, and for common household objects rather than special children's toys or materials. Some of the activities are intended to relieve you of concentrating on your child while you are especially busy; activities that are separate, though similar, to your own, and absorbing enough to keep your child involved by himself for a while.

The routine implied in this chapter may seem unfair to working parents who, after all, do not spend all their days at home. But fortunately or unfortunately, those who work full time often have to get household chores dones as well. The suggestions offered here will be usable, if less frequently used.

As with every other part of this book, caretakers of all sorts and ages, whether older brothers and sisters, grandparents or baby-sitters, are invited to use whatever appeals to them. There are many more suggestions than you will need, or than the most vigorous child or adult would attempt.

GETTING UP

Pulling themselves up from the pillows and into focus once again, parents and children face the morning. It is few people's favorite hour. And it is no time for games. You have to get dressed; you have to get organized. The suggestions here are only for using the physical routine of grooming and the mental activity of anticipating your day to advantage.

During the process of getting dressed, a child is made aware of hands, feet, front, back—all of himself. That awareness is called body image. A body image can be like the ugly duckling—lumpy, large-nosed, feet-in-the-wrong place. Or it can be like the swan—all together and moving neatly.

An adult's image of himself has grown from his sense of his body in childhood. That sense is partly intellectual—knowing the parts of you, how they fit together, what they can do. But it is emotional, too—feeling that the whole of you works well and is likeable. As a child greets himself in the morning, is polished up a bit and clothed pleasingly, he is both learning about himself and forming an opinion of himself.

The mental ability to anticipate and to plan grows from childhood, too. The more a child can participate in knowledge of the day ahead and in what you both intend to do about it, the greater his sense of competence and control. Children can be violent on the subject of what to wear. One boy must wear his old floppy hat everywhere. One girl won't put on a striped shirt without a tantrum. Such violent feelings may lead to war—a war parents feel they have to win. Children feel strongly about their clothing for the same reasons adults do. Think of yourself trying on clothes in a department store. You look at yourself in the mirror. The outfit is just "not you." You can't wait to take the offending garment off. Although a child's "me," his sense of self, is brand-new, it may be surprisingly rigid. If he is not clothed in his own image, he is literally not himself. The feeling may make him quite uncomfortable.

Try to let your child choose what he wears each morning. If you don't like the result, there's no law that says you can't say so. If you do enjoy his choice, your specific compliments—*the colors match, blue jeans are good for outdoors*—will help to form his taste and judgment.

What if you can't stand letting a child choose his own clothes? Whether it's because little girls who wear masses of costume jewelry embarrass you, or because wearing dressy clothes to the playground is impractical, there is a compromise that might work. Lay out two or three different outfits for your child to choose from. Lean a little toward your child's preference; for instance, one piece of jewelry; a new, but not party, outfit. Then stick to your guns. You are being reasonable.

What about that old hat? Or the ragged baby blanket that must always be dragged along? Such items may be so important to a child's sense of being his own person that you will have to stand them—at least for a while.

Oscar-the-Grouch wears his favorite raggedy hat.

DRESSING

As you dress your child, put his actions into words. *Give me your foot* and *put your arms up* help a child learn the names of body parts and to feel where hands and feet are at that moment. As a child gets older, mention less obvious body

parts: *Let me get these sleeves above your elbows. Is the collar too tight around your neck?* To see how confusing a child's body can be to him at first, ask a toddler to turn his back to you. He is more aware of his front than of his back; he may find the task impossible. Many toddlers also confuse "tummy" with "behind." Dressing out loud lets a child "find" the parts of himself and relate them to one another.

One of the more boring aspects of parenting is the constant tying, zipping, buttoning—and yanking and struggling—of dressing and undressing children. Teachers, faced with scores of children to bundle and unbundle daily, have devised these methods for outdoor wear:

Jackets: Lay the jacket out on the floor in front of the child. The lining should be facing up, with the collar toward the child. He leans down, puts his arms in

How to put on a jacket:

Ernie points to Bert's chin.

the sleeves, and then stands up and flips the jacket back over his head. Believe it or not, the jacket is now on correctly.

Boots: The child puts a plastic bag (food-storage size) on each foot over the shoes. Then he pushes his shoes into his boots. The plastic is more slippery than sneaker and shoe soles, so that four- and even three-year-olds can get their own boots on and off.

For indoor clothes, there are no such clever inventions. As your child learns to dress himself, act as assistant. Hand him clothes opened up and oriented correctly; start his feet into his pants, but then require that he be less than limp: *"push your feet in," "pull your pants up."* Scrunch shirts into a doughnut (the neck is the hole), stretch the neck a bit, and start it over his head. He can get his own arms in. Reach into a sock, grab the heel and pull it upwards out through the

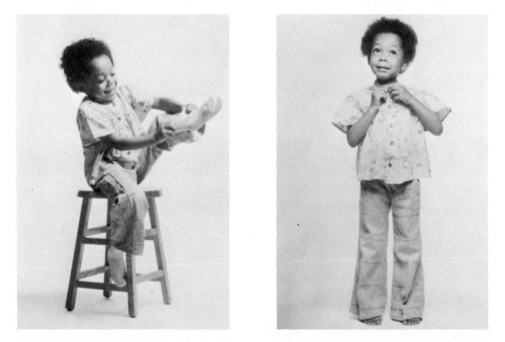

top of the sock. Put this half-inside-out sock on his foot. He can peel the top up over his foot and ankle.

Once in a while, if you're in a mad rush, it's okay to give more help.

BACKWARDS AND INSIDE OUT

As you've no doubt noticed, children can make no sense of the orientation of their clothing on their bodies. If their shirts are not on backwards or inside out, it is purely accidental. To help a child get his shirt right side out and facing front, make a polka dot with a laundry marker on the inside of the front neckline. The shirt will be on the right way only if the child can see the mark as the shirt goes over his head. The same thing can be done with pants and overalls, shirts and dresses.

Fasteners: There are commercial frames and even dolls that are equipped with oversize laces, zippers, and buttons to give a child practice with fasteners. These get a lot of use in a school, but may not interest a child for long enough to be worth the expense. Instead, make your own out of discarded clothing. (Tack an old shoe to a board for lacing and unlacing; staple a cut-out placket from a pair of pants for zipping and unzipping, from an old shirt for buttoning and unbuttoning; put a dog collar around a stuffed animal for buckling and unbuckling.)

Shoe Mixups: There is no foolproof way to keep the right shoe on the right foot because children fail to see (or even feel) the difference. Most children can't tell left from right consistently until they are six or seven years old. You will either have to line the shoes up correctly right in front of your child's waiting feet, or use this "match the dots" method: with a waterproof marker or laundry pen, make a dot on the inner sole of each shoe, placing it at the inside edge. When the shoes are lined up correctly, the dots will be next to each other.

Match shoes by matching dots.

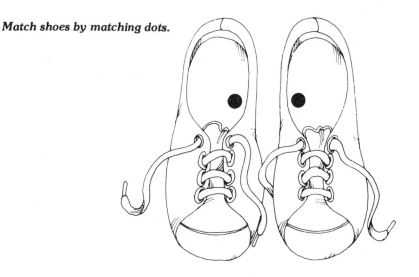

The "rabbit ear" method:
Hold each lace as a loop—or rabbit ear—
and then tie another half-knot identical to
the first.

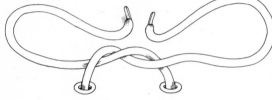

By the way, until they are at least six years old, don't expect children to tie shoelaces. When the time comes, the easiest way to tie a bow is the "rabbit ear" method.

To keep shoelaces tied without struggling with the knot later on, tie only the loops a second time.

What if your child is perfectly happy to have you dress him all the time? You're probably stuck with it for a while longer. Being dressed is a pleasant baby time, and he's not willing to give it up. Try compromise deals: after he gets his underwear on, you'll help with the rest; if he gets the shirt over his head, you'll get his arms in.

What if your child won't let you help at all, but starts each morning with rage as he fails to cope with his clothing? Offer practice with fastening the fasteners that frustrate him. Offer assistance such as neckhole stretching, sock preparation and shoelace loosening. But try not to help too much. This sort of child will soon learn to get himself into his clothes, since it is obviously important to him. Until then, grit your teeth and wait it out.

To show that we are allowed to be likeable—to ourselves and to others—spend a few minutes admiring yourselves in the mirror. While you fix yourself up, let your child fool around with his looks, too. With a glass of water and a comb, he can make his hair look different. It doesn't take much additional energy to remark on what the mirror shows—a cute nose, white teeth, or whatever "beautiful"

effect your child has achieved. The idea of this is not to teach vanity by suggesting, "Oh, you are the most gorgeous child and you will grow up to be a model," but, "I like the way you look. Do you?"

FACE GAMES

An infant's early interest in and affection for a parent's face is often expressed by touching. Though two-year-olds can be trusted not to jam a hand down your throat or get your nose in a death grip, they still like to pat your face, to give it different expressions by tugging at the corners of your mouth, to "work" your eyes by moving your eyelids up and down.

There is an old game that might have arisen from this sort of affectionate exploration of a parent's face: You pull the skin of your throat, and out pops your tongue. You pull on your left earlobe, and your tongue moves to the left. Pull your right earlobe, your tongue moves to the right. Then push your nose upward: Poof! Your tongue pops back into your mouth. Try this game during dressing time or play at making mock facial expressions (especially sad ones accompanied by crocodile tears). Kiss by rubbing noses and by patting cheeks. All these ways of exploring each other's faces are reassuring ways to show affection.

PARTS OF THE BODY

There are some body parts children are particularly fond of talking about, such as belly buttons, bottoms, and genitals. Whether you use pet names like "tushy" or "pee-pee," or scientific names like buttocks and penis, acknowledge that these are parts of his body, too. The words arise frankly in the course of everyday matters—asking a girl if she'd like to wash her own genitals since the soap may sting, but adding that you'd like to wash her behind to be sure it's clean.

Sometimes children are active in calling attention to their private parts by being public about their nudity. No need to encourage exhibitionism, but it's nice to admit that a child's whole body is indeed pleasant to behold: you like it fine, and now would he please get some clothes on.

EXERCISES

Some parents do morning exercises. Some children like to copy them. If you aren't too out of breath to manage it, chant what you're doing as you move: knee up, knee down; leg back, leg front. Young children will get confused, swinging arms while you're kicking legs. Slim and supple they might be, but this business

Exercise 2

Exercise 3

of getting one's body into the right place at the right times is harder for them than it is for you.

Here are several exercises * that are good for you and your child to do together:

1. Balance on one foot, letting your child hop at first to help keep his balance, but later encouraging him to stay put—and, you hope, upright!

2. Hold your hands out to your child as though to pick him up. Let him grab your fingers or your thumbs and jump up as you lift him to your chest. If his grip weakens, your free fingers can grasp his wrists to help out. This strengthens your child's (and your) arm and hand muscles.

3. With your child facing away from you, hold him with the same hand grip (as shown), then have him lift his legs straight up in front, open, close, and lower them again. This is one of the few exercises that really works for abdominal muscles—and ultimately for good posture.

BIG BIRD SAYS

For people who don't exercise in the morning, this is another way to combine the words for body parts with specified movements and positions: Play "Big Bird Says." *Big Bird says wiggle your toes* (into your socks). *Big Bird says bend your elbow* (so I can get you out of these pajamas). *Big Bird says hold your head up* (so I can get you into your shirt). Give your child a chance to be Big Bird, or choose his favorite Sesame Street character.

Another way to play is standing in front of a full-length mirror. You can stand behind your child and make the movements, too, to help him. As your child

* Exercises developed by Bill Thompson, co-author of *The Every Body's Book*.

learns new words, you can turn the game around so that he tells you what to do. *Shake, wiggle, swing, stamp* are words for movements. *Up, down, high, low, sideways, backwards* are words for positions and directions.

WINDOW VIEW

As you go about these early morning routines take a moment to look out the window together. What do you notice? Help your child make observations with you. The sidewalk is wet (it rained during the night). The trees are moving (it is windy). Three people are carrying umbrellas (they expect more rain). Perhaps what you notice and what you infer from your observations will change your plans: no picnic in the park today! Observing, drawing conclusions, and acting accordingly are powerful training in problem-solving.

Often your child will notice things that are not important to you. You glance at the sky, he sees the garbage truck. Use whatever comes up to make predictions and influence actions: *I wonder if it comes every morning just when we get up. Let's look for the garbage truck tomorrow.*

SESAME STREET NEWS

Help your child to observe the weather each day, and perhaps report it to you by pretending he is Kermit the Frog reporting for the Sesame Street News. Open the window and feel the air together. If you can see people from your window, look at how they are dressed. Older children can "read" a thermometer. Use all the evidence to figure out what to wear outdoors that day.

Guy Smiley gives the weather forecast for Sesame Street.

By the way, this is not just an intellectual exercise. Letting a child observe the weather and predict what clothes will keep him comfortable, even if he is wrong and suffers temporarily from heat or cold, teaches planning and common sense. There is a catch: you must let the child make mistakes. If his discomfort upsets you, bring along the heavier jacket or lighter shirt when you go outside.

LISTENING

Close your eyes, both of you. Listen. The morning has its own sounds: Daddy showering; birds singing and toilets flushing; dogs barking, garbage-can lids clanking, water boiling, toaster popping. Let your child be Sherlock Hemlock and figure out what is going on by the sounds he hears. Help him out when he falters.

If you play this game over a period of time, each of you telling the other what you hear, your child's ability to listen and to interpret sounds will grow sharp. At first he hears a "bang." Then he knows it is a door slamming. Then he predicts: *Jessie is slamming the door; the school bus will be here in a minute.*

Sherlock Hemlock, the world's greatest detective, listens for clues.

PLANNING

First we'll have breakfast; then we'd better do the shopping. What day is today? Monday? Then we have to return library books, too. Talking to yourself as you think out your day is not a sign of craziness, but a valid method of communicating the future to your child. If he picks up on something, make use of it. Let him mark Monday on the calendar with a crayon. If he wants to go to the playground, fit it into the sequence of events for him (after shopping, before library). Although this planning is informal and conversational, your child is learning to envision the future—and sometimes to reshape it to his own needs. Both skills empower him because he participates in what is ahead.

What if you are too distracted or grumpy in the morning to be social? Then don't try. Any of these ideas can be used some other time when you are in the mood.

CHORES

Even a very young child can help with morning cleanup if your expectations are matched to his capacities. Don't expect a child to be organized. A child who is told, "Clean up your room," literally cannot locate a starting point, much less a process that will end in the goal of a clean room. Break down each job, and wait until one thing is done before you ask for the next thing: *Put your clothes in a pile here* (wait); *Carry the pile to the laundry basket.* Don't expect a child to be coordinated. Most children can't even empty a wastebasket without making a mess. Find jobs that don't require accuracy (carrying the wastebasket to the door), or find a technique that the child can handle (emptying a wastebasket one item at a time). A child may love to go through the motions of sweeping or wiping, but fail to appreciate the point of the activity. All a child's vigor may still leave jelly on the breakfast table. Don't expect thoroughness.

Make work a social event, an opportunity for togetherness. Few children will work in isolation from you. You wash, he rinses. You pick up clothes, he picks up blocks. You dust the top, he dusts the bottom. If you are feeling relaxed enough, conversation and singing go well with routine chores.

At this age, you are not teaching a child his responsibility to his family. You are showing him what a family is: a group of people who work together for one another's benefit and pleasure. The roots of responsibility grow nicely from this cheerful seed.

If work is so pressing or so disagreeable that you feel antisocial, best not to ask for help that day. If you are sometimes irritated with a young child's clumsiness and slowness, if you feel you would rather do it yourself, skip this section of the book. Look at "Quiet Times" for quiet activities that will keep your child happily busy and out of your hair while you get your work done. There are so many ways a child can learn a particular skill that there is no reason to put yourself out for a method that annoys you. When you need a job done fast, do it yourself.

What if your child refuses to help out? He may not see a difference between work and play. He may only be refusing a game that doesn't appeal to him just then. If you were washing dishes in suds or cutting out cookie dough instead of making beds the game might strike him as more fun. Try again another time with another game.

"HELPING"

Think before you ask for help. Do you really need it? Fetching and carrying can save you a lot of work, but a three-year-old's "helping" with the ironing is no help at all. Pride comes from feeling needed. Choose help that you will really value. If you know your child can't really be of help, ask for his company instead. He can't fail at keeping you company. And if your child insists on "helping" at a task beyond his skills, try breaking the job into smaller bits—sweeping one little corner or holding the dustpan while you sweep into it. Often the biggest help is simply that your child is constructively occupied so you are free to work.

JOBS FOR A THREE-YEAR-OLD

A three-year-old can usually:

Sponge up a spill (you finish the wiping)

Clean silver (a few pieces, preferably spoons)

Wash windows (you count the squirts with him)

Wipe dishes (unbreakable ones)

Put things away (one category at a time, and in a specific place)

Dust (small, simple spaces like a windowsill)

Sort laundry (all the white clothes, all the socks)

Fold clothes (handkerchiefs, napkins)

Vacuum (the fluff under the radiator, the cereal that spilled)

Clean fingerprints (you prepare the sponge)

Wash dolls' clothes, toys or unbreakable dishes in suds (you pour the soap and rinse)

Scrub bathtubs (they can get inside to do it)

Point out that there are some things three-year-olds can do more efficiently than you can because they are smaller.

STORAGE

Organized storage helps a child develop classification skills. Classification is basic. It is how we know that we will find milk in the dairy case or that buttons are in the notions department. Adults make sense of a multitude of objects by assigning each to a class, and organizing them accordingly. You can make classification clearer to a child by the way you store his toys. A toybox is not organized. Dolls and doll clothes are mixed up with blocks, puzzles, crayons, construction sets, vehicles, batteries, dress-ups and bubble gum wrappers. They are not even all toys.

Divide playthings into categories that make sense to you. ("Things to build with" is as clear as "Crafts." "Doll play," "Dress-ups"—the way you choose to classify makes no difference.) Use bags, boxes, shelf or drawer space for storage. Then when your child wants to take something out or you want him to put something away say, *"The blocks are next to the other construction sets." "Put your doll's dishes in the box that holds her clothes."*

PICK-UP WORDS

A child can pick up new words and useful ways of thinking as he picks up around the house. All he needs is for you to use informative language. *Put your underwear in your top drawer* gives a child more information than *Get these things out of here.* You have specified an action (*put* rather than *throw*, *drop* or *drag*); named the object (*underwear* rather than *things*); and given a location (*top drawer* rather than *out of here*).

Save stooping and climbing by asking your child to be the delivery person. He reports for work, you give him an assignment. *Deliver the newspaper upstairs to my bedroom. Put it on the bottom shelf of my bedside table. When you come back, please deliver my sewing basket to me.*

This sequence is long, and hard to remember. Only you can judge when your child can keep so much in his mind at once and do each part of the assignment in order. Some children have a good auditory memory; they easily recall what they have heard. Others ask *What?* all the time. They hear you, but they can't recall many words at a time. Start with one instruction. Keep it short. Repeat it if he needs to hear it again. Even as his auditory memory improves, try to stay aware of how long your sentences are and how many actions you are describing.

MAIL

When does the mailman come? If it is at the same time each day, your child can learn to recognize that time on the clock. Say he always comes at ten o'clock. Draw a clock face with the hands in the right position. Shortly before ten o'clock, watch the clock together. Point out when the hands on the clock are in the same position as the ones you drew, and say, "That's ten o'clock." Each day, your child can clockwatch and predict the mailman's arrival. This is not yet telling time, of course, but it is a familiarity with the configuration of a clock face that will make things easier in the future.

There are some jobs children can do when the mail arrives. Sort the letters (they come in envelopes) from the fliers and newspapers (they don't come in envelopes). Open the envelopes with a dull knife. Save colorful ads in a shoebox for future cut-and-paste activities.

Try teaching your child to recognize his last name on the envelopes. If the word is pointed out often enough, most children can learn its whole shape long before they can actually read. See if your child can find envelopes that have the same kind of stamp. If he can already compare sizes well, he can stack envelopes from biggest to smallest. Help him sort the mail that is for Daddy or Mommy, or another member of the family. Perhaps he can actually deliver the mail to the right person later on. Or your child can count the letters you receive—just as The Count counts the letters he sends to himself on Sesame Street.

TELEVISION

To avoid the irritation of endless dial-twirling with the volume at high blast, you have to show a child how to choose the channel he wants, and how to control the noise. First, see what numerals your child already recognizes. Many children learn a few channel numerals just from having the stations announce themselves so often.

If your child doesn't know any numerals, teach him the one or two numerals he may be turning to most often.

Now get a television guide, and look up a favorite program. Wait until it's time for the program to begin. Let your child set the channel dial (show him what indicates that the dial is in the right position). Then turn the set on. Presto! There is his favorite program. The accuracy of all this will no doubt impress your child, and he will get pleasure from setting the dial instead of twirling. Of course, this is not to suggest that children should control their viewing! *You* must decide how much television your child should watch, what times of day, and how much freedom you will allow in the selection of programs. (We recommend Sesame Street!)

RADIO

Setting the dial on a radio is harder than on a TV—too hard for most children. But a radio is excellent for learning volume control. Find some music you like, and let your child play around with the volume knob. Ask him to turn the sound (or noise) "louder" or "quieter."

Find a talk show. Go into the next room. Ask the child to turn the sound louder so you can hear it, or quieter so you can't. Let him trade places with you and give you instructions so he gets the idea that sound diminishes with distance. All of this experimenting will help your child understand how to control sound levels.

SOUND GAMES

Set a windup alarm clock to only a few minutes ahead. Hide the clock. When it rings, ask your child to find it. This game gives a child good experience in locating the source of a sound.

If you have a tape recorder, here is something you might try: load a fifteen-minute tape into a cassette tape recorder. As you work, let your child record the sounds of the vacuum cleaner, running water, flushing toilet, passing trucks, barking dogs, slamming doors. Show him how to rewind and play back. What was that noise? Ask your child to tell you what the noises are as he plays them back. Sometime later, replay the tape again and see if he can still identify the sounds.

When a child gives a wrong answer to a question, what should you do? Disagree. He thinks that noise is the vacuum? You think it's the dishwasher. A disagreement is quite different from accusing a child of being wrong. Yet sometimes a child is wrong and needs to know it. Saying "What else could it be?" might be a good reply.

Oscar blows his own horn too loudly for Judy Collins.

TELEPHONE

Ever since long-distance dialing was invented, children who fool around with the telephone have caused catastrophes. The ability to properly dial a phone, however, can be a valuable skill for a child when he can understand that the telephone is not a toy. You may want to teach your child your own phone number, and your community "emergency number."

Letting a child dial a local number now and then under your supervision may keep him from experimenting on his own. After a child knows his numerals from 0 to 9, write down for him one telephone number you dial often. (Write it down all in numerals, since the letters on a telephone dial are confusing to children.) Show him how to dial the first numeral or the last one. Sometimes it's hard for a child to grasp that he must move his finger all the way around to the "stopper" when he dials. If he has trouble with that, he can practice with the receiver still in place. Each time you make this particular call, let him dial the numerals as you read them off; then let him try to dial the whole number in order by reading the numerals himself.

Let your child hear the results of getting the number right.

HOUSEHOLD APPLIANCES

Other appliances a child can use safely *with supervision* and instructions are toasters, washers and dryers, dishwashers and vacuum cleaners. Warn of dangers.

Caution:
- *Explain that there should be no wet hands while using appliances, no sticking utensils into toasters, and discuss other precautions you might take for granted. Demonstrate by having your child hold his hand over the toaster to see how hot it gets. Listen to a sneaker tumbling in the dryer.*
- *You plug the appliances into the socket, and explain to the child that this part of the job is yours only.*

Show how things work: set the dryer for five minutes, then wait until the machine turns off. Set the washer, then let your child turn it on and off several times. On some washers you can feel the water temperature to demonstrate the effect of the temperature dial. Adjust the toaster to "dark" or "light" and watch the results together.

Although you will have to supervise the use of most appliances for years to come, the child who can make his own toast and start his family's clothes in the dryer is way ahead in competence and independence.

LAUNDRY SORTING

Think through all the sorting tasks you do yourself when you do the family's laundry. White clothes here, colored clothes there; clothes for folding, clothes for ironing; towels to this closet, sheets to that one; children's clothes in this pile, adults' clothes in that one. The easier sorting jobs can be done by children.

Easiest sorting: Put all the socks into a pile (the child only has to know what a sock is, and sort it out from non-socks). *All the white clothes, all the towels, and all the underpants* are similar tasks.

Harder sorting: Match the socks into pairs. (The child has to find "socks that are the same" by color and by size. He has to understand "pair" to mean two-that-are-the-same.) Other sorting jobs that are about this hard would be *Sister's shirts, kitchen towels, the baby's clothes.*

Hardest sorting: Find all the laundry that belongs upstairs. (The child has to know an awful lot about the way you run your household.) This is an example of the kind of job that may be too hard for a preschool child.

If you're making a game out of it, you might sing the Sesame Street sorting song—with three red socks and one white one.

> ### *ONE OF THESE THINGS*
>
> One of these things is not like the
>   others.
> One of these things just doesn't belong.
> Can you tell which thing is not like the
>   others
> By the time I finish my song?
>
> If you guessed this thing is not like the
>   others,
> If you guessed this thing just doesn't
>   belong,
> If you guessed this thing is not like the
>   others
> Then you're absolutely right!

Copyright © 1970 Jonico Music, Inc.
Music by Joe Raposo—Lyrics by Bruce Hart. Used by permission.

"ONE OF THESE THINGS IS NOT LIKE THE OTHERS"

Even if your child is not participating, you can help him learn more about sorting by remarking on the job at hand. Let's say he can't sort socks. Do it yourself, but do it out loud: *Is that a red sock you have? Here's another red sock. See, they match. They're a pair. Oh, this is a long sock, it must be Daddy's. We'd better look for some more long socks. Yes, here's another long one. It's the same length. That's another pair.*

Silly as you may sound to yourself, you'll find that soon your child will anticipate your actions and reach for a matching sock himself. He has learned the attributes—color, size—by which you are sorting and matching to make up pairs of objects.

What if your child nags and whines to go out as you go through your morning cleanup routine? If none of the helping or playing activities suggested here are working for you, there are only two choices left. Put up with the whining, or leave the work behind and get out of the house earlier. You can't satisfy everybody all of the time.

What if your child insists on active or messy play just when you are trying to get the house straight? Be firm about what bugs you the most. You have a right to live without paint puddles on the floor first thing in the morning. But how about leaving one area *un*tidy? A child's room or a family room could be cleaned only at the end of the day, leaving freedom in the meantime to build, pedal a tricycle, and make a mess. Better that than a child with "nothing to do."

SHOPPING LISTS

If you make a grocery list, your child can help you take inventory. There are several thought processes you are using that can be shared. You may be planning hamburgers for dinner. You think to yourself, do we have ketchup? Relish? Rolls? You are recalling the class of items that *go with* hamburgers. When you check to see if you have these things, you are classifying another way: relish and ketchup are in *jars, kept in the cupboard*. Rolls are *bread, kept in the refrigerator*. Let your child think what goes with what, and then check in the right place to see if you have it in stock.

Do we have enough? *Half a bottle is enough. One, two, three, four, five rolls is enough*. Judging quantity and counting are valuable experiences, too.

You can show the importance of planning. On Sesame Street, the King invited all his subjects to a picnic, and told them all to "bring something to eat." Since no one bothered to plan the meal, everyone came with hot dog buns.

Little by little, children also learn in which stores various categories of goods will be found. Even though a child can't read yet, a shopping list that is organized by type of store—and read aloud—will help him understand what is to be found in a *hardware store, drugstore, grocery store* and *clothing store*.

GOING OUT

When it is time to get out of the house to do errands, or just get some exercise and relief from indoor work, there is a particular richness of casual opportunity for learning games. The activities in this section vary from conversational to physical, and take you all along your way to wherever you are going. It should be noted that just as there are particular hazards inside your home—from electrical outlets to poisonous substances—so there are particular hazards outside your home. To teach rational fears of real dangers to our children is healthful.

We should teach them not to put their hands toward unknown dogs, not to pick up dirty objects from the street, not to go after bees and wasps, and not to accept invitations from people they do not know. These are healthful cautions that safeguard children from real dangers.

Any parent also warns children to "look both ways before you cross" or "wait for the green light." But children understand these warnings in childish ways. A child may understand a safety jingle as a magic incantation. He recites the magic words, then plunges into traffic. Or he may wag his head to one side and the other as though that were a magic ritual, then walk right into an oncoming car.

Intersections that are protected by lights, pedestrian zones, and crossing guards are perceived as dangerous. Unprotected intersections may be seen as safe. Moreover, it takes a child many years to understand that he is to look for the green light that is straight ahead of him, and not one of the many other lights that are in his field of vision.

When you teach your child to cross streets, avoid pat recitations of rules or traffic jingles. Instead, watch traffic and listen for approaching vehicles. See if he can tell you whether a car is going slow or fast, is going to turn or not, has come to a full stop. Ask his judgment before you cross a street together. Is a car coming from that side? Is one coming from the other side? Can we cross now?

SHOPPING ROUTES

As you plan your errands, you are mentally ordering time and space into an efficient sequence of events. You are deciding in which direction to start, in what order to do the errands, and what route you will follow. Although a young child can't perform this complicated planning yet, he can absorb a good deal of the concept behind it if, again, you talk as you plan. Much of what you say reveals relationships in time and space: *We'll pick up the fish at that store next to the barber shop. We can stop at the cleaner on the way home. Let's buy your new sneakers this afternoon after we go to the playground.*

If your child says *NO! I want my new sneakers RIGHT NOW!*, you can point out that the shoe store is nowhere near the other stores you must go to this morning. It would take too long to go in both directions.

There may be a temptation to turn these casual talk-aloud activities into a question-and-answer session. *Where will we buy milk? What goes with hot dogs? What store is next to the supermarket?* Few people enjoy being tested. You are not trying to find out what your child knows, but to inform him of the ways in which you use your knowledge to keep your life in order. Thinking patterns are contagious if you reveal them to your child.

HURRY, HURRY

To you, hurry means an efficient combination of better organization and faster movements to reach a goal in a shorter time. To a child, hurry means "act frantic." He may move as fast and jerky as a silent movie, but he is only getting nowhere fast. To help a child hurry, organize his movements for him: *Go to the closet. Get your boots. Bring the boots here. Sit down. Put out your foot. Put out your other foot. Okay, let's go.*

One reason hurrying can cause panic and tears is that children may fear they will be left behind. Perhaps you can remember this from your own childhood. It is time to go, but you can't find your shoes. The car engine starts before you have climbed aboard. Panic. Since children might assume parents can forget, misplace and abandon their offspring, do be careful not to say things like "hurry up or I'll leave without you." It's much more reassuring to say: "I can't leave without you, so would you get that coat on?"

ON THE WAY

Sometimes walking with a child under four is awful. He drags behind so that you are nearly walking backwards to keep track of him, or he plunges into the street, or collapses in rage in the middle of an intersection because he is suddenly "too big to hold hands." There's no changing the difference in walking style between adults and children.

Compromises relieve the tension and tend to encourage reason. Choose safe places where your child can run ahead—like from the corner to his home. Plan to go slowly through the most enticing part of your route. Try letting the child who won't hold hands hold your clothing or pocketbook instead. Make an issue only of necessity: he must walk directly home when your arms are full of packages or the baby is screaming for lunch; he must hold hands at the really scary intersections. As rigid rules foster resistance, so flexible ones encourage compliance.

To vary the pace and keep your child headed in the right direction, you can play a follow-the-leader game—taking turns, of course. Take a giant step over a puddle. Run to the end of the block. Walk slowly, fast, hop on one foot. Say what you're doing as your child copies your actions, and encourage him to do the same. When you're sick of this game, or notice that people are staring at you, use the words to tell your child what to do by himself for the rest of the way.

STREET PATTERNS

Children are pulled by the configuration of the landscape around them. They hippity hop the sidewalk squares, circle the hydrant, bump their hand against every post in the railing. If time permits, letting the landscape pull your child this way and that serves as a perfectly good learning experience. It is a physical way of getting the feel of shapes and patterns, and of learning balance and strengthening muscles.

HAND SIGNALS

By four or five years old, most kids get interested in the idea that you can control others' actions by hand signals. They notice policemen bringing huge trucks to a halt, or they see someone commanding silence with a finger to the lips. Hand-signaling a child as you go down the street can be a good game. Use a palm-up hand for STOP, a crooked finger or a beckoning gesture for COME. Make up whatever signals you like for fast, slow, turn, hop, run.

Don't be the boss the whole time. Let your child have his turn.

WINDOW-SHOPPING

Window-shopping is a great pleasure and an intelligent pastime. You wish you had this, your child wishes he had that. (You have different points of view.) Window-shopping this way can help you make the point that neither adults nor children can always have what they see and want—but that people of any age can enjoy wishing and sharing their desires.

Do you see those red shoes way in the back of the window? (He has to locate the object with his own eyes.) I feel like eating all the chocolates in the window. (Some candies are called chocolates.) Do you like the flowered dress or the striped one? (He must identify an object by its patterns.) Do you remember that fire engine we saw in the toy store window yesterday? (He must remember a past event.)

WHAT DO YOU SEE?

When the walking atmosphere seems calm and conversational, play a game of noticing. *What do you see? I see a policeman. What is he wearing? White gloves.*

What's that noise? His whistle. If this conversation leads to talking about why the policeman wears gloves and blows a whistle, fine. If your child's attention is distracted by a jackhammer, fine too. *What does a jackhammer do? Why is the man wearing a hardhat? What will he find under the street?* Noticing leads to curiosity, and curiosity leads to knowledge.

You can also use what you notice for pretend games. You notice a woman carrying a very heavy box. Imagine together what might be in it, and what the woman is like, and where she might be going. Or you see a sneaker on the sidewalk. Who might have lost it, and how, and what is happening now to the single-sneakered owner?

WHICH WAY?

As your child becomes accustomed to the routine of errands, see how well he has learned his territory. Let him lead you by the hand from one stop to another, or tell you which way to go next. You can clarify his sense of direction by mentioning names or numbers of streets, pointing out landmarks, and using the words right and left (though he probably won't understand these concepts yet). You may notice that your child finds his way almost exclusively by landmarks; he does not yet carry a map of his territory in his head. Until a child "sees" the lay of the land as though he were above it, he can become lost by straying only a few feet from his accustomed route. One way to help a child understand space better is to occasionally vary your routes to the same destination. Other activities that help a child develop mapping skills are on pages 97, 130 and 140.

SIGNS

Whether you do errands on foot or by car, you are obeying signs and symbols that your child can learn the meaning of. Show him the words ENTRANCE and

EXIT, or IN and OUT at the supermarket. Maybe he can recognize the words in other stores and choose the right door; or look for the same words in parking lots so he can choose the right path. Let him look for the word EXIT on the highway, and in department stores and apartment buildings. UP and DOWN, STOP and WALK are fairly common signs too.

SIGHT WORDS ON THE STREET

BUS STOP	ONE WAY	MAIL	HOT
TELEPHONE	SUPERMARKET	OPEN	STREET
STOP	WET PAINT	CLOSED	WALK
DON'T WALK	DANGER	COLD	OUT
EXIT	SCHOOL		

The point here is not just to recognize a few words in print, but to understand the utility of written language: a sign tells us what to do.

Many of these "sight" words are taught on Sesame Street and are very useful for your child to know.

Your child can learn to recognize words by the shape of the whole word. He does not have to know how to spell them. This is particularly easy when the words are seen in their proper context; i.e., the word STOP on a stop sign, or the word EXIT over a door.

GROCERY SHOPPING

There are a number of ways to play classification guessing games in the supermarket. Say you are at the dairy case: *What can we find here, milk or spaghetti?* That's the easiest game. A harder game is to ask: *Where is the milk, near the butter or near the tomatoes?* An even harder game is to simply ask where the milk is. Here the child has to organize the form of his answer for himself—*near the butter, in the dairy case,* or *in the back of the store.*

If a child answers incorrectly, by the way, you needn't pounce on his mistake. Once in a while, go ahead and look for spaghetti in the dairy case. Experience is a good teacher.

Label Matching

Save sample labels from items you buy often. Keep the side panel of a rice box or the paper label from your brand of canned beans or the wrapper from your usual soap bar. When you shop, give your child one or two of the sample labels and ask him to find you the box or can that is the same.

For the youngest child, point to two choices and let him show you the right one. Older children can search the shelf area themselves or choose from more alternatives. This game is very good practice for finding patterns that match.

Ernie has found the bananas in his supermarket.

As your child becomes more adept at handling items in the store, he can help you out in ways that require new learning. He can pick out the *largest* cereal box, *three* cans of tomatoes, *square* crackers, or *Crisco* brand oil.

Asking

Knowing how to ask for information is an efficient learning tool. Where you are well known in a store—and if your child is not too shy to do this—let him ask the clerk where to find the soy sauce, or whether he'll have fresh strawberries this weekend. Listen for the answers yourself, and see if your child relays an accurate answer to you.

Getting Change

Paying for and getting change from the purchase of small articles introduces children to the idea of equivalence. This is a difficult idea for preschoolers to grasp. Explain that five pennies are equal to one nickel; two nickels equal a dime. Buying small, inexpensive items provides the clearest lessons in coinage.

Carrying Packages

Children are less likely to be tiresomely playful on the way home from shopping if they have a package to carry, too. Ask the clerk to put something of medium weight and size into a separate bag for your child to carry. Onions or bread are good choices. Be sure to express your gratitude for the help.

Putting Away

Children can learn quite young to be of help to you by putting some groceries away. As usual, a good deal of guidance is needed. Limit the task, and describe it carefully: *Take everything out of this bag, and put it on the table. Could you put the dog food under the sink? Put the cheese in the drawer in the refrigerator. Take all the fruits to the sink. I have to wash them.* As you put things away together, be aware of the words you are using. "Let's put all this stuff away" says less than "Let's put the dog food cans under the sink with the dog bowl."

Unpacking groceries can involve matching, sorting, classifying and counting activities.

Matching: One egg to one hole in the egg container is one-to-one matching. So is one cookie for each child.

Sorting: Emptying bags of all the groceries *except* "all the cans," or "all the milk cartons" is sorting.

Classifying: Putting the cleanser with other cleaning solutions, bologna with other sandwich meats, cinnamon with other spices is classifying.

Counting: "One, two bottles of milk; one, two, three cookies for you," is counting. When a child is just learning to count, be sure he touches each object and moves it into a group as he counts, "five, five apples." Otherwise, he may be just reciting numbers and not learning the idea that the words describe a quantity of objects. Simplify counting also by arranging groups of objects in rows or similar simple patterns rather than in circles or "bunches."

Eleven eggs and one cookie.

Caution:
- *Some cleaning agents you buy at the supermarket are poisonous, and shouldn't be handled by children at all.*

Although the whole process of shopping for groceries and putting the goods away afterwards offers many opportunities for learning, the combination of shopping and child-watching may not be every adult's idea of a good time.

Some children are lousy shoppers. There's that kid who brings the can display crashing into the aisle. There's the one who nags to leave, to eat, to go to the bathroom, to climb into the cart, to climb out again. There's the one who runs wild all over the store so you have to worry whether he's been lost or kidnapped. And there's the routine tantrum thrower.

If you have a child who is not good company when you shop, tell him so. Make it clear you would rather do it alone. Ask a friend to keep an eye on your child (in the playground perhaps, or at home) while you do a few errands. You can reciprocate when your friend needs some time alone. Save heavy shopping for the weekends or a time when someone else can take over child care for a while.

The Count counts eggs.

Joe Mathieu

What if your child asks embarrassing questions in public or makes insulting comments in front of strangers? At the checkout counter, it's common for children to ask where babies come from, to point out a person's large behind, or to ask why that man has no arm. You can't act as though you didn't hear because your child will repeat himself in an even louder voice. And you can't launch into a big discussion on the spot. Be assured that no one is as shocked as you are. Be frank, be brief, and acknowledge the truth.

Where babies come from is an interesting question; you will have time to talk about it when you get home. Yes, that person is nice and big. Yes, the man has only one arm. Later you can explain more to your child. When questions about handicapped people come up, don't make the mistake of assuming that all people with differences are ashamed. Stress instead that no one likes being talked about in public. (Your child would not mind someone noticing his green shoes, but might not like strangers to point and say, "Look at that kid in green shoes!")

What if you discover your child has taken something from a store? Don't leap to the conclusion that he is a thief. Young children don't actually "steal," because they don't yet have a concept of buying. The man in the store is nice. He gives all those things to Mommy. That is what stores are for—to give you what you want. If your child casually takes goods from a store, simply say, "Oh, we didn't pay for that. We have to give the store money for each thing we take. Let's go back and give money for the candy bar." (Of course, if you don't want the child to have the candy, explain your feeling and return the candy bar.) There is no reason even to use the word "steal."

The child who is hazardous when let loose from the grocery cart and must, therefore, ride in the seat, may be content to stay put if he can be the navigator. Let him point which way to turn to get to the meat counter, the vegetables, the checkout area. The game is most effective when you really do as you are told— even if you end up temporarily in the wrong place.

Older children can drive the cart by pushing it for you if they are neither rash nor careless.

LABEL PICTURE "READING"

If you buy a lot of canned or frozen foods all at once, let your child identify what is in each container by "reading" the picture on the label. These pictures are, after all, symbols. They stand for the actual stuff that is in the container.

Sometimes labels show not what is in the container, but what it will become: Mashed pumpkin will become pumpkin pie, powdered gelatin will become gelatin dessert. Helping a child use the label to predict what a substance can be transformed into is valuable too.

WHERE FOODS COME FROM

There's a true story about a three-year-old city child who, with his family, was visiting a farm in Indiana. He ran into the kitchen with a freshly pulled carrot in his hand and said, "Mom, you won't *believe* where I got this!"

Where do eggs come from?

Where does milk come from?

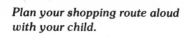

*Plan your shopping route aloud
with your child.*

Fishermen have to catch the fish before it gets to the market.

In these days of packaged foods, the source of what we eat can surprise—and sometimes shock—a child. Carrots grow underground in dirt. Meat is really animals. Milk comes from cows, just as it comes from the breasts of women. An egg comes out of a chicken. Some eggs have chickens inside! These facts, once so rudimentary to children, now strike them as miraculous, yucchy, or untrue.

Besides explaining the source of common foods, try to let your child see for himself: beet seeds grown in a pot, a friend nursing her baby, a whole chicken as you cut it into portions, a bird's nest with eggs that hatch into baby birds.

Many cookbooks have recipes for making common foods such as bread, butter, soup, cheese, pickles, peanut butter, and jelly. If you're not big on cooking, even the simple experience of squeezing your own orange juice offers a homey, old-time security. It isn't magic. We can "make" food ourselves.

MEASURING

Save cash register tapes for measuring activities. There are several ways to use them. You can compare lengths: *Is this tape longer or shorter than this one?* Or compare a tape to another object: *Is this tape longer than your arm? Shorter than your foot? The same length as a spaghetti box?*

Just for fun, stick or tape or glue the lengths of cash register tapes together into one long piece. Roll it up. Add to the roll each time you get another piece of tape. Eventually the roll will be long enough to measure whole rooms with. It would also make an excellent supply of scribble paper or a prop for any pretend game that requires "tickets."

See page 167 for other grocery "trash" to save for creative activities.

Adults are able to think of "how long" or "how heavy" in terms of units—more inches means longer, more pounds means heavier. Young children cannot measure things by units. Their idea of measurement is based on simple comparison. The new shoe is longer than the old one, the teddy bear is bigger than the baby, my suitcase is heavier than yours. There is a specific order in which a child learns to compare the sizes of objects.

First, he learns "same as": Ask him to find two cans that are the same size, then a "different" size. Next he learns larger and smaller (or lighter and heavier, thinner and thicker): Ask him to find a can larger than this one, or smaller than this one. Then he learns the concepts of largest, smallest (or lightest and heaviest, or thinnest and thickest). Get out three cans and help him arrange them in order from smallest to largest.

The big step to using units will not come until your child can use numbers because our adult sort of measurement is actually a numerical comparison: a six-foot man is six times longer than a ruler.

See pages 75 and 141 for other measuring activities.

Oscar-the-Grouch's country cousin comes for a visit.

VISITING

Although this section is about the social event of adults and children getting together, you deserve your own social life without children in tow.

Using baby-sitters is healthful for both of you. You need to get away from your child sometimes, and your child needs to learn to function during your absence.

Check the competence of a potential baby-sitter by calling other families he or she has worked for. Ask the baby-sitter questions that will reveal his or her style: *Do you play with children? What kinds of play do you like? How have you dealt with crying? Fussy eating? Wildness?* (It is only fair to warn a baby-sitter of predictable problems.)

Write down what you expect done: dishes washed, bedtime story read, night-light left on, window opened. Show the location of important things: the telephone, Band-Aids, supper. Write down the doctor's telephone number, and a number where you can be reached.

When you find a baby-sitter who pleases both you and your child, stick with that one if possible. Adjusting to one person after another is trying for everybody.

Most normal children are sometimes frightened at being separated from their parents. The loss, even for a few minutes or hours, is felt almost physically, as though part of the child were missing. (You may recall this feeling from childhood, or you may have felt something similar the first time you left your newborn baby.) Children begin to feel less separation anxiety as they become able to do simple things for themselves. The ability to feed oneself (like putting together a jelly sandwich) or soothe oneself (like being allowed to play records or rest on Mommy's bed) make a child feel less helpless, less lonely. Be sure your baby-sitter does not hamper your child's abilities. With your child present, explain: *He can bathe himself, he can pour his own milk, he is allowed to use the quilt on my bed.*

A child who remains inconsolable long after you have left him with the baby-sitter is not trying to control you. He may be afraid that you could leave him forever. To help such a child, give him brief and very reassuring experiences of separation. Play hide-and-seek around the house. Arrange for five-minute or fifteen-minute absences: *You will stay with Grandma while I get some gas in the car. Mrs. Henderson will stay with you while I take the laundry down.* Visit other people's homes, and leave just to put a dime in the meter, buy an ice cream at the corner. These very short separations demonstrate that you are to be trusted. You will come back exactly when you said you would.

Adult Visits

If you take your child when you visit an adult friend not accustomed to children, prepare the child for it. Explain that your friend has no children, no toys, and perhaps no peanut butter, either. Look around for a toy to bring with you. Choose one that he has forgotten about, or an all-time favorite. The toy will have to compete with the novelty of your friend's bric-a-brac. Bring a book, crayons and paper, and bring a snack along, too. Don't plan for long visits at first.

Stay longer than planned only if all three of you are enthusiastic about the idea. A parent pleading "just a while longer, Dear," is as irritating to a child as "just a little more, Mom," is to you.

Politeness

Only the simplest social graces are possible for preschool children. When an adult comes to visit, learning to say hello and use the person's name are more important for your child than shaking hands or making formal introductions. Many children are too shy (frightened) of new adults to be even this direct or gracious. That shouldn't prevent you from being polite to your child. If he is clinging to your skirts, or covering his face, or even if he has just fled the scene, you can say, "Hello, Mrs. Friend, this is my daughter Jane."

Simplicity relieves the tension, and provides a model for the easy way to meet new people. It doesn't matter that Jane can't say hello yet. The same goes for the child who only gives a glare in the newcomer's direction, or roars at her, or makes sure to bump her as he dashes by. The behavior can be talked over later, but for now plain politeness will work better than a lecture to an already angry child.

What if your child disrupts adult visits? Is he doing it on purpose? Maybe he wants all the attention. (And he is probably getting it. Even your annoyance is an attention that may be preferable to being left out.)

Before you try to solve this problem, examine your own motives honestly. Often we secretly want our child to be the center of attention. We start a visit in a good mood—showing him off, thinking he is cute, boasting in his presence. While we soak up our friend's admiration, the child comes to the logical conclusion that he is the purpose of the visit. Everyone is so interested in him. If this seems to be what is happening, sacrifice the admiration and treat your child more offhandedly from the first moments of the visit.

Big Bird has to learn that sometimes it's not polite to interrupt.

Be more practical about visiting times. Invite friends at nap-time, during your child's favorite TV show, or while he is visiting a friend of his own. Don't emphasize your interest in your child. (Don't ask him to dress up specially, or show off his new trick.) Do emphasize your interest in your friend. (While your child is resting, your friend is going to tell you about her vacation. You really want to hear her.)

What if children interrupt while you are talking on the phone? It may be because they are jealous. The phone call has taken you away from them. Save your lengthy calls for times when your child is away or asleep. If your call is important, prepare your child by telling him whom you are calling, why, and for how long. Ask if there is anything he needs before you start the call. If you like, let him say hello and then hand you the receiver. If he presses his demands loudly during the call, sometimes it may be easier to explain again that you can't make him a bologna, pickle, and mayonnaise sandwich while you are talking. (If he has been quietly crayoning and only wants to show you the picture, it is less trouble to look, respond, and then get back to your call.) After the call, perhaps you should remind the child that he could have waited until you finished your call. It will take quite a while to teach your child that interrupting phone calls is not allowable behavior, but the message will eventually penetrate.

One more word on socializing with other adults: much as you and your child may both share the notion that no one is as wonderful as Mom and Dad, forming relationships with other adults is important to a child's development. Never mind that your mother-in-law is too free with the cookies, or that your husband's old school buddy plays rough. The very fact that Mrs. Jackson fusses over dirty fingernails (and you don't) introduces your child to a new idea: different people impose different restrictions; different people allow different freedoms. Getting used to these differences—and finding pleasure in them—helps your child to feel comfortable for short periods away from your side.

Child Visits

When you go to visit a child's friend, bring along a toy your child doesn't care for anymore. His friend may be intrigued with it, and more likely to share his own toys.

When a child's friend is coming to your house, you may wish to put away toys your child does not want to share, and leave them hidden during the visit. This is not selfishness. Certain of a child's toys are so closely identified with his sense of self that he cannot allow them to be used by others. You might feel the same outrage if someone were to use your underwear, or help himself to your toothbrush. There are many possessions adults do not share with visitors.

Many visits between preschoolers escalate into wildness. At the first sign that play is getting out of control (crashes, high-pitched voices), step in. Offer a snack. Ask one of the children to help you with something—finding a certain record, arranging blocks, washing the doll's clothes. Or demonstrate a simple game: put

Ernie and Bert share a chair.

an empty can on the floor for them to roll a ball at, or give them a carton to throw a beanbag into. Hide a teddy bear in the room, and let them look for it. (Make it easy so they don't rip the place apart.) All of these suggestions give a child an organized way to wind down from wildness. See Chapters Three and Four for quiet, creative activities several children can enjoy together.

Cleanup

Two kids in two hours can leave a colossal mess. If you wait until the friend goes home to say, "Now get this place cleaned up," your child will feel mistreated. After all, it took two to mess it up. Instead, plan a cleanup time fifteen minutes before the end of the visit. All of you clean up together. This technique has an added advantage: it gives fair warning of the end of the visit. If this strikes you as too blunt or too impolite a way to treat guests, alleviate the pain by offering a snack after cleanup.

Even Oscar sometimes cleans up his own mess.

What if your child never gets along with a friend during a visit? He fights, never shares, can't take turns. Try a different sort of visiting. Ask his friend over to watch a TV special, or to take a walk, or to have lunch. Then the friend goes home. Or try this: Invite a friend for a clay party, a coloring party, a cut-and-paste party. Provide enough materials for both children. When the children are finished with the activity—whether it's five or fifty minutes later—the party is over. The friend goes home. Both methods avoid use of the child's toys, define the activity and make the visit short.

TAKING TURNS

Help your child learn to take turns by teaching him simple reciprocal games. You hide an object, he finds it. Then he hides it, you find it. Set up a large wastebasket as a target. Take turns throwing balled-up pieces of paper into it. Throw or roll a ball back and forth. Place two lengths of string on the floor to form a "river" to jump over. You set the width for him, he sets the width for you. Take turns pulling a card from the deck, and saying whether it is red or black (or hearts, spades, diamonds, clubs; or the numerals if he is ready for that).

If there is one of these games your child enjoys, suggest it to him when he has a friend over. Taking turns is much easier when the game is an old favorite.

You will not always like the children your child likes—the bully, the baby, the boaster and the cusser. Will such friends be a "bad influence" on your child? There is a tough fact to face here: your child is nobody's victim. He has chosen this friend so he can participate in the friend's personality and behavior. The friend is an expression of himself. He does not have to act so big with his babyish friend. He does not have to take responsibility when the bully is his boss. Or he does not have to be so good with the wild kid or the cusser. Removing the friend will not remove your child's need. Let him be a baby more, or let him be bad and angry more. He is doing the best he can to fill his needs; he could use a little help.

What if you *still* can't stand your child's friend? Then state the truth. *I don't like Sally's swearing. You can see her in school, you can play with her outside, but I don't want her in the house where I have to hear her swearing.* If this information is instantly relayed to Sally (or worse, to her parents), take the bull by the horns. Tell Sally or her parents that swearing bothers you, but you really think the two children should be friends if they like each other; that this seemed to you the best solution for everyone.

JUNK TOYS FOR OUTDOORS

Children may have a more difficult time socializing with their own contemporaries than with the older generations. Because of the difficulties, outdoors is the best early meeting ground for children. Whether it's a backyard or a playground, outdoors is more neutral territory than inside your home. To encourage more play, less argument, supply quantities of old or broken toys (a folding shopping cart or child's wagon helps haul them to the playground). Even a wheelless truck or the last few pieces of a construction set will provide novelty to other children. Surprise everyone with a collection of Popsicle sticks or frozen-juice cans for the children's sandbox, or with lengths of clothesline to drag behind their trikes. These quantities of novel objects offered in neutral territory ease the tension of early group play.

Caution:
- *Avoid swallowables, splintery or sharp objects, cans with jagged edges.*

FIRST PLAY

At first, children play side by side, but not together. One builds blocks, the other pushes cars but, literally and figuratively, no path connects the building to the vehicles. Play, at this point, is keeping company. Later—perhaps school age—children begin to play cooperatively. The building becomes a garage, the cars drive in and out of it. The transition from keeping company to cooperative playing is not smooth. It may look like this: Johnny builds a castle in the sandpile. Susan kicks it down. Such overtures may be invitations to play, just as the wrestling and teasing between young adolescents is a cautious prelude to boy–girl relationships. In a moment, Johnny may help to kick the castle down and Susan may help to rebuild it.

RESOLVING CONFLICTS

When two toddlers both want the same toy, both tug. One tugs harder and gets the toy. The other lets go and cries. By five or six, an experienced child, faced with the same conflict, can draw upon a host of alternatives. He can hit, bribe, threaten, beg and steal; he can distract, trade, share, take turns, appeal to an adult, and even appeal to reason or to justice. How has he learned such a flexible and large vocabulary of alternatives? The most direct methods—hitting, steal-ing—are learned without much adult help. But the negotiations by which he settles conflicts—the deals and compromises that are a mark of his maturity—are learned from adults and from older children in the course of everyday events.

The following are examples of common types of negotiation: *You always get the front seat—That's not fair* is an appeal to justice. *I'll give you the truck if you give me the bulldozer* is a trade. *There are enough crayons for both of us* is sharing. *When you finish that picture, let me use the crayons* is taking turns. *If you take a nap, I'll buy you an ice cream* is a bribe. *If you don't eat that spinach, there'll be no dessert for you* is a threat. *You can't use my lipstick, but you can use the powder* is a compromise. *Swallow your medicine so you can feel better* is an appeal to reason.

Listen to yourself as you attempt to resolve conflicts with your child. You may find you would like him to learn some kinds of negotiations rather than others.

Parents who consistently defend their children against the abrasions of others may prevent the growth of negotiating tactics. Unless you really want a child who always runs to you for help (*Mommy! He took my wagon! Mommy, he won't let me play with him!*), let a certain amount of conflict prevail during the sandbox years. Offer suggestions but defend your child only when he is certain to get himself clobbered with a heavy object. Pushing, shoving, and sand in the hair are helpful experiences. They prove there must be a better way.

BATHTIME

Some things, probably most things, are not learned from lessons. You don't teach balance to a baby learning to walk. You can't explain to him that walls are solid. He feels these things out for himself. Even after a child can understand

language, you don't teach him the fact of gravity, the meanings of human facial expression, or the attributes of sand. They are learned intuitively by dropping many things, by watching many faces, by playing in the sand. Free exploration is a powerful learning tool. Any infant mammal—a rat, a puppy, or a baby—deprived of opportunity to explore, grows up not only less knowledgeable but less intelligent than others. Although specific bathtime activities are suggested here, for the most part let your child be. Warm baths are lovely, slow baths are luxurious, and water is itself entrancing. Sure, supply things to play with in the bath; of course, be around for safety's sake and company; and wash your child at the end of the bath. But for most of the time, let him explore water as he will.

Bathtub Accessories

These are common nonbreakable objects that are particularly fascinating as bathtub toys:

Drip-type metal coffeepots (the bottom is good for filling and pouring, the top and middle sections let water drip through at different rates, and all the parts fit together).

Plastic basting tube (remove the rubber bulb if your child squirts water on the floor. Water will still stream out the small end).

Plastic eyedroppers.

Plastic containers of any size and shape (look for small plastic bottles, larger detergent and food containers. If you punch holes in the sides of a large container, water will spurt out like a fountain).

Sponges.

Corks, wooden spoons, wood scraps, plastic egg cartons, capped plastic bottles (they all float; some act as rafts).

Lengths of plastic tubing (sold for aquariums at pet stores and good for bubbling underwater).

Eggbeaters.

Suction cups (the ones that are used to tip children's arrows; they stick to the tiles and tub sides).

Since we are recommending so many awkwardly sized and shaped bathtub toys, here are some storage suggestions:

Nylon net bags, sold either as shopping bags or for holding lingerie in the washing machine.

Small plastic baskets, sold as laundry baskets.

Plastic milk bottle boxes, which your grocery or milkman may or may not give or sell to you.

Water Words

Pour, spill, sprinkle, splash, spurt, squirt, drip, dribble, flow, flood, trickle, spray. Each of these words describes a different way that water behaves—and each word sounds like what it describes. When you use them, you increase both a child's vocabulary and the accuracy of his thinking on a particular subject, water.

Hot and Cold

Let your child help adjust the temperature of his bath. Show him the *H* and *C* on the faucets and explain that they stand for HOT and COLD. Teach him he must always turn the cold water on first. Then let him hold his hand under the cold water, and adjust the hot until he gets the temperature he likes. Let him try to get the water hotter or colder. This is more complicated to him than to you. Most likely, he will add more hot water to make the water hotter, more cold water to make it colder. He won't understand that one could also decrease the cold water to increase the temperature, and vice versa. Also, in spite of the arrow your faucet may have to indicate direction, he will quickly get confused as to which way is off, which on. Needless to say, he should experiment with the faucets only when you are there to supervise.

Thermometer

A thermometer is too difficult for preschoolers to read, but they are able to observe the mercury (or red dye) column rising and falling. Use a baby's bath thermometer. Hold it under the stream of water as your child adjusts the temperature (this may be easier at the sink than in the bath). Ask for predictions: *Will the line get longer or shorter when you turn on the hot water?* Once he learns that "longer" (or higher) means hotter, you can explain better why you take his temperature when he is sick, and how you can tell how warm or cool it is outside just by looking at a thermometer.

Caution:

- *Both the glass and the mercury in thermometers are dangerous. Supervise your child's thermometer experiments.*

Bubble Baths

Some bubble bath solutions are drying to the skin; they may cause itchiness or even rashes. Try a bubble bath out once, and watch for reactions before you do it again. If your child tolerates the solution well, a bubble bath now and again is a pleasant variation on daily bathtime. It offers a new "stuff" to explore; it gets a child clean without scrubbing; and it says baths are for pleasure.

Scented Soap

Though more expensive than popular-brand soaps, scented soaps offer a particular learning experience. Perhaps for a special present, buy a few bars of soap with different, distinctive scents—lemon, pine, rose. Let your child sniff each bar. Tell him the name of each as he smells it; let him choose which he wants to bathe with. After he is familiar with all three, see if he can sniff out pine or lemon or roses with his eyes shut.

Floating

Give your child the top of a plastic egg carton to use as a raft. Give him a variety of objects to load into it. Some should be light, like plastic animals. Some should be heavy, like a full shampoo bottle or a metal truck. As he loads the raft, see if he can guess when it will sink (*Will it sink if I put the hairbrush in? If I add the soap?*). Try the same sort of game by floating an empty bottle, then filling it

with water until it sinks. Such experiences teach the rough notion that weight has something to do with floating and sinking.

Preswimming Activities

Fear of water prevents many children from enjoying beach and pool, and later interferes with the process of learning to swim. The bathtub, being a friendly, comfy warm sort of place, can be a good spot for preswimming activities that can help your child feel more sure of himself in larger bodies of water.

- Let your child blow bubbles through a plastic straw. Ask him if he can do the same thing with his mouth. Blowing bubbles with his mouth will get at least part of his face into the water.
- While your child covers his eyes, put a small object (a marble, a plastic flower) in the bottom of the tub of clear water. See if he can put his face in the water and find the toy. He has to open his eyes under the water to find it.
- Crook your arm comfortably under the back of your child's neck. Let his body float free. If he is relaxed, you can move him a bit in the water to get him even more used to the sensation of floating.

Caution:
- *Keep an eye on bathtub play. Young children shouldn't be left alone in the water.*

Bathtub Fears

Unreasonable as it seems to adults, a lot of children are afraid they will be sucked down the bathrub drain (and sucked into vacuum cleaners, or flushed down toilets, too!). Other children fear that the rush of water coming from the tap cannot be stopped; it will rush out and overflow all over. Both are normal (and normally transient) fears. For such children, don't pull the plug until they are safely out of the tub. And don't leave the water running while you leave for a few moments. Stay in the bathroom to "protect" your child, even though you don't share his fears. Both fears can be helped by experiences that are not scary: turning faucets on and off, for instance; and when the bath is empty, finding out that a doll or a little plastic animal cannot fall down the drain.

Do not, however, try to allay these fears in a child who has never expressed them. You could arouse an anxiety that didn't exist.

"Give Me Your Foot"

After an interval of relaxing and playing, it is time to get down to the business of washing. Ask for each part of your child's body in turn. Ask him to look up, so you can reach his neck; turn around, so you can get to his back; stand up, so you can wash his legs; lift an arm, so you can wash under it. Not only does this help a child learn the names of parts of his body, it also gives him a sense of control. His body is not grabbed; it is his to offer.

What if your child is genuinely annoyed by your physical attentions as you bathe him? Respect his feelings. Except for face and neck, a good soak in the bathtub removes most of the dirt. The rest comes off on the towel.

Teach your child to wash his face and neck with a damp washcloth in front of the mirror and under your supervision.

Shiny Clean

Good grooming habits arise more easily from pleasure than from necessity. It is usually a matter of indifference to a child whether he is clean or dirty. But the process of becoming clean—the warm water, good smelling soap, fluffy towels, caresses and compliments—impress on a child's emotions the niceness of cleanliness.

Add to the pleasure whatever you can—baby powder for its scent and softness, a dab of perfume once in a while. Please your child with hairstyles that appeal to him, with nightclothes that feel luscious to the skin. Buy pretty or even novelty toothbrushes, and find a toothpaste that tastes good to him. And when all is done, compliment him; he is so shiny clean.

Nudity

Unless you yourself feel uncomfortable about the matter, baths for two young children of the opposite sex are all right because they are informative. The preschoolers get a chance to look at each other's different genitals in a casual, everyday context. Sexual curiosity is a fact of life, and you may find such casual encounters helpful in satisfying that curiosity.

No one can decide for you whether or not you will appear nude in front of your children. There are legitimate warnings from psychologists both about too much exposure to adult nudity, and about too little. Here are the arguments so you can consider the issues in the light of your own modesty (or lack of it) for yourself:

Children who never see nudity in early childhood are ill-prepared for the shock of sexual difference. They assume everyone is made like they are. They may come to another conclusion, too; since parents hide their bodies, nudity must be wrong or bad.

On the other hand, children who are exposed to parental nudity continually and intimately, such as in baths with the parent of the opposite sex, or naked cuddling together, may leap to just as unwarranted a conclusion: the parent is offering sexual attentions to the child.

Either extreme can place a great burden on children and may hamper their ability to deal with their own sexuality later.

Many parents are able to find a good compromise with incidental nudity that a child normally encounters as he wanders in and out of bedrooms and bathrooms.

Shampoos

What if your child is terrified of shampoos? Or screams when his face is washed? His panic is real. He feels as if he is suffocating when you cover his face with the washcloth. He feels as if he is drowning when you pour water over his head. Wash a frightened child's face at the very end of his bath. Use a small square of sponge, or the corner of a washcloth. Rub only a small area at a time without ever covering nose, eyes or mouth. Even better, let your child look in the mirror and try to do the job himself.

You could substitute "dry" shampoos, sold in drugstores, for regular shampoo (although this is only a temporary solution). Dry shampoos are rubbed into the hair and simply brushed out. Or use no-tears shampoo, but at the kitchen sink instead of in the bath. Your child can either lie down on his back on the counter with his head over the sink, or sit in a high chair with his back to the sink. Wet his hair with a sponge. Use the sponge to rinse the soap from around his face. Rinse the rest of his head from a plastic pitcher or with a sink spray attachment.

Whether you use the counter or the high chair method, let your child hold a towel in his hands to wipe his face with when he wishes. Encourage him to keep his eyes open (as long as his head is tipped back so that soap drains away from his eyes), so that he feels he is in better control of what is happening to him. He could also hold a folded damp washcloth over his eyes, and peek out from under it from time to time.

Mop-up

If all these pleasures and experiments have left you with an inch of water on the floor, join the club. It happens in the best of homes. Next time, try less water in the bathtub. Pull the shower curtain nearly closed, and be sure it hangs inside the tub. And if the flood comes anyway, keep two large floor sponges and a plastic pail at hand. Kids can clean up water, too.

MEDICINE CHEST

The medicine chest is a dangerous place to keep medicine. Even a toddler can climb the sink to get to the "candy" aspirin. Use the medicine chest for innocuous items such as toothpaste and bandages. Put medicines up high on a closet shelf, or even in a locked box, until you are sure your child has grown out of the temptation to taste forbidden pills. Keep razor blades in a safe place, too. Don't forget that the solutions used to clean toilet bowls and unclog drains are lethal, and so are dishwasher detergents. Even powdered cleansers are dangerous. Don't store any cleaning solutions under the sink. Of course, this advice will also free up space for storing bathtime toys!

MEALTIME

A large chunk of each day in a three-year-old's life is centered around food. He accompanies you as you shop for it and prepare it. Much of the time, his mouth is full of it. So, even though grocery shopping has its own section in this chapter, mealtime contains an unusual number of activities.

Parents with small kitchens may find all this activity impossible. Without ample floor space or generous counters, it's just too hard to share the kitchen with young children. Nevertheless, read through the ideas. They may not work out for you in the kitchen at mealtimes, but you may be able to adapt them to other times of the day or other parts of your home.

Grover tosses a salad.

Toward the end of the section are suggestions for the meal itself, from table-setting to ways to help a child through the physical and social demands of the family meal, to after-meal games. Not every family has the luxury, of course, of sitting down to a meal together every day of the week; but perhaps you should try to do it as often as possible. The give-and-take as food is offered and conversation shared is experience in simple socializing.

As is often the case, new learnings involve new risks. If you let your child set the table, there will be broken dishes. If you let him help with mixing, there will be spills. How far you wish to go in allowing the games and learnings suggested here is up to you. No single experience is irreplaceable; and for any experience, many other activities elsewhere in this book can substitute.

The risks you really cannot subject your child to without your best efforts to protect him are burns and cuts.

Stove Safety

Safety is better taught by carefully managed experiences than by lectures and warnings. Take the usual precautions. Use back burners as often as you can. Turn handles toward the rear of the stove. But also demonstrate the heat of cooking to your child. Move a pot lid slightly to one side and let your child see the steam emerge (watch out for steam burns, though). Show your child how hot a frying pan is by carefully letting a few drops of cold water drip onto it. The almost explosive sizzle and pop will impress him. Develop a loud warning system for the times when you must carry hot pots or boiling foods from stove to sink. Shout "CLEAR THE WAY!" or "HOT FOODS COMING THROUGH!" A gamelike quality to the ritual will encourage your child to scurry out of harm's way.

Electric burners are especially dangerous to children. Kids understand well enough not to touch them when they are red, but many children have been badly burned by touching the burners when they are hot, but black. Show your child that you are turning off a red-hot burner. Let him watch as the color fades. Then hold his hand high over the heat from the burner so that he can feel that it is still very hot.

Dangerous objects such as knives are better used by your child openly, under your supervision, than used for his secret experiments. If you would like to teach your child to use a knife safely (after he is four years old), show him how to hold one to cut soft things—hand on the handle only, cutting down through the object toward the table or counter top. Give your reason: Cutting with knives is not *bad*, but it is dangerous. It is your job to keep him safe.

Kitchen Jobs

Jobs a three-year-old might be able to handle in the kitchen are:

Arranging bread, crackers, or other simple foods on a plate. (Try baked potatoes, too, as a safe way to teach a child how to use potholders. Dump the potatoes out of their baking dish first, so that there is no danger of a burn.)

Sharing out portions (one cupcake for each person, two carrot sticks).

Preparing salad, especially tearing up lettuce leaves and mixing the undressed greens. (This is best done with hands, well washed, of course.)

Slicing soft foods—such as cooked potatoes for potato salad, bananas for dessert—with a table knife.

Stirring ingredients for puddings, gelatin desserts, boxed cake mixes.

Pouring premeasured ingredients into a bowl or pot.

Spread, Slice, Chop, Beat, Measure

These are kitchen jobs that help a child learn to coordinate his ten sticky, stubby fingers:

Peel the skin off a very big carrot (or just scrub, if carrot is young). Then let

Buffy Sainte-Marie finds kitchen jobs that Big Bird can do.

your child continue to peel all he wants. He can eat the slivers he makes. Instead of bread sandwiches, offer firm crackers like Melba toast rounds or thick rye crackers. Let your child use a butter knife to spread them with something soft— room temperature butter or cream cheese, apple butter, or peanut butter.

Children can chop a few pieces of something like apple in a chopping bowl. The chopped apple makes a nice snack. Beating eggs is an old childhood favorite, but use your biggest, heaviest bowl and only a little egg or batter.

As you measure out ingredients, think of ways your child could participate. If he can't pour milk yet, he could get his eyes to counter level and tell you when the milk has reached the top mark in the measuring cup. If he can't do the final measuring of sifted flour, he might be able to manage the rough measuring before sifting. And he can count teaspoonfuls with you, feel the weight of the roast, and say whether one bunch of carrots looks like enough for everyone. If you give your child these experiences early, you can count on real help in measuring later.

What if your child is so clumsy or so messy that you can't stand his preparing foods? He can use the practice, but you can use substitutes for food. Let him beat soapsuds in a metal or plastic bowl in the sink. He can practice spreading paste on small bits of cardboard with a butter knife, chop play dough in a chopping bowl, and slice up clay bananas. If you object to using your own kitchen tools for craft materials, tag sales (garage sales) and thrift shops are good places to look for inexpensive, used kitchen tools.

What's Cooking?

When food is cooking, but your child can't see into the pots, play a scent discrimination game. Ask, *What's cooking?* Some smells are learned easily—

Guy Smiley, Sesame Street Game Show host, introduces a TV cooking game.

Super-Grover's super sense of smell sometimes gets him into trouble.

bacon is an easy one, and so are onion, hamburger, and spaghetti sauce. If your child can't or won't guess—or if he answers wrong—sniff the pot together (being careful not to get steam-scalded noses!) and take a peek at what the food is.

Some children love to sniff at things, and can become adept at identifying many smells. Try having your child close his eyes and sniff at herbs and spices. Distinctive ones to start with are garlic salt, cinnamon, and tarragon. The easier way to play is to name the smell he is to identify, then give him a choice of two. The harder way is to ask him to name each substance as he sniffs it.

Sugar and Salt

When you adjust the amount of sugar in lemonade or the amount of salt in a soup, let your child taste it and then act on his judgment. *Is the lemonade too sour? Does it need a little sugar? Is the soup salty enough?* Then let him taste the juice or soup again after an adjustment has been made.

Sharpening any of a child's senses sharpens his ability to take in information from the world around him. Asking for his judgment lets him use the information he takes in.

What Happens Next?

What happens next is an association game to do with cause and effect. *I'm whipping the cream. What happens next? I'm putting butter in the frying pan. What happens next?* If predictions like cream becoming stiff or butter melting are beyond your child now, play the game with more obvious cause-and-effect relationships, and use easier words. *I'm opening a can of soup. Guess what we're having for lunch?*

Shape Sandwiches

Use sandwiches or toast to teach a child shapes such as circle, square, rectangle, and triangle. Tell him you're going to have toast triangles this morning. Let him see you cut your toast. Ask him what shape he wants. Show him that you can cut rectangles (three thin ones make this harder shape more obvious), or squares. You can even cut circles with a cookie cutter. Use the same words to describe the shapes of other foods, such as cookies and crackers, carrot slices, pieces of cheese and cake.

Color Cubes

Vegetable dyes are relatively inexpensive colors for experimenting. Empty an ice cube tray and refill it with water in the kitchen sink. Let your child use the tiny drip bottles that some vegetable dyes come in to mix drops of color into the ice tray compartments. When you have a moment free from your kitchen work, mention the name of a color he has made, or suggest a mixing experiment. *Let's put a drop of red into the yellow cube and see what happens.*

Caution:
• *Some children may be allergic to food colorings, either on the skin or eaten.*

Water-Glass Sounds

Quite delicate experiments with tone discrimination can be done if you have a group of several identical glass tumblers or highball glasses. Start with two. Set the experiment up next to the kitchen sink. Fill one glass two-thirds full of water, the other only one-third full. Let your child hit the rim of each with the edge of a butter knife or a pencil. Which glass makes a higher sound? Give your child a small pitcher of water and experiment with him to see if he can get both glasses to sound the same by adding water or by pouring some out. Let him fool around until he discovers that the more water, the higher the sound; the less water, the lower the sound.

Bottle Game

If you see that your child enjoys pouring water from one container to another, try this experiment: Find an eight-ounce plastic baby bottle and a half-pint-size food container. Both hold eight ounces of water. Fill the containers with water colored with a few drops of vegetable dye. Pretend it is juice. Ask your child which one he wants—he can have the one with more juice. Young children will think the baby bottle holds the most juice; it is "bigger" (taller) than the other container. Pour the juice out of the food container. Let your child see you pour the remaining colored water from the baby bottle into the food container. *Now is there as much juice as you had in this baby bottle?* (He will perceive it as less.) Pour it back again. To your child, the juice has become more again, since the column of liquid is higher.

Your child won't yet give up this apparently unreasonable opinion, but many such contradictory experiences will finally make him question his perception of size.

The reason, by the way, that young children can't compare volumes is that to do so they would have to consider two dimensions simultaneously: the base of the bottle in relation to the height of the bottle. The ability to think relatively doesn't develop until a child is into elementary school. During the preschool years, children learn to compare either the width of objects or the height of objects, but cannot consider both dimensions at once.

Just for fun, try convincing your child that a friend of his can be both bigger and younger than he. To young children, "years old" is a measurement of size; many are in fact bitterly disappointed when they fail to become "bigger" on their birthday. The misunderstanding is caused not only by our sloppy use of the word big (*Oh, you're three? why you're a big boy now!*), but by the child's difficulty in considering two dimensions that vary in relation to each other. Just as he is certain a taller bottle holds more than a shorter one (no matter how wide each may be), so a bigger person must be more years (no matter what anyone says!).

Busy Beans

There are times when children insist on being underfoot, and you have no job you could stand them sharing. Here are a few activities that might keep a child busy at the kitchen table or on the floor in a corner for as long as half an hour:

Get out an empty egg carton and several dozen beans of different varieties— kidney beans, chick-peas, limas. Mix them all up and let your child sort them into compartments in the egg carton.

Using the dried beans or different shapes of macaroni (elbows, bowties, shells and wheels), let your child make designs.

If he knows any letters of the alphabet, straight and curved macaroni shapes can be used to form most of the letters.

Spill a layer of raw rice into a roasting pan. Your child can draw pictures in the rice by pulling his finger through it.

Sugar cubes make good miniature building blocks.

Sound-Discrimination Shakers

Use either empty cylindrical cereal boxes or any other small boxes to make sound-discrimination shakers. Collect identical containers until you have at least three. Put a dozen dried beans in each of two containers, a tablespoon of rice in the other. Close the lids (but don't glue them for this game). See if your child can find the two that sound the same by shaking them. He can peek inside after he has guessed.

If you accumulate as many as six containers, you can make three pairs for a matching game. Vary the sounds by using a pencil stub, a few coins, sand, dry leaves—each time putting the same object or substance into two containers. *Before you test your child on his ability to match them, however, shake the boxes yourself to be sure you can easily hear the differences and match the pairs.*

Jellies and Glops

Substances with a peculiar feel to them can keep a child busy while you cook. Two particularly peculiar ones are double-strength gelatin, and moistened cornstarch. Mix two envelopes of unflavored gelatin into a cup of cold water. Heat in a saucepan until the gelatin melts. Add another cup of cold water, and pour the mixture into a pie plate. Chill it in the refrigerator until it hardens. The result is a big round of rubbery, transparent gelatin that can be lifted from the plate in one piece, cut, torn, jiggled and mushed by your child.

Or put a few tablespoons of cornstarch into a cup and add cold water, drop by drop, until the cornstarch is a thick paste. When the paste is squeezed in your child's hands, it will feel dry and crumble. But as he relaxes his grip, it will liquify and ooze from between his fingers. Both these satisfying substances are not harmful if eaten, and they are easy to clean up.

Snacks

There is probably no such thing as a child who prefers only three meals a day. Stomach capacities are small, muscular activity is high, and the need for multiple pick-me-up snacks is real. Besides the usual sandwich or fruit, here are some snack ideas that supply good nutrition, are fun to eat, and easy enough for many children to prepare by themselves between regular mealtimes:

Shelled hard-boiled egg: Let your child slice it in an egg slicer, and pour a little mound of salt onto his plate to dip each slice in.

Cold cooked beans: Your child can spear them with a fork—dipping each first into a puddle of ketchup.

Cheese cubes and crackers.

Crackers and peanut butter.

Celery sticks, carrot sticks or other raw vegetables dipped in room temperature cream cheese.

Miniature boxes of raisins.

Setting the Table

Think of a table as a game board. The object of the game is to place the counters (napkins, plates, forks) in certain positions (places) for a certain number of players (the family). The game involves several mathematical skills.

When a child can say "one plate for Daddy, one plate for me," he can match "one to one." Ask him to put on the table a plate for each person, or a plate for each chair. Let him continue to match one to one with a napkin for each plate, a fork for each napkin.

Counting is only a harder kind of matching; a numeral is matched to each object—one for the first plate, two for the next. As your child puts the plates out, count for him as he places them. Later, count the plates with him before he places them. Later still, ask him to count out the plates himself until he has reached the correct number.

Until a child is at least of school age—and usually much older—he can't remember much more than plate, napkin, glass, fork, knife, spoon. Good practice at remembering even that much is to check the table after it is set. "Is there a glass for each person?"

One More Place: Don't forget that when you have a friend over to share a meal, there is *one more* place to set. When a member of the family is not at home, there is *one fewer* place at the table. Arithmetic is born!

Simple Setting: To make table-setting simpler for young children, adopt temporarily a symmetrical table arrangement. The plate goes in front of the chair. The napkin goes on the plate. The silverware goes on the napkin. The glass can go in front of the plate. The usual arrangement of silver and glassware is too hard for a three-year-old because it requires the concept of right and left. If you insist on it, you'll end up rearranging the table every time he sets it, and he will not get the sense of a job well done.

Positions: As you hand other items to your child to put on the table for you, use the words that describe where to put them.

The salt and pepper go *in the middle* of the table. The platter goes *in front of* Mommy. Put the ketchup *between* you and Susie so you can both reach it. Move the glasses *far from the edge* so they don't get spilled. When you first give instructions like these, you may find your child doesn't really understand them. Show what you mean.

Extras: Different meals call for different utensils and condiments. Figuring out these extras that go with certain meals is a kind of problem-solving; it may be too difficult for a child under five or six. Try and see: We're having hot dogs for lunch. Do you remember what you like to put on your hot dog?

Napkin Folds: Practice shapes with paper napkins. One day they could be left as big squares, the next day folded into small squares. They could be triangles, they could be rectangles. This is how to tie a soft paper napkin into a bunny rabbit:

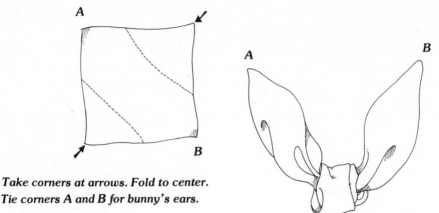

Take corners at arrows. Fold to center.
Tie corners A and B for bunny's ears.

What if your child can't wait for dinner? Assume that he's right—he can't. The reason may be fatigue rather than hunger, but the reason doesn't matter. Feed him dinner earlier. One method that works for some families is to cook the day's meal for adults, and use the previous day's leftovers for the children. Stews, bean soups and such are the most convenient for this double-duty cooking.

Another way is to serve the children's meal early, composed of quick, healthful foods. They include: cheese, peanut butter, pasta with crumbled hamburger or cheese, raw vegetables and fruits, a hamburger or pizza with meat on it.

Whenever you can—Sundays, perhaps—serve the family dinner in the afternoon when your youngest children can hold out longer.

Favorite Foods and Nutrition

A child who thinks edible substances are limited to french fries and hamburgers can get to be a nuisance. Try to avoid the problem by offering your child a wide variety of foods from the time he graduates from baby food.

One of the principles of good nutrition is to eat a variety of foods, so you help establish good eating habits by encouraging experimentation early. Forget the notion that children only enjoy bland flavors. Try ethnic foods if they are available where you live—any dried bean dishes, fried plantain, and bean sprouts. Experiment with flavorings such as chili powder, curry, soy sauce, garlic, and oregano. A child of five, experienced in a wide range of flavors, textures and appearances, may not only love clams, camembert cheese, and moo goo gai pan, but be pleasingly enthusiastic about trying new foods wherever he goes.

Bob and Maria bake bread in an Indian oven in New Mexico.

Families who consider themselves part of an ethnic group can make the most of it through their cooking. Whether we are experts in refried beans or pasta or pumpernickel, the food a family feels best with becomes an important part of a child's identity. When you prepare your own ethnic foods, mention it to your child. *"This is the same soup my grandmother used to make."*

How Much?

New knowledge sticks best when children can use it in important ways. When you dole out food, ask your child "How much?"—and then suggest to him: the *biggest* hamburger? Only *a few* peas? A *spoonful* of potatoes? Your child will be learning many different ways to describe quantities, and he can use the new knowledge to judge for himself—and to inform you—how much he can eat.

What if your child wastes food? The fault could be yours, or it could be his. It is his fault if his eyes are too big for his stomach. But it is your fault if you are deciding for him what, and how much, he ought to eat. If his own judgment is faulty, serve him smaller portions accompanied with a promise to save him plenty of food for second helpings. For the child who never cleans his plate, who leaves his vegetables, or only picks at his stew, ask before you serve. Try very hard to respect his judgment. Malnutrition by choice is rare. Violent opinions are common. Very many children have small stomach capacities. The more you make an issue of eating, the more a child's stomach tightens, the more his throat constricts, and the more unpleasant mealtimes become for both of you. If you are worried about your child filling up on starchy foods and neglecting proteins and vitamins, don't buy all those starches in the first place. Your child can eat only what you make available to him.

May I?

By asking for what he wants to eat, a child learns to specify time, position, sequence, and amount. Encourage him (by example and by questioning him) to ask for a *second* helping rather than just more, a *small* potato rather than "that one," his meat in the *middle* of his plate, rather than "there," and only a *few* peas, salad *later*.

The most common food dislikes among children may be based on looks as well as taste. "Mixed up" foods like stew seem messy to some children. These children may eat better if ingredients are separated—a carrot here, one piece of meat there, and a small potato on the other side of the plate. The cabbage family, including broccoli and cauliflower, are often disliked, and so are asparagus and spinach. The very few vegetables that children may like, such as green beans, are sometimes preferred raw or only slightly cooked. If a child is receiving supplementary vitamins, you don't have to worry too much about his dislike for vegetables. Many vegetable haters have grown up to be vegetable lovers. Also, children's nutritional needs are different from adults'. Children need more protein, as in meat, than we do. And because of their high energy use, they require far more carbohydrates such as potatoes and breads than we do.

The Milk Hater

It has been discovered only recently that many of the children who hate milk are actually allergic to it. They get tummy aches from drinking it, and their digestion of milk is so poor they don't benefit from it. Even children whose digestion of milk is normal may be sensitive to off-flavors caused by getting milk too cold (as when it sits outside the store for an hour on a very cold morning) or too warm (as when it sits on the table until dessert time). Spring milk may have an unpleasant garlic flavor caused by the wild onions cows may be eating in the pasture.

Rather than fighting with a milk hater, substitute some other drink for liquid and some other source of calcium, such as cheeses and green leafy vegetables.

Serving

As a child's manual skill improves, he can cut up simple cakes for the family or spoon out mashed potatoes and pudding desserts. Both jobs call for judgments of size, quantity, or proportion—*a big piece for you, a small piece for me; two*

Big Bird feeds Snuffle-upagus spaghetti —Snuffie's favorite food.

spoonfuls for Susie, one spoonful for you; cut this piece in half so you each have the same amount.

All children share certain misconceptions about quantity. Before four-years-old, and often even after, a spread-out group of objects appears to a child "more than" the same group when it is pushed close together. Prove it to yourself: take five pieces of bubblegum (or pennies, or chocolate chips) and spread them out into a long row. Take five more, and put them closely side by side. Which group does your child want? He will reach for the "biggest"—the more spread-out group.

Even if your child can count, and you have him count out both of the groups, he may still insist the spread-out group has more chocolate chips. Learning to count does not teach a child that the number he has counted up to tells him "how many," no matter how the objects are arranged in space. This realization (seldom learned until the age of seven) is called conservation—the number of objects is conserved (stays the same) no matter how the objects are arranged. Conservation is learned by repeated experiences of both counting and arranging.

When you are counting food items with your child, let him handle and arrange the carrots, cookies or cheese cubes as he counts.

Since "spread out" looks like more to children, and "close together" looks like less, use the misconception to arrange food appropriately on a child's plate. For the child who asks for more than he can eat, spread the food out thinly all over the plate. For the poor eater, scrunch food together in a couple of little piles.

Manners

As you observe your slovenly three-year-old at table, gobbling, dripping, yelling, grabbing, try calmly to figure out what irritates or repulses you the most.

Start teaching manners there. *Janet, I think you can learn to eat now without putting your face down in your plate. Hold your head up and see if you can carry the fork up to your mouth.* You might tell William he can blow bubbles in his milk at lunchtime, but that when the family is eating together, the noise is unpleasant.

When teaching manners, avoid insults like *Fred, you eat like a pig.* Also avoid generalizations like *People do not suck their spaghetti up.* What "people" do is less important than how you personally feel about it.

Dinner Conversation

As you may have noticed, children are not born conversationalists. They interrupt. They don't follow the subject. They have no sense of give and take. The ability to converse develops slowly, urged on by good examples and plenty of reminders. Say you are talking about the boss. Your child says, *I hate her!* You say, *Do you mean my boss?* No, he means Susan. Susan broke his truck. Tell your child you'd like to hear about that, but right now you're talking about your boss. Does he remember your boss, Mrs. Soandso? Do make an effort to keep your story short, because your child will not be able to go for long without interrupting with another non sequitur. Pick up his thread for him: *Now tell us about Susan.* Help him see that conversation is supposed to lead somewhere. Tell him about the time your uncle helped you fix a broken toy, or some other related incident.

For some reason, young children find it difficult to talk in a normal voice. Or rather, shouting seems normal to them. If you try to talk over their voices, or yell

A Monster Family dinner.

FAMILY DINNERS
ARE REALLY GREAT.
WE EAT THE FOOD
AND THEN THE PLATE

to them to be quiet, dinner time becomes one long crescendo. There's nothing for it but to remind a child over and over that he's shouting; that you can hear him perfectly well if he uses his talking voice. To remind without yelling yourself, touch him to get his attention. Use the momentary silence that ensues to say your piece.

Squabbling

Civilized meals become harder to manage when you have more than one child. The reason is simple: The kids are competing for your attention, and getting back at one another for each success. Kicks under the table, teasing, put-downs and complaints exhaust and enrage the whole family. Here is a suggestion for one way of handling the problem. Discuss the matter openly. The fact is, you might say, you don't enjoy any of your children when they are squabbling. It spoils your dinner. Perhaps you will not eat with them when they act this way. The next time, no matter who starts what, no matter whose fault it is, you will pick up your plate when things get unpleasant and eat in peace and quiet elsewhere. Do as you promised. You may find that a peacefully shared parent is preferred to no parent at all. (Don't forget that parental squabbling at mealtimes is just as upsetting to kids!)

Table Games

Here are a few quiet, interesting games that can be played at the table after the meal is eaten.

Feelies: Hide an object in your lap (a spoon, a jar top). Pass it from person to person under the table. Everyone is allowed to feel it, but not to peek at it. Then each child gets a turn to say what the object is.

I see something: Think of an object on the table that is within your child's view. Say *I see something (sharp, pointed, and you can cut with it; red, juicy and good to eat)*. Your child looks for something on the table to match your description. Don't forget to give him a turn, too.

Same and Different: Put three objects next to one another (two spoons, one fork). Ask which ones are the same, which is different. For older children, use two objects that are only the same in certain ways (a china cup, a china plate) and ask what's the same about them or what's different.

Say more: Choose an object on the table (a pickle). Say something about it (*it's green*). The next person has to say something else, and so on around the table. Such a description goes: *It's green, sour, bumpy, a vegetable, good to eat, goes with hamburgers, used to be a cucumber, grows on a vine, is shaped like a hot dog, is wet and rolls.*

BEDTIME

Bedtimes—whether for the afternoon nap or for the night's sleep—are among the most difficult times of day for many parents and children. This section deals with ways to ease your child into rest or sleep with both traditional bedtime "rituals" and a few new ideas.

In general, one of bedtime's difficulties is that you and your child may not see eye to eye on the subject.

You can easily tell when you are tired, and when you are sleepy. Children do not always recognize when they are tired, and often resist the sensation of sleepiness. Helping them to fatigue is tricky. Going to sleep means being separated from you, and from the interests and activities of daily life. To some children, it also means a kind of "giving up," which leaves them vulnerable and anxious. There are children who deny that they *ever* sleep.

When your child acts tired (overexcited, easily frustrated, cranky) you can say *I think you must be tired; everything seems so hard for you. If we read together* (or whatever relaxes your child) *maybe that will help you to feel sleepy.*

When your child looks sleepy, offer to help him fall asleep. The idea is to

Ernie keeps Bert awake by asking him questions.

acknowledge his physical state and to support it, rather than to accuse him of it. Accusation only leads to fiercer denial of tiredness or sleepiness.

Sometimes you only wish your child were tired because *you* are tired. Tell him you are tired. He must go into his room now so you can rest. There is no sense in insisting that he go to sleep. That's something people can't do on command.

Some kids are nappers, some aren't. No yelling, pleading or forcible restraint will get a nonnapper to sleep in the afternoon. He simply needs less than others, and he always will.

Make it clear if it is not for your child—it's for you. Say, *I need to be alone; I need a rest; I need a quiet time. While I am in my room you may* (and here give a short list of alternatives according to his age) *color with crayons; look at these books; play with your doll.* To be sure he doesn't leave his room and get into trouble if you fall asleep, hang some bells on his door. They will wake you when the door is opened.

If the reason you want your child to rest is because he gets too crabby otherwise, you can still explain in terms of your own point of view. You can't stand his crabbiness when he gets no afternoon rest.

Besides naptime and bedtime, you may need other "time outs" during the day.

Tell your child when you feel tired, have a headache, want to be alone, can't stand the noise. Tell your child when you are furious with your best friend, or upset about something. In time, your child will learn to tell you how he feels, too. The difference is no one's fault; it is simply a practical matter that both of you can make allowances for. When he is cranky, you can leave him alone. When you are in a bad mood, he can keep out of your way. The idea of retiring into privacy for a while need not be confined to regular bedtimes.

Bedtime Ritual

Almost everybody, if he stops to think about it, has a bedtime ritual. You may feel unsettled and unable to sleep unless your teeth are brushed, the door shut, the children checked. Children's bedtime rituals are not so practical, but they are even more urgent. As your child begins to develop bedtime preferences, try to make them part of an inviolate routine. Tucking in, drinking water, turning on a nightlight, checking for hidden monsters, kissing goodnight and a ritualized bedtime wish like "sweet dreams" are all normal, needed routines.

Bedtimes are occasionally good times for a comfy chat. You might want to bring your coffee with you. Get an extra pillow so you can lie back, too. Go over the day together. Nice things happened—remember the puppy with the curly tail? Bad things happened—you were so mad at me this morning! Tomorrow is another day. Maybe you'll see that puppy again. Maybe we won't have an argument about how much milk to pour on the cereal.

Wish together, too. Perhaps your child wishes he could have that puppy with the curly tail. Perhaps you wish you had a house of your own so it would be easier to have a dog. Neither of you may get your wish, but shared longings build sympathy, and ease us into rest.

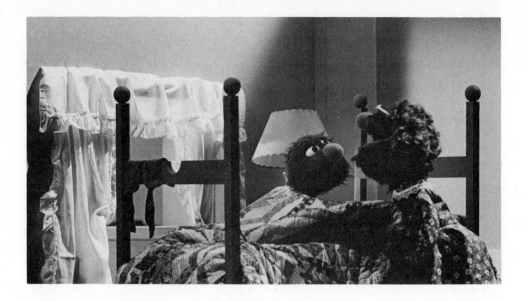

Because taking leave of today is so difficult, it may relieve your child to plan tomorrow. Talk about what you will do together—not to excite him, but to let him know there is a tomorrow.

Flashlight Games

To help a child deal with darkness, here are some bedtime games that let him control light and shadow. Give your child a flashlight. Turn the room lights off. Ask him to find the chair, a picture, his own feet by pointing the light at it. Let him put his fingers in front of the light beam to make shadows. Ask him to make a shadow of his whole hand, or of his finger. Can he make the shadow wiggle or jump? Teach him how to hold his hands in different ways to make the animals shown here.

After a child learns how to make these shadows, show him how to make the duck "quack," the eagle "fly," and the dog "bark."

Photo Albums

The family photo album makes a terrific bedtime storybook. *Remember Uncle Jack? This is a picture of him on the beach the day he got lost and.* . . . The stories might be about relatives, when you were a child, about the day you got married, your child when he was a baby, or about his last birthday (*See, there's the cake. It had gumdrops on it*). There is no story as gripping, as gratifying, as the story of one's own family.

If you like, you can select your child's favorite pictures to arrange in a special album. You can write under each picture a short version of the story that goes with it.

Picture Reading

Restless children, or very young ones, may not be able to sit still for even the shortest storybook. This doesn't mean they are not ready for books. Forget the words. Look at the pictures. Point to something you think will interest your child (*Look! A truck!*). Add dramatics (*RRRRRRRRR! Here comes the truck. Beep beep, watch out!*). Your child may pick up from here and make his own sound effects, pretend to steer the truck, leave to get his own toy truck, or turn the page to see what else is in the book.

Since this kind of reading allows a child to remain active, make noises and pretend, he can get hooked on books years before he is ready to sit still and listen quietly.

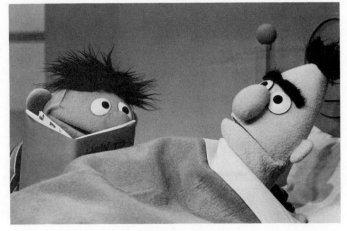

Every night Ernie reads Bert a bedtime story.

Good Books

Any book is "good" if a child finds it gratifying. A child may love a book because of a single picture in it—a fireman rescuing someone or a monkey doing a trick. You may never know why the emotional content of that picture is so important to him, or even what content he sees. But his pleasure in the picture makes the book a good one for him.

This is true of the story too, or of a single episode or even a phrase in a book. A child may fail to grasp the plot at all, yet want to hear over and over again about the elephant who fell in the lake, or that the Little Engine said, "I thought I could I thought I could I thought I could . . . "

If your child settles on a few books he wants to hear or to look at over and over again, let him. Repetition now will not restrict his literary tastes later. In fact, freedom to be in love with a couple of books now will help him love many books later. If you can, buy these few favorite books for him.

It is easier to love one's own book than the library's. But use the library to supplement your family's supply with more books than you can buy. Librarians will recommend those childhood favorites that are considered classics, help you choose stories that are at your child's age level, or locate for you more books on a child's favorite subject.

For your own sake, avoid books that you find difficult to read (stories in verse are awkward for some) or that take more than ten minutes to read (unless divided into chapters), or that bore you after the first reading. No matter how hard you try to be "nice," your child will detect your groans when he asks for those books. The best children's books have usually managed to please adults as much as they please children.

Bedtime Rhythms

The repetitive rhythms of nursery rhymes seem to have soothed many generations of children to sleep. They also help children absorb the basic rhythmic patterns typical of our language. To emphasize the patterns of these and other childhood verses—and to bodily soothe your child, too—hold his hand in yours and quietly keep the beat of the verses by moving your hands up and down. Other rhythmic bedtime activities that relax children well past infancy include patting or rubbing your child's back, rocking him in your arms, or singing him to sleep.

Snow White and the One Hundred Dwarfs

Some adults are very good at making up bedtime stories for their children. For those who feel stumped, however, here is one particular story a grandfather told over and over again with unfaltering success. It goes like this: "Once upon a time there was a princess named Snow White, who came upon a tiny house in the dark forest. In the house lived one hundred dwarfs, and their names were . . . " The storyteller then invents funny names until the listener falls asleep.

Things to Take to Bed

To fall asleep is to leave the real world. It means leaving parents. It even means "leaving one's senses" both literally, in that one can no longer see or hear or feel; and figuratively, in that one becomes a victim of the "craziness" of dreams. Perhaps this is why children insist on being accompanied into sleep by some object from the real world. The object may be a baby blanket, a doll or stuffed animal, or even something as incongruous as a bulldozer.

Whatever your child's choice, you will only increase his nervousness at bedtime by trying to talk him out of it. You may be able to help him more by hanging a favorite picture on the wall right near his pillow, putting stickers he likes on his bed, letting him hang on to the book you have read to him. A nightlight may help reassure him that when he does wake up, he can instantly see again the real world he has left.

That particular doll or animal or blanket that accompanies a child to bed may have a crucial role in his development. As an infant grows into toddlerhood, one of the more difficult tasks he faces is to separate himself from his parent. Though we can't read a baby's mind, his behavior hints that he doesn't yet think of himself as an individual. His functioning is so dependent upon the adult who cares for him that it is to him as though they were one. Only gradually does a baby realize that the crying that indicates his hunger and the hand that provides the bottle emanate from two different entities: me, and other. We can at least imagine that this feels both painful and exhilarating. Unity is lost; autonomy is gained. But not all at once. For a long while yet the child is torn between the urge to function on his own, and the need for unity with his parents.

This is his problem: how can he walk away from his parents, say *no* to them, and still have them always with him? By making a clever substitution: a baby blanket, a rag doll, a stuffed animal that serves as a soothing, caressing, but portable mother or father. The child may suck a corner of the blanket, or tug a fringe of yarn hair through his fingers, or hold the animal to his face when he

Ernie always takes his Rubber Duckie to bed.

needs solace. He may feel desperate if he is without it, and he may linger anxiously near the washing machine when it is laundered.

Such an object is called a transitional object because it serves transition between infantile dependence and the more secure independence of the four- or five-year-old. If your child has such an object, respect its importance.

Ticklish Games

Visiting uncles, parents who haven't seen their children all day and older brothers and sisters often share a common bedtime mistake. They tickle, they pillow fight, they tell monster stories, they play games of horsey and chase and grab. All these games are exciting and fun, but they are all a little scary, too. Tickling may result in a sensation similar to being suffocated. Roughhousing can hurt—and at the very least it makes a child all too aware of his own weakness compared to big people's strength. As for scary monsters and chasing games, there's enough of both in a child's own bad dreams. Save these games for earlier in the day, when a child has the energy and time to deal with their possible ill effects. Make bedtime a calm time.

Role Reversal

If you don't understand why your child has such trouble getting to bed, or what he might need to help him, try reversing roles. You are the babyish child who nags, asks for ten glasses of water, whines to stay up later, or teases and acts wild. As your child plays parent, you may find out two things: first, how he perceives your bedtime behavior (*I said get to bed this instant or I'm going to spank you good!*) and second, what he might prefer as bedtime behavior (*I'll leave the lights on, I'll give you crackers to eat)*. At the same time, your child is seeing your enactment of how he behaves. Both revelations may help you and your child to modify your actions by imagining the other's point of view.

Bedtime Treats

A frequent tactic of the harassed parent is to encourage a child to go to bed with the promise of a reward. It's important when offering a reward for you to distinguish between a treat and a bribe—and decide for yourself.

What is the difference? A treat is given unconditionally; a bribe is given on conditions. If ice cream is promised in advance, but only on the condition that the child behave well, then it is a bribe. If the ice cream is promised in advance without conditions, then it is a treat. If a privilege is offered "if you go to bed on time," it is a bribe. If a privilege is offered "because you have been so nice lately about going to bed on time," then it is a treat.

Less equivocal bedtime rewards include a piggyback ride to bed, or a favorite story.

Frequent Awakening

Children who wake up and call for their parents many times during the night may be checking that they are still around. Sometimes you can guess at the reason: the family is going to move, and your child is afraid of being left behind; a parent has recently been hospitalized, and could suddenly leave again; or there has been a fight, and a parent has walked out in anger. Sometimes you can't figure out the fear at all. But if you suspect such a problem, try these ways of alleviating your child's fear: Suggest he call to you when he wakes up, and you will call back to him to let him know you are there. Don't yield to his wish to sleep in your bed with you, but leave his door open and a hall light on. He can get out of bed and check that you are there.

Frightening dreams, bedwetting, and even sleepwalking are other sleep disturbances that children may experience. If you or your child are concerned about such problems, consult your doctor.

Nighttime Fears

Fears of thunderstorms, darkness, kidnappers and monsters can be alleviated, but not cured. Adults, after all, may still wince at the crash of thunder, feel creepy feelings in the dark, worry about kidnappers, and prefer to watch Frankenstein in company.

Share your fears together. You don't like thunder either, but you know it can't hurt you. You sometimes feel as though something is behind you in the dark, but really there never has been. There are bad people in the world, but you do this and that and the other to keep your family safe from them. And scary monsters? Well, they are scary to think about, but you have only seen pictures on television and in books. You have never seen a real one. These statements will not banish fear entirely. But the combination of your willingness to share your fears and the good sense with which you have coped with them is more reassuring than saying, "Don't be foolish."

Dreams

Children have not yet developed the boundaries that separate for them their internal from their external lives. To them, a dream is as real as anything else. Ask your child where his dreams come from. He may solemnly point to the window or underneath his bed. Perhaps he will say they come out of his eyes. Ask him if he can touch his dreams. He may be surprised at the question. Of course he can touch them! Because dreams are so real to children, they may be genuinely furious or desolate to discover the tiny monkey you gave them during the night is nowhere to be found in the morning. And they may be terrified of the witch behind the curtains even after you have "proved" she is not there. Explain dreams to your child this way: Ask him to close his eyes and think of a doll he wants badly, or a dog that really frightened him. Can he see a picture inside his mind? That is what a dream is like—pictures that the child himself is thinking.

3 Quiet Times

THE ACTIVITIES in this chapter are quiet, calming things to do to fill up intervals of unclaimed time.

For instance, when your child is bored on a long bus ride, waiting to see the doctor, feeling restless until Grandma arrives, there are dozens of absorbing games to help the minutes pass. The suggestions require no equipment other than what you might find with your eyes as you look around you, with your hands as you reach into your pocket, or with your imagination as you search your own mind. A few of the activities require preparation, but usually no more than remembering to bring along a pad and a pencil. They are all peaceful activities that won't bother other people in public places.

You might also use these suggestions to create intervals, especially to calm your child down when he is feeling wild or distressed.

Before getting into the games themselves, however, a word should be said about one all-time favorite quiet activity—cuddling. Have you noticed how toddlers in the midst of play will return to their parent and lean close for a moment as though to refuel before taking off again? Though not so obvious with preschool children, the need to gather strength from babyish times still exists. Hugging,

cuddling, lap-sitting, leaning—and the confiding conversations, the soothing songs that go with it—are ways children fuel themselves to meet the relentless challenge of growth. Cuddling isn't a weakness; it's a source of strength.

When the need arises, feel free to hold your child in your arms while you watch television together or read a book. When your child is tense or overtired, calm him in your lap. Preschoolers aren't too old for rocking, either. And when you are waiting for the dentist or the doctor, a good cuddle wouldn't hurt.

Music is good accompaniment to cuddling. If you like to sing and hum, do it. A repetitive song, sung in a slow rhythm, will be most soothing. Or turn on the radio or the phonograph to listen to music together. Children, far from enjoying only kiddy songs, often like listening to classical, rock, soul or country music—especially if they are sharing the moment with an adult.

When the two of you are relaxed, just sitting together quietly, confiding feels natural. Perhaps you regret you blew your stack over something so small as a broken cup, or know that sooner or later you have to tell your child that his aunt is really sick, or want to say how much it upsets you when your child makes so much noise in the car. There is no rule that parents must always be strong, or right or perfect. It is more helpful if they are always human.

And when the interval is filled with peace, remember back to your own childhood; tell your child something of how you felt then. Don't always look for entertainment value, but sometimes talk about hurts and wishes, times you cried yourself to sleep, scary dreams and firm beliefs—about what you thought God looked like, how you thought the wind was made, what you thought your dog was telling you—that turned out to be untrue. Knowing you were once similar to him, your child will feel safe in revealing his own childish ideas. This is a way the generations come to know each other, and to understand their connectedness.

Lily Tomlin, as Edith Ann, has a quiet moment during her visit to Sesame Street.

TALKING GAMES

There is only one way children learn to put their ideas, observations and feelings into words—by talking. Conversation with an adult is, of course, part of most of the hundreds of activities in this book; but this section concentrates on games that require various specific language skills, from clear articulation to learning important new words.

The richest range of thought and feeling you can express to your child will most likely be in the language you speak best. The emotional and intellectual abilities that come with communicating comfortably and skillfully in any language are very basic.

Many of the talking games that follow are designed to practice visual and auditory memory. Why is it important that a child see again in his mind what he has seen with his eyes, or hear again in his mind what he has heard with his ears? To learn to read, a child must already have developed the visual skill to remember the shapes of letters, and the auditory skill to recall the sounds they make. These are the skills you are teaching him now.

To get the feel of these skills yourself, think of what happens when you have made out a grocery list but forgotten to bring it with you. Often, you can "see" the list in your mind, and still use it to buy your groceries. Or as you go out the door your child calls out a last-minute request. If it doesn't penetrate then, a few minutes later you may "hear" what he said again. Both visual and auditory memory are eminently practical life skills.

Oscar's Can

This game is similar to an old one called Grandmother's Trunk that you may have played as a child. Ask your child to copy whatever you say. Start with an easy statement: "I put a frog in Oscar's can." If he can copy that, add on to the original statement to make it longer: "I put a frog and a mudpie in Oscar's can." As your child gets better, add descriptive words too: "A slimy snail and a purple snake." And take turns; your child will have to remember the same list whether he is the cat or the copycat.

There are many ways you can vary this copycat game to teach slightly different skills, according to the ability of your child. For instance, use it for rhyming (a snail and a pail on a horse's tail), or for consonant sounds (a button, a ball, a bear and a bowl). You can also use "Oscar's Can" to teach the sequence of the alphabet and of the numerals from one to ten.

Chants

The role of rhythm in learning may be imperfectly understood, but it has been practiced as a memory aid for as long as anyone knows. Rhythm has traditionally been used to help children memorize the alphabet, count, and recite the days of the week or months of the year. Even adults use rhythmic devices to recall the number of days in each month or a confusing spelling rule. Advertisers depend on the "stickiness" of rhythmic jingles to make you remember their products. And Sesame Street uses jinglelike rhythms—some new, some old—to teach many of

On Sesame Street, numbers are often taught accompanied by catchy jingles. "Let's sing a song of five" is heard as this picture is shown on the screen.

the things that children first learn by rote. You can do the same, whether you are reciting with your child the traditional alphabet jingle or trying to remember to stop at the cleaners on the way home. (Try it: *Stop at the CLEANers, stop at the CLEANers, stop at the CLEANers, on the way HOME.*)

Snapshot Memory

Before you set out on what you know will be a long inactive ordeal of riding or waiting with your child, choose a bunch of snapshots that were taken recently. They should all be ones that were taken while your child was present. Later, when he is bored, take out the snapshots. Ask him to tell you who the people are, where the picture was taken, and what was happening. Jog his memory when he needs help: *Look, here's Henry in that awful hat! Remember, he kept pulling it over his face every time we tried to take his picture?* Or for a younger child, *Here's Daddy. Can you find Daddy?*

Landmarks

If you travel often along the same route, there may be landmarks you or your child have pointed out. Perhaps you pass a certain statue, and then your bus turns past the park. See if your child can predict the next landmark. Help him out by using words that express a sequence: *Look, there's the horse statue. We'll pass the park next. Do you remember what we always look for next?*

Mental Pictures

Tell your child to look around him and notice as many things as he can. Ask him to close his eyes. Does he have pictures in his mind of what he saw? Can he tell you what he saw? If this game seems to baffle your child, make the instructions more specific: *Look at those two trucks. See what colors they are. Now close your eyes. What colors are the trucks?*

What's Missing?

Dig into your pocket or pocketbook and take out three objects (a key, a comb, a matchbox). Put them in your palm or lap, pick each one up in turn, and check that your child knows the name for each. Then while he closes his eyes or looks away, remove one object. Now let him look again: What's missing? As your child gets better at this game, make it harder by adding more objects or by removing more than one object at a time.

I'm Thinking of Something

This game is akin to riddles. You describe an object ("I'm thinking of something red and round"), and your child guesses what the object is. The skills required are quite sophisticated. Your child has to hear the words red and round, imagine *redness* or *roundness*, then match his mental image with a real object somewhere within his view.

The easiest way to play is to show your child two objects that you feel you can easily describe—a key and a cookie, for instance. Say, *I'm thinking of something you can eat. Is it the key or the cookie?* As he is able to recognize and name more abstract qualities, such as color and shape, you can use those words in your description. Eventually, expand the number of objects he must examine to everything that is on the table, or in a magazine picture, or within his entire view. By the age of five or six, a few children are able to play "I'm Thinking of Something" with objects that are not in view: *I'm thinking of something that has four legs, a tail, and says meow.*

Be generous with adjectives when you talk with your child, and use the same adjective in many ways: Sharp knives, sharp noises, sharp tongues, sharp minds. Sweet candy, sweet talk, sweet faces, sweet dreams. And soft voices, soft pillows, soft colors, soft hands.

When someone describes a cloud or a hairdo as "fluffy," you know what they mean even though a cloud and hair are very different from each other. Moreover, you can say "fluffy" to describe a quilt, a cake, a kitten or a flower. In each case you mean something slightly different—a fluffy cake neither looks like a kitten nor feels like a quilt.

You have learned to abstract in your mind the quality of "fluffiness." How does this complicated skill come about? How do children develop it? Simply by hearing objects and experiences described often and well.

Questions, Questions

Ask your child to think of something in the room, but not to tell you what it is. Then ask him questions about it. Is it something to eat? Is it near the door? Does it have writing on it? (Try to ignore the fact that your child is staring hard at the object all this while. This may be the only way he can keep it in his mind.) If your child wants to switch parts and be the questioner, fine. He may only guess wildly. (Is it the couch? Is it the door?) Let him play his way while you continue to play your way. In time, he will begin to notice and to use question-asking strategies. The ability to ask relevant questions is an essential skill for your child to develop for problem-solving.

Think of a Number

After your child has not only learned to count, but can actually tell you how many objects there are in a group, see if he is able to play this hard number game. Say a number between 1 and 10. Ask him to say a number that is higher or lower. (If the words higher and lower confuse your child, try more and less, or bigger and smaller.)

The Count counts some friends.

Nonsense Rhymes

The purpose of rhyming games is not to teach your child poetry, but to help him listen for particular sounds in words. Rhyming is an exceptionally difficult task for young children—not because they haven't spontaneously rhymed from the time they could babble ma-ma, pa-pa, but because they have a hard time understanding what the word "rhyme" means.

Most children will begin by rhyming nonsense words. You say *mitten*, he says *pitten*. (Often it's even easier to use many-syllabled sounds like *elephant, pelephant*.) This is a perfectly acceptable start.

Most children will prefer yummy or yucchy sounds best, like *fooey, gooey, mooey, shooey, pooey*. It's still rhyming. The task of searching for a real word to rhyme with one you choose is far more difficult than making up nonsense sounds. To do it, a child must review many possible rhyming sounds, but select and say aloud only those that are real words. You can help your child learn to select by saying three words (hat, cat, mitten) and asking him to tell you which two words rhyme. Or you can ask your child to say a word, and you must think of one that rhymes.

On Sesame Street, Don Music composes songs with rhyming lyrics that don't always make sense.

Beginning Sounds

Finding a word that begins with a particular consonant sound is similar to finding a word that rhymes (ends with a particular sound). It is best to start this game with what are called sustaining consonant sounds—those that make a noise when spoken and held, even if they are not followed by a vowel: *M*, *N*, *L*, *R*, *S*, and *F* are all sustaining consonants. Consonants such as *B* or *T* are more confusing. You can't say them without adding some sort of vowel sound after them, as *buh* or *tih*.

Bert and Ernie hold the first letters of their names.

Again, children may start with nonsense words. You say, *think of a word that starts with ssss, like sit.* He says, *soo* or *sil* or anything that comes into his head. Help him along: *Yes, soo like soup! Sil—or how about silly?* By the way, you needn't wait until a child has learned either to name the consonants, or to couple the name with its sound. The point is only to help him hear the sound that starts a word, and choose other words that start with the same sound.

Herbert Birdsfoot and Grover demonstrate how rhyming words are made by changing the initial consonant.

Feeling Sounds

Just for fun, and for a little more awareness of his own speech, let your child feel voice sounds. Have him put his hand loosely against your throat. Make a low growly sound. He will be able to feel it easily. Make a high squeaky sound. The vibrations are quicker, harder to feel. Let him feel his own throat as he makes different sounds.

Now experiment with the sounds of speech. Some sounds are voiced (the vowel sounds) and some sounds are made without any voice at all (as *P, T, S*). Sounds that are not voiced are made by expelling air. The child can feel the air coming out of your mouth with his hand. Voiced sounds can all be felt at the throat.

B is for butterfly.

Whispering

Listening to whispers requires hard concentration. And learning to whisper so others can understand you requires careful articulation of the sounds in words. Both skills are important enough to overlook a certain impoliteness in whispering in public—as long as you don't use the game to make remarks about people! Whisper a question in your child's ear (*What do you want for dinner?*). Tell him to whisper his answer back. If all you receive is an enthusiastic wet whooshing in your ear, whisper back that he is talking too fast. Let him try again.

What if, when you play these games—or even in ordinary conversation—your child says "what?" all the time? He may, of course, have a hearing difficulty, and your pediatrician can check that out. But he may also have a more subtle disability that is more difficult to diagnose. For instance, his auditory memory may be so underdeveloped that he forgets the first part of a sentence by the time he hears the last part. This and other difficulties in processing sounds can be tested by a specialist in learning disabilities. Your school or doctor can recommend such a specialist.

If the trouble seems only mild, help your child in these ways: Touch him to get his attention. Stoop down to his level, and look him in the face when you talk to him. Keep your sentences very short. Be absolutely sure to *give him only one piece of information at a time*. And when he says "what?" repeat your words slowly to him.

Luis and his young friend communicate best face-to-face.

FINGER GAMES

When we ask a child to tell an M from a W, or a C from an O, we are asking something quite difficult. Turn an M upside down, and it becomes a W. Close the curve of a C, and it is an O. The differences are small and subtle. Touching and manipulating small objects seems to help children learn to see the differences between similar shapes. The touching games and finger games that follow are one example, and so are any games that involve arranging macaronis, toothpicks,

Sesame Street detectives are
hot on the trail of
the fugitive M.

By turning himself upside
down, M disguises himself as
a W.

paperclips and so on into various patterns. As a child's hands become accustomed
to feeling out and arranging different shapes, he becomes literally able to
"handle" the more abstract tasks of recognizing and drawing the letters of the
alphabet.

Touch and Tell

Pick up several objects that are at hand (a block, a ball, and a pencil; or a key,
a rubber band, and a penny). Let your child see the objects and tell you what they
are. Then have him close his eyes, handle the objects, and identify each one by

touch alone. If he has trouble, play the game with only two objects that feel very different from each other. Point out the differences: the ball is round, the block has pointed corners; the ball is squishy, the block is hard. Make the game harder for children who are good at it by choosing more, and similar, objects (a crayon, a pencil, a lollipop stick and a twig).

Fishing

Put a dozen small but familiar objects into a paper bag. Your child can go "fishing" with his hand in the bag. When he catches a "fish" he has to call out its name (a paperclip fish, a pencil fish, a lollipop fish). If he's wrong, he has to throw the fish back after he's taken a look at it. The game simply continues until he has fished the bag empty! Several children can take turns playing this game.

Mystery Envelopes

This game requires preparation, but it's fun to do once or twice. Choose six or seven small flat objects such as a washer, a key, a coin, a paperclip, a rubber band, a bit of string. Put each object into an envelope and seal the flap. Get out a soft pencil, too. When you want to play the game, hand your child one envelope at a time. Let him feel it with his fingers and try to guess what is in the envelope. When he's finished guessing, lay the envelope flat on a table and show your child how to rub the pencil over the object inside until he can see its image. Did he guess right?

Finger Letters

Children who already know several letters well may be interested in trying to form the shapes of them with their own fingers. Draw the letters for the child to copy. The letters that lend themselves to this game are $C, D, I, L, O, P, T, U, V, X$, all in capitals.

Say the name of a letter your child knows. Form it with your fingers, and let him copy you. If you child doesn't know any letters yet, don't try this game, as it may confuse him. He can't find an O in your fingers until he knows what he is looking for.

Touch Discrimination Game

If you have a bunch of fabric scraps at your disposal, you could set up this interesting but more difficult touch discrimination game. Choose pairs of scraps that differ in texture: two bits of felt, of velveteen, of rayon, of burlap. Put one piece of each fabric into the bag and find another that "feels the same." (Don't include too many choices.) You may play the same game using familiar objects. Blindfold a child, and put something—a comb, a mitten, a shoe—in his hand and ask what it is. Maria plays this game with young friends on Sesame Street.

Touch Writing

Have your child close his eyes and open his hand out flat. With your finger, draw on his palm the shape of a letter he knows. Ask him to tell you which letter it was.

If your child doesn't know any letters yet, play the game with two shapes, a circle and a cross. Draw the two shapes with a pencil first, and be sure your child knows the names. Then draw one shape in his palm and see if he can tell you whether it was a circle or a cross.

For older children or those who are super-good at this game and know almost all their letters, here are the hardest ones to distinguish: those that have the same number of strokes but differ in shape, such as L, T, X, Y, V; those that differ only in direction, such as W and M or lower case $p, b,$ and d; or those that differ only slightly in shape, such as $J, U, C,$ and O. (Try these hard versions out on yourself first to be sure you are drawing the letters in the simplest, least confusing way.)

Sign Language

An absorbing and quiet activity to do with your child is to speak with him in sign language. Explain that this is one way to communicate. People who can't hear speak to one another with their hands. Pointing out objects around you and nodding and shaking your head, combined with the small vocabulary illustrated below, is sufficient for some lively conversation. Teach only two or three signs at a time, and experiment with those before going on to others.

I

love

you

Linda Bove of Sesame Street communicates these words with sign language:

strong

listen

Little "People"

With a few touches of washable marking pen, fingertips can be transformed into tiny puppets. Two dots for eyes, a curvy smile or a straight frown, and you're set to go. Set up a simple situation for your child: *Charlie here* (your index finger) *is going shopping with Susie* (your child's index finger). *What is Susie going to buy?* Let your child lead the way from there. He will probably use a squeaky voice, and will get into the play better if you do, too.

Another way to play impromptu puppet games is to simply walk your fingers along as though they were two legs. You can go "shopping" through the pages of a magazine, or use the furniture as imagined rivers, mountains or caves. (Try climbing steps, walking backwards, running and jumping.) If your child finds this two-fingered walk difficult, he can accompany you as a spider walking on all five fingers.

Traditional Finger Plays

There are many wonderful old finger games that, while very difficult to explain in writing, are quite easy to learn by watching. If you don't know "Here's the Church and Here's the Steeple," "This Little Piggy," "Where Is Thumbkin?," "Itsy Bitsy Spider," ask around among other parents, or children of about first-grade age.

Or show your child how to twiddle his thumbs, interlace his fingers, hide his thumb inside his fist, compare hand sizes, or any of the other small delights you may remember from childhood. All of them, besides being curiously absorbing, help a child to become aware of where his fingers are in relation to one another.

PENCIL AND PAPER GAMES

These games can be played on any sort of paper. Keep some of the used envelopes you would ordinarily throw away, or cut up grocery bags into smallish pieces. For convenience when you are away from home, buy the smallest size note pads and take one along with you. A washable ink marker is often the best writing instrument for a young child. The point doesn't break, the ink flows effortlessly, and the dark line is easy for a child to see.

If your child can't handle either a pencil or a marker, he wouldn't be the first one. Finger dexterity comes slowly for many children. Forget the small pads and the fine writing instruments for now. Instead, use big sheets of paper (newspaper, opened-out paper bags), or a large chalkboard. Buy thick chalk or jumbo crayons. Try the games suggested in this section on a large scale, particularly the simplest ones like "Copylines" and "Paths." Let your child hold the crayon or chalk in his fist if he wants, rather than in the "proper" way with his fingers. And if even on a large scale these games are too frustrating, encourage him to scribble, even by scribbling along with him if necessary.

Scribbling is a much-maligned activity that actually practices important rhythmic arm and hand motions, develops awareness of size, direction, shape, and position. Look carefully at your child's scribblings and save samples of his work from time to time for comparison. You'll notice that some scribblings are circular, others are back-and-forth or up-and-down motions. Some scribbles are small, and some are large. Perhaps you'll see experiments with series of short lines or dots. You will even notice that scribbles sometimes cover the entire page, and other times are confined to the center, or to a corner. You may still not be able to appreciate scribble-scrabble as art, but it is a perfectly acceptable learning technique.

Occasionally a child who loves pencil and paper games becomes interested in writing letters of the alphabet. Should you teach your child the upper- or the lower-case alphabet? Although both may be taught simultaneously in school, and lower-case letters are really more common than upper-case, most children can learn to draw the shapes of the capital letters more easily. Your own job will be less confusing if you start with capitals.

Only after your child knows upper-case well should lower-case letters be introduced, starting with those that look different from each other, like A and a. But by this time your child will probably be in school anyway.

As far as the exact strokes and forms of each letter are concerned, different schools may use different methods. If you feel nervous about teaching your child the "wrong" way, but would still like to continue, call the school where he will be going and see if you can borrow a kindergarten workbook or writing worksheets.

Letters into Words

If your child is one who early on becomes interested in writing, you may wonder if you should teach him to read. Be encouraging, but be careful *not to expect more of him than he can perform*. Children who don't read early (by kindergarten or early first grade) seem to catch up with the early readers within a couple of years. The fact is that what takes great effort to teach to a four- or five-year-old is much easier to get across to a child of six or seven. It is really a question of what you and your child enjoy doing together, rather than what will be of advantage to him at school.

No one knows why, but the first form a child draws is almost inevitably a circle. Even stranger, the circle is then often elaborated into a figure called a mandala— a circle with a cross running through it. Just as intriguing is the next childhood attempt: a circle with rays emanating from it, which is used to represent the human face with hair, the sun, and even hands. We don't know how to interpret these mysteries, but it is exciting to watch their development in your own children.

When a child draws his first human figure, it is likely to look like this:

The head is the center, to which arms and legs are attached (the arms and legs are simply extended "rays"—or modified hair). There is no body. It is probable that this does not reflect lack of drawing skill, but is an accurate representation of a child's body concept. Around school age, a body is often added, though arms may still emerge from the head. And probably not for years will a child "see" the human body as possessing either neck or shoulders, nor feel an urge to represent a face in profile.

Same/Different

The basis for any activity that could be called prereading or prewriting is the ability to distinguish between shapes, sizes and directions. For instance, *d* is different from *p* only in position; the shape is the same. We adults have made these distinctions so automatically for so long that we are not aware of the skill. But if we are faced with learning a new alphabet—Hebrew or Arabic—we suddenly become aware of how carefully we must note sameness and difference in the learning process. This is why the Sesame Street game "One of these things is not like the others" has been a consistent element in the program from its earliest days.

Even if you can barely draw at all, you can probably manage to put together some simple games of same and different. The idea is to draw four figures, three of which are exactly the same. Vary the concepts by asking your child the question both ways: *Which ones are the same? Which one is different?* The examples shown are easy to draw, but stress the kinds of differences your child will have to notice as he begins to name and write letters of the alphabet.

As you play this game, you can let your child just point to the answer, but be sure you then follow up with words that describe the differences. When he has a firm grip on the words, he can explain his answer himself.

The games of "Copylines," "Paths" and some of the dot games that follow are designed to help a child trace with his hand a pattern his eyes have observed. For certain children, this is enormously difficult. The same children may find it hard to walk along a chalked line, throw or catch a ball, and learn to write. The difficulty, called poor eye-motor coordination, is very common. Luckily, eye-

"One of these things is not like the others." David asks the children to point out the trash can that is different in size.

motor coordination can be much improved by any activity that requires a child to use both his body and his eyes in a coordinated way.

Copylines

Make a straight line. Can your child make a straight line? Make a curve. Can he copy you? Try a wavy line (call it a snake), or a zigzag (that can be grass), or a bunch of U's connected to each other (the ocean, this time). Or draw two parallel lines and let your child add vertical ones to make a fence or railroad tracks (he should try to make all his lines the same length). All of these line games are rather fun for odd moments, and excellent prewriting practice as well.

Paths

Draw two straight lines parallel to each other and about an inch apart. Tell your child your drawing is a road, and his marker is a car. Can he drive down the middle of the road without ever hitting the sides?

Make the same drawing, but curvy this time. Tell your child it is a river, and his marker is a boat. Now the path is harder to follow because he must anticipate each curve and aim his marker accurately.

As your child can maneuver these paths without bumping into lines, you can make them harder by making them narrower and by increasing the number and the sharpness of the turns your child must negotiate. If the game gets boring, spice it up with other bits of crude drawing—Grandpa's house at one end of the road, the zoo at the other.

Dot to Dot

Draw two dots about an inch apart. See if your child can draw a line to connect them. If he can, there are a number of dot games he might enjoy.

Draw three dots to form a triangle. Can he guess the shape? Let him join the dots and see. Do the same with four dots to form a square. Then show him a trick. Join the dots with crossing lines to form an X.

Draw dots to form the straight-line letters of the upper-case alphabet: *A, E, H, I, K, M, N, T, V, W, X, Y, Z.* Be sure you use only letters he knows well, one at a time, and show him what letter he is to form from the dots you have set up.

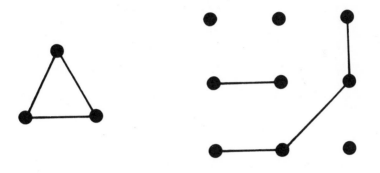

Dot Grids

Make a grid out of dots—say three dots across and three down for a total of nine dots; or for a younger child, two dots by two dots for a total of only four. Now join a few of the dots yourself to make a pattern. As in the illustration, your lines can be vertical, horizontal or diagonal. Make the same grid for your child, and see if he can draw lines to form the same pattern you made. The skill he develops from this game will help him to notice and to copy the configurations of letters and numerals.

A child's drawing of the number 2 and his two friends Ernie and Bert.

Dot Counting

Use dots (or small circles) for various counting games. For instance, draw three dots in a row and count them together. Then draw three dots in the form of a triangle, and count them again. Draw the same three dots, but this time far apart in different corners of the paper. Count them again. Though a young child will not learn this yet, eventually it is important for a child to realize that no matter how you arrange three dots, their number doesn't change. (Children who find this confusing can practice using pennies or beans that they can move into different patterns themselves.)

To teach a child numerals, write the numeral 3, for example, and then have him count with you as you draw three dots. Write the numeral again, and let him draw the dots.

To practice counting, draw three circles. Draw the same number of dots in two of the circles, but a different number of dots in the other circle. Can your child count and tell you which circles have the same number of dots?

Circle Pictures

Draw a circle for your child. Make two dots for eyes. Can he make a mouth? Can he add hair? Make another circle. Can he turn it into a lollipop? Draw a rectangle. Can he make it into a bus (or a wagon)? These games, simple as they seem, require an important intellectual skill—the ability to connect parts to make a whole. As a child adds a mouth to make a face, a stick to make a lollipop, wheels to make a wagon, he is showing that he knows how different parts relate to make a whole object.

Pumpkins

Draw a generous-sized circle (a couple of inches across) and say it is a pumpkin (or use a real pumpkin if you like). Now this pumpkin is having his birthday today, and he feels very happy. With your child either advising or drawing, make the pumpkin a smiling face. Draw other pumpkins, make up other situations, fill in other facial expressions. Turn the mouth down, add tears. Try a zigzag mouth or pointy teeth for anger. If there's a mirror nearby, both of you can try on different expressions yourselves. Watch your eyebrows particularly and try to copy them.

*Children can try dramatic
expressions and see them in the
mirror.*

MAGAZINES

Strange as it may seem to adults, children have to learn to "see" pictures. A child who can easily identify a photograph of a horse profile may not recognize it at all if it is sketched out in a few lines, if only the rear end is shown, if it is embedded among other details, or if it is drawn from an odd perspective. Looking together at many kinds of pictures in magazines or elsewhere, pointing out what you see, explaining it, is actually training in perception.

Through your ability to interpret, your child will learn to single out the bird's nest in the tree, to recognize a cartoon-type or a human stick figure, to name a horse by the look of its tail, and to recognize a skyscraper, whether the picture was taken from the street below or the sky above.

Although many specific activities with magazines are suggested here, the most basic and most frequent one should be to leaf idly through the pages, looking at this picture and that picture with your child.

What if your child can't sit still, can't concentrate, tears magazines to bits? There are plenty of children who are propelled by an inner restlessness to be in nearly constant motion. Sitting still is hard for them, concentration even harder. They are pulled into action by whatever captures their eye. It is as though a step says, *Jump off me*, a ball says, *Throw me*, and a magazine says, *Tear me to shreds!*

A nearly empty room, clear of pictures, toys and other distractions is helpful. So is quietness. So is the comforting confinement of a lap and a firm arm to lean on. You might also find it helpful to substitute some of the more active tearing and cutting activities also suggested below in this section.

Pat the Kitty, Eat the Cake

The vividness of magazine photographs makes them perfect for pretending. When you spot a picture of a kitten, pat it. Call, "Here kitty, kitty, kitty!" Ask your child to pour some pretend milk into a bowl, and put the dish in front of the kitty so it can eat. (Turn the page.) A birthday cake! Well, blow out the candles! Slice a piece for you, a piece for your child. Yummy! (Turn the page.)

Surprisingly, children of only two, who may neither talk well nor listen patiently, may enter into this sort of reading with great good humor. And you may find in their reactions more knowledge than you knew they had.

What Happens?

A photograph is a moment caught and held. Something must have happened before it was taken, something must have been about to happen afterwards. Even though you know most magazine photographs are posed, wonder aloud where the boy is going on his bicycle, why the baby is crying, what is in the bag the woman is carrying. There are no right answers to questions like these. Their purpose is only to tease out a pattern of wondering, thinking, proposing an explanation or predicting a consequence.

Search

Occasionally you will come upon a drawing or photo that shows a great many details—a city scene, a crowded room, a landscape. Locate some small detail yourself, and point it out to your child (*Look, children are playing ball behind that*

Can you find the embedded hats in this picture?

tree). Ask him to search the picture and tell you what he can find. Use your finger to concentrate his attention in a certain area. Use words as pointers, too: *Is anybody looking out the window of the red building?*

Children often have trouble seeing details against a crowded background. (You may have noticed this when you've asked your child to find a sneaker in a messy room.) The details are said to be "embedded"—just as a written word is embedded in a whole page of type. This activity can also be done as a game, such as, "I see something" on page 83.

Find the Cars

If your child often remarks on certain categories of objects (leaps on every car ad, calls every male a Daddy), go through magazines looking only for that category. The category itself is not important—whether it is food, Mommies, dogs, or trucks depends on your child's interests. What is important is that your child is keeping one class of objects in mind over a period of time and in the face of many distractions as he searches page after page of the magazine. To understand more about why organizing objects into groups (classifying) is important, see Chapter Two. For more methods of instructing children in classifying, see the Index.

The Cow Says Moo

As you notice different people, animals, food, and vehicles in magazine pictures, try to couple each picture with a bit of information: *The cow says, MOO. What does the man do? He puts gas in the car. Where does the butter go? In the refrigerator.*

For years and years, pictures will be an important source of information for your child. Not only will he learn to interpret and store the information contained in the picture itself, but with your help, he will learn to ask questions in order to obtain more information. Naturally, the information can become more telling than what the cow says, but the strategy is the same.

Silly Pictures

Save up your old magazines for cutting and pasting. Leave one large, colorful magazine uncut. Then cut out all sorts of pictures from the others: chocolate pudding, babies, kitchen pots, flowers, wheels. Let your child glue the small pictures onto a large picture in the uncut magazine. The results are pleasing, or funny or morbid: a tree full of puddings and cakes, a horse on top of a car, or a baby in a kitchen pot. Don't be alarmed at the grisly side of a young child's sense of humor; three-year-old slapstick is normally awful stuff.

Matching Ads

Many magazines are filled with colorful ads for food, some of which you may have in your own kitchen. Keep your eye out for your own brand of detergent, oil, pudding, cereal, coffee and so on. Look out for good pictures of oranges, carrots, and bananas, too, if you keep these produce items on hand. You or your child can cut out the pictures and save them in a bag or box. When you have accumulated a half dozen or more, spread the pictures out on the kitchen table or counter (or floor, for that matter). Take out the actual products that match them, and see if your child can pair each picture with the product.

What if your child can't cut with scissors? Cutting is a particularly hard skill, and plenty of children fly into a rage when they tear the picture by mistake or cut off some vital part of it. First, buy your child a good pair of scissors. The scissors ordinarily sold for children are so dull, so stiff, that even an adult would find them frustrating. Department stores and cutlery stores sell excellent blunt-ended children's scissors in the same high quality as adult sewing shears. The cost is high, but they will be used for many years.

If even good scissors don't help your child, put them away for the future and show him how to tear instead. Many children who can't handle scissors can use their fingers quite dexterously to tear paper into complicated shapes. Let your child practice first on construction paper (it has no grain or direction to its fibers, so it tears well in any direction) before he goes on to magazines.

The rest of the activities in this section require some work on your part, but are valuable if you have the time or inclination. Puzzles require cutting cardboard, and both puzzles and scrapbooks turn out best if you use the dry-mount method of glueing. Before describing the activities, here is some technical information that will be helpful:

How to Cut Cardboard

It will hurt your hands to use scissors on cardboard, and it won't be a clean job anyway. A matte knife (hardware stores call it a utility knife) or a hobby knife is actually easier and makes a clean cut, even in inside spaces. Use a breadboard or other piece of wood as a cutting surface. Lay the cardboard flat on the board and pull the knife blade along the line you wish to cut, without using very much pressure. Go over the line a second time to get all the way through the cardboard. Don't be stingy with blades; change them often, just as with razor blades.

How to Dry Mount

Water-soluble glues like white glue or paste tend to pucker paper and give you a bumpy job. Rubber cement works much better. Using the brush that should come with the cement, spread a thin, smooth coat over both the cardboard and the back of the paper that is to be glued to it. Let both surfaces dry. (This takes only a couple of minutes.) Position the picture where you want it above the cardboard, then lower it down into place until the surfaces meet. Pat it down with your hand. Excess rubber cement can be rubbed off cleanly with your fingers.

To dry mount:

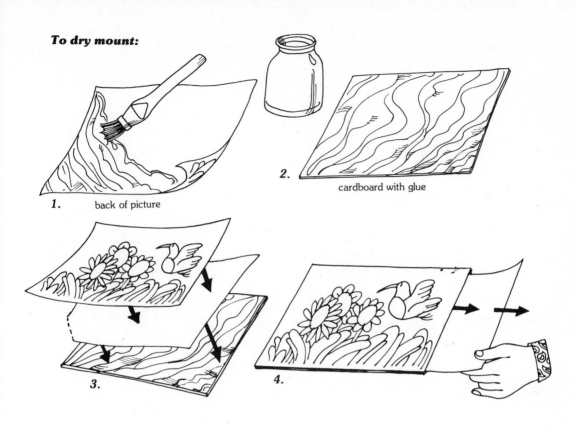

1. back of picture

2. cardboard with glue

3.

4.

If you're cementing a big piece of paper onto the cardboard, it will be hard to position it because once the two glued surfaces touch, they glom onto each other and can't be slid about. There is a clever way to cope with this. When the glue is dry it will only stick to another glued surface. Cover *all but one corner* of the cardboard with a plain, unglued sheet of paper. (Snip off one corner first.) Position the picture with glue on the back, and let it stick itself to the one exposed corner of cardboard. Now gradually slide the extra plain sheet of paper out from under the picture, which will then stick neatly where you wanted it.

Scrapbooks

Scrapbooks can contain any collection of pictures your child likes (labeled in clear letters if you have the time). They can be all one subject: cars, animals, food, toys. They can be different subjects that go together in some way: a country scrapbook, a city scrapbook, a scrapbook of objects you have in your own home. An alphabet book could couple a beginning letter with an object that starts with that sound. A number book could have a numeral and objects to count on each page. Books on colors and shapes are other ideas.

The illustrations on the next page show how to put together a dozen or more sheets of paper to make a scrapbook. If you would like a cover, construction paper is satisfactory. (Use a paper punch to match holes in notebook paper, or stitch or staple the cover together with non-notebook paper.)

If you don't want to make a scrapbook, stationery stores sell a variety of term paper binders that will hold unlined notebook paper; or you could use any of the

various spiral or stitch-bound binder notebooks sold to schoolchildren. An ordinary school ring-binder notebook is especially good if you want to be able to change the pages around or add new ones.

To cut out magazine pictures more easily, turn to the centerfold of the magazine. Take out the staples. Now you have a stack of separate magazine sheets from which it will be much easier to cut.

To glue cut-out pictures onto your scrapbook pages, use the dry-mount method with rubber cement (page 116) for the neatest job. For a less fussy job, use drops of white glue on enough spots on the back of each picture to hold the edges down. Don't try to smear the whole back of the picture with glue or the paper will pucker.

Picture Puzzles

As you leaf through magazines, keep your eye open for simple, clear photographs of everyday objects (check that the whole object is shown). When you're done with the magazine, cut these pictures out, cutting off the background if it is confusing. Dry mount each picture on a shirt cardboard. Then cut the cardboard up into three or four varied sized and shaped pieces to make a puzzle.

For the youngest child, cut the following in the most logical way: a two-piece puzzle in which the child must match the back and front halves of a car or a dog; or a puzzle in which the wheels of the car are separate pieces, or a house must be fit back into the surrounding landscape. For older children, cut the puzzle into more pieces and along less logical lines, so that the picture as a whole is less evident when the puzzle is taken apart.

CARD GAMES

Although the process is somewhat tedious, homemade cards for various games can be more intelligently planned and more interestingly designed than store-bought sets. You will need heavy paper or cardboard in squares or rectangles of equal size. Use shirt cardboards, construction paper, poster board, or manila paper for the cards themselves. Cutting the paper or board is the most tedious part of the job. Use a ruler and pencil to mark the squares. Cut paper with scissors, but use a matte knife (see page 116) for cardboard, running the blade along the edge of a steel rule if you have one, or trust your own hand if you don't. (Using a paper cutter is the best method of all—if one is available.)

The simplest games for the youngest children require as few as half a dozen cards. But while you're at it, make sixty or even more cards so you have them at hand for new games as your child is ready for them.

If you are making a game that uses pictures, dry mount them onto the cards with rubber cement (page 116). If you are making a game that uses objects, glue them onto the cards with white glue, applied liberally.

Family Cards

If you don't feel like making cards at all, there are a few games that can be played with snapshots. Look through family snapshots for clear pictures of each cousin, aunt, uncle and grandparent your child knows. Include pictures of your immediate family, too. Then use the set of photos for sorting games based on family relationships. One time, help your child sort out all the cousins in the family (including himself!). Another time, find which children go with which parents. (It might surprise your child to learn that you and Aunt Sally are children of Grandma and Grandpa.) Still another time, sort out who married whom. If you like, it might be fun to arrange all the pictures in a pyramid shape to show the whole family tree.

Mystery Cards

This game has to be made from snapshots. (Use black-and-white film to save cost.) The photos don't have to be mounted on cards. Take pictures of objects around your home from odd angles (an opened soda bottle viewed from directly above), or from very close up (six inches from a plate of spaghetti), or showing only part of the object (the coiled wire hanging from your telephone). Then take a second set of pictures of the same objects from normal distances, normal perspectives and showing the whole object.

The point of the game is to identify "mystery" photos (close-ups) with the "normal" pictures (regular distance).

For older children, don't bother taking any "normal" pictures. They'll have

A closeup look at fish scales.

Fish scales as part of the whole fish.

more fun just puzzling over the mystery ones. Older children might also have fun thinking up ideas for these photos—especially if they think they can trick a younger brother or sister.

Matching Pairs

Collect pairs of identical pictures to mount on cards. Several issues of the same magazine (ask friends to save their copies for you) will yield pairs of identical baby ads, cars, foods, and so on. Two copies of the same old shopping catalog will give you pairs of just about any object your child is interested in.

Play the game by spreading out one card of each pair (no more than three cards for a young child). Then hand your child one of the remaining cards, and ask him to find the card that is the same. Keep handing out cards for him to match until you or he is tired of the game. (If your child can't find the match, don't be afraid to do it for him. Your help isn't cheating.)

Feelie Cards

Pairs of cards made with small objects instead of pictures could be helpful to the youngest children—as long as they are old enough not to try eating the objects. Good items to glue onto the cards (use white glue) are leaves, beans, macaronis of different sorts, buttons, paperclips, stamps, bits of gift wrapping, ribbons, cloth scraps, cotton balls, toothpicks, safety pins, washers, screws, nuts, and so on. Again, make the cards in pairs.

This card set has the advantage of being very concrete; your child can feel as well as see the objects. Although you can make the game easy (matching pairs of cotton ball or bottle cap cards), you can also make it very difficult (matching pairs of fabric scraps or matching pairs of different raised patterns of gift papers).

Older children might enjoy making this set of cards for a younger brother or sister.

Lotto

Pairs of pictures can also be made into lotto games. Mark a shirt cardboard (or any heavy paper) into six rectangles. Glue one each of six different pictures onto the cardboard. Make as many of these boards as you have pictures. The matching mates to the pictures can be made into cards for the lotto game.

Each player gets a lotto board of his own. Taking turns, each player draws from the deck of cards, shows everyone the picture, and calls out what it is. Whoever has that picture on his own board gets the card and places it on top of its match on the board. The player who is the first to cover all the pictures on his board is the winner, and can shout out LOTTO!

The game can be played by as many people as there are boards. If you're not using all the boards, keep the cards that go with the unused ones in the deck anyway. It won't hurt for your child to practice scanning his board for each card that is picked up.

If you have made a set of "Feelie Cards," there is another version of lotto that could be fun. Give your child a few cards to spread in front of him. Put identical beans, paperclips, buttons and so on in a paper bag. Let him draw from the grab bag and see if he can find objects that match his cards.

Caution:
• *Don't give small, swallowable items to very young children.*

Dress-box Board Game

When you happen upon a sturdy dress box, make it into a board game based on matching. The inside of the top is the board and the whole box can be used to store the game parts. Draw a curving path from one end of the inside of the top to the other. Make the curve short and simple for a young child, longer and more mazelike for an older child. Mark the path off into spaces as shown in the illustration.

Now decide the goal of this board game. It could be to learn shapes (circle, square, triangle) or colors (red, yellow, blue) or three new numerals or letters of the alphabet. Using the three shapes, colors or symbols you wish to teach, distribute drawings of them about equally among the squares on the path as shown. Decide which is the beginning of the path, and which is the end. Mark the beginning with an arrow (or whatever you wish) and the end with a "reward" symbol ("home," a star, a picture of a cookie).

To play this game, you need either a set of cards (four each of the three shapes, colors or symbols) or a spinner. The spinner we show can be attached right to the board itself with a brass paper fastener, or mounted on a separate piece of

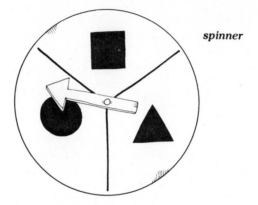

spinner

cardboard on which you've drawn pictures to match those on the path. Use toy cars, plastic figures or just some buttons as playing pieces. Each player starts where the arrow indicates, takes his turn spinning the spinner or drawing a card from the face-down deck, and then moves his piece to the next square that matches the card or spinner picture. Whoever is the first to arrive on the last space on the board is "home"—the winner.

Young children often have trouble accepting rules and turn-taking. Eventually, the desire to play the game usually overcomes these problems.

What if your child cheats? There's hardly a three-year-old in the world who doesn't. But it has nothing to do with dishonesty; he simply doesn't yet understand the nature of rules. To him, a rule is a declaration: YOU CAN'T STEP ON THE LINES. The rule can be changed by a new (or louder) declaration: STEP ON ALL THE LINES. Rather than fight against nature by insisting on "proper" ways to play, you might have fun together exploring all sorts of possible rules.

Take out a checkerboard or a Chinese checkers set, or any game board. Ask your child to tell you how you must move your pieces, marbles or checkers. Then ask him how he is going to move his. At first, his ideas may seem silly, but after a while you may notice that your child is actually working within certain boundaries he has noticed: patterns of lines, squares and holes, numbers and directions of moves within the patterns. He is not consistent yet, but he is experimenting with the invisible and arbitrary self-limitations by which we rule our games.

Caution
• *Don't give small, swallowable items to very young children.*

Sorting

Once a child can match *identical* pictures or objects, he may be ready to group objects in other ways, by sorting through cards.

Although sorting tasks can be quite absorbing to children, they can easily become too confusing. A child's intellectual ability to group objects, for instance, may be much better than his perceptual ability to scan a large number of cards and find the one he is searching for.

Say you want to sort cars from animals. Start with between three and six cards. Hold up one card. Say, *This is a car. I'm going to make a pile of cars over here.* Hold up the next card. Say, *This is a dog. I'm going to make a pile of animals over here.* Let him try the next card, which should be either a car or an animal. Ask, *Is this a car or an animal? A pig? That's an animal. Put it in the animal pile.* If he hesitates, show him what you mean.

Once over this hurdle, try spreading the cards out for him to scan. Help him by asking for a particular card, by pointing, or even by holding one up for him to notice. As he improves, add cards, add more groups to be sorted, and add extraneous cards—ones that don't fit any group. He has to learn to ignore as well as to notice.

Color Sorting

Collect pictures of many objects that match one another in color only. For example, green leaves, a green dress, a green car and the Green Giant; a red flower, red cherries, a red tricycle.

Play the game by letting your child sort the cards into stacks according to color. (Only a few three-year-olds can name colors accurately. Since you may be using this game to teach colors, use nonconfusing ones such as very similar shades of blue, bright red, yellow and green; not orange, pink, pale blue, muddy green. Teach your child one color, such as red. Be sure he can sort out all the red cards from all the others before you ask him to learn a second color and sort the cards into two stacks.)

Make this game harder for the older child by using colors with more subtle differences (pink, orange, purple) or very different shades of the same color (pale blue, navy blue, turquoise, royal blue).

Fancy Classification

The simple sorting games above are the basis for learning that an object can be grouqed with other objects in many different ways (or *classes* of objects). For instance, a red dress could be classed as "something red," as "clothes," as "soft," as "not alive."

As you begin to accumulate many cards for different games, sit down one day and look them over carefully. Look for pictures that could be sorted in several different ways. Make a game of it by spreading the cards out and, working together, divide them up now one way, now another. Keep the game informal so your child can come up with new ideas like "everything with buttons on it" or "all the pictures I like."

Noisy Cards

This is a game of matching a consonant sound to a picture of an object whose name starts with the same sound.

Go through your picture cards, choosing several pictures for each of the consonant sounds you are sure your child knows. Check that your child uses the same word to name the object! Make new cards on which you print the consonants you're using. Spread out the picture cards, then hand your child a consonant card. Shout out the noise it makes. Then he can choose pictures that start with the same sound, and shout the word out noisily, too. (This is *not* an easy task for preschoolers!)

S *is for sneaker.*

Number Cards

Since it is hard to find pictures that show a specific number of objects, you will have to make number cards either by drawing on them yourself, or by glueing objects to them.

With a pen, draw polka dots in the patterns illustrated here. The patterns differ so your child will be forced to count instead of just matching the "look" of the patterns. You can also glue small buttons or beans onto the cards with white glue,

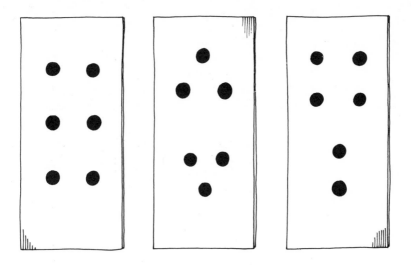

again following the illustration to get the patterns right. Many children will find it easier to count the raised objects. Now make a second set of cards with the numerals 1 through 10 written on them.

For a child just beginning to count, play this game with only the dot or bean cards, and only in the numbers 1, 2 and 3. Give him a card, and let him choose from those that remain a card that has the same number of beans. Let him use his fingers to touch the beans as he counts out loud (in unison with you if necessary). Add other cards with more dots or beans as he is able to count further. Don't rush it; you're looking for real counting, not a haphazard recitation or guess.

Little by little, introduce your child to the numeral cards, again starting with 1, 2 and 3. Give him a numeral card (you say the numeral aloud) and let him choose a bean or dot card that contains that many. You may find that your child can do this intuitively, without counting, by now. Most people can recognize a number of objects without counting them up to five, and frequently higher. This is good news, not bad—and your child will still get counting practice on the higher numbers. Arranging the objects into smaller groups makes it easier for a child to keep his place in counting beyond 12.

When your child has learned numbers and numerals from these homemade decks, he may be ready for real playing cards.

Deck of Cards

A regular deck of cards, even if some are missing, is a good learning tool. Use it to demonstrate that the numeral stands for the number of hearts or spades on the card. (Show him just the numeral, let him guess how many hearts there will be. Then cover the corners, let him guess the numeral.)

Use the picture cards for helping your child see the small differences first between kings, queens, and jacks, and then the really tiny differences between each of the four kings, the four queens, the four jacks.

Use the different suits for sorting games. Try just red cards from black cards, then try diamonds from hearts, spades from clubs.

When your child is familiar with the cards in a standard deck and can call out the names and numbers, you may be tempted to teach him actual card games. But there's little sense in trying to play skill games competitively with young children. First, they are no match either for you or for older children. Second, they can't obey the rules. And third, they don't really understand when a game is finished, much less how it is won. If you need still another reason, witness your child's fury when he is accused of losing!

Trading

One noncompetitive card game for young children involves simple card trading. Lay out ten or so cards in front of each of you. Say, *Let's see, you can have two of my kings. What will you give me?* Or you can say, *I'll give you an ace if you'll give me a two.* Or later still, *You can only have my queen if you have a pair of fours for me.* Then he negotiates a trade with you.

Cleverly, this innocent game accustoms your child to the idea of card game restrictions, while avoiding the difficult concept of winning. (If you help an older brother or sister understand the devious nature of this game plan, he might be willing to adjust his point of view and play peacefully with a younger sister or brother.)

Go Fish

This popular-with-kids game is easy enough for preschoolers who know their cards, but it's too difficult physically if the child must hold his cards in his hand. You can't expect preschoolers to play card games that require them to fan the cards in their hands. They can't do it.

To play Go Fish with a young child, deal five cards, face up, to each of you. Put the rest of the deck face down between you. Take turns asking the other player for a card that matches one of yours. If he doesn't have it, you must "go fish" in the deck, taking only the top card. If you get the card you wanted, you can repeat your turn. Again, this version is noncompetitive since you can see each other's cards, but it is hemmed in by more restrictions than Trading. The game ends when all the cards are matched up in fours.

ON THE ROAD

Children are seldom good travelers. They can't sit still, they get bored easily, and they don't understand why it takes so long to get anywhere. Nevertheless, the suggestions in this section should help you not only get through the potential ordeal of being on the road with children, but even give you high moments of enjoyment together and longer intervals of peace. Some of the activities are especially valuable ones, too, and adaptable to airplane, bus and train travel as well as the family car. A few general suggestions are in order here.

Unlike you, the grown-up traveler, a child on a trip hasn't the foggiest notion where he is or how to get back to where he started if he happens to lose his family along the way. A child may reach the ripe old age of ten before he realizes that the road you always take to get to Aunt Martha's house is the exact same road you take to come home again. He sees the sequence of landmarks on your route in a different order coming and going—therefore, they seem like two different roads! This anxiety about being "lost in space" contributes to carsickness, wildness, whining, hunger, thirst, calls of nature, and other bothersome travelers' complaints.

This basic anxiety is increased when (as must occasionally happen) the adults themselves get "lost." Lost is an awful word to children; it means the toy that was never found; it means the family that never got home again.

When traveling, reassure your child that either you:
    a. Know where you are going, or
    b. Know how to ask for directions, or
    c. Know how to read a map.

Your child has no other sense but yours to trust.

For long trips, both food and diversion will be necessary.

Travel Tips

Good snacks to bring along for car, bus, train and airplane trips are apples, cubes of cheese, carrot sticks, bite-size cocktail crackers, grapes and raisins. You won't avoid mess altogether, but these are about the least sticky, least crumbly foods you can find.

When a trip will take over a half hour, stash a few of the following gadgets in pocketbook or glove compartment to distract your child if he begins to act restless: a box of paperclips (show him how to make a necklace with them); assorted ceramic magnets (sets of various shapes are sold in novelty and toy stores); pocket-sized magnetic checkers or chess (to fool around with only); a penlight (especially if you are traveling at night); wildlife stamps; address labels or other gummed shapes plus scrap paper to stick them onto; a comic book of some character your child watches on television.

Caution:
• *Don't give small, swallowable items to very young children.*

When the trip is over, reclaim the gadgets—or what is left of them. They are not a gift, but a way of helping your child through the confinement and tedium of travel. He can have them back next trip.

Many of the talking games on pages 95–102 are also good diversions for boring car trips. I'm Thinking of Something, Nonsense Rhymes, and Beginning Sounds are especially good. Wherever we suggest several levels of difficulty within the same game, it can be played with children of different ages if they are willing to take turns.

As for carsickness, there are medications for it (ask your doctor). And don't forget the frequent stops along the road and a good rousing song once in a while. Remember to take a pillow and blanket for nap-taking.

Paper Plate Toy

A particularly pleasing car toy can be made from a paper plate, a magnet, and a variety of small metal items. Buy the heavy dinner-type paper plate with a high rim and rigid construction. Buy a reasonably strong magnet (the smallest horseshoe magnets sold for children are too weak to use for this toy). Collect small metal objects around the house: paperclips, wing nuts and washers, hairpins (which can be bent into interesting shapes), small springs and gears from broken toys. Test them all to see that the magnet attracts them.

Caution:
• *Don't give small, swallowable items to very young children.*

Now put them on the plate, and show your child that he can make all these metal "characters" move by running the magnet underneath the plate.

If he would like a more interesting environment for his metal characters to move about in, you or he can draw a road, a river or a house right on the plate. You can even make a paper-cup house (tear a piece of the cup out at the rim and then glue the cup upside down onto the plate) that his characters can move in and out of.

Find the Numeral

Choose any numeral your child already knows. Look for it together along the road. Your child can spot it on license plates, route and mileage signs, billboards, gas stations. This practice is especially helpful because the same numeral will be written in many styles, sizes and colors—yet it will always mean the same thing.

The same game can be played with letters of the alphabet, but be careful to choose very common letters like S, or the vowels.

Trucks and Cows

Choose some object that is often seen along the road (trucks, cows, gas stations, emergency telephones) and start a "collection" by counting each one you see. When you have gotten to more cows or trucks than your child can count, do his counting for him so he can hear the pattern of the numbers and say it along with you. Eventually this will help him memorize the teens, and learn the pattern of counting from 20 to 100. One day you may regret you ever started this game, as a ten-year-old can bore you for hours counting every telephone pole.

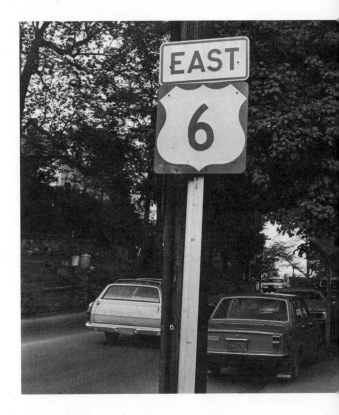

Stars and Golden Arches

All along the highway, there are symbols your child can learn to recognize. Look for famous golden arches, or stars on signs. Point out new symbols he has not noticed—the sign that means "school crossing," or "no fires" or "Garden State Parkway." It doesn't matter which signs he "reads" as long as your child is experiencing the good feeling of understanding what a symbol means.

Curves and Crossings

Among the most logical symbol systems ever invented is the plain old road sign system. You see a curved arrow, you know you are approaching a curve. You see a cross, you know a crossroad is ahead. Point these signs out to your child, explain them, watch together to see how the road does exactly what the sign predicted. Soon your child will watch for signs himself, and inform you of what is ahead.

Your child may also be able to understand the center line symbols, though they are harder. Point out to him and explain the meaning of solid and broken lines. Perhaps he can spot areas where you are allowed to pass another car, or even notice when a driver has disobeyed the rules.

Young children have only the slightest comprehension of space and time. Five minutes into a four-hundred-mile car trip, a child may ask, "Are we there yet?" When he does arrive eight hours later, he asks to go back home for a minute to get his hat. He has failed to connect time with distance. The problem is simply not solvable for many years, though the map and clock activities below lead toward the eventual solution.

Trip Map

Before you go on a trip, get a good map of the area you are about to travel. (If you belong to an automobile club, the trip plans they provide are excellent.) Mark out your route on the map with a broad-tipped marking pen. Make big circles around places where you will stop for gas, lunch or to see a sight. Circle landmarks, too (tunnels, bridges, rivers, mountains) if you know their location. Write some explanation in each circle for your own reference later.

Fold the map so the day's route is visible, then tape it with freezer tape so your child can't open it all out again. Then as you drive along, from time to time show your child where you are on the map, and which circle is coming up next. Tedious as car trips are for children, this activity gives them some sense of progress and also breaks the route into shorter segments that they can manage to get through one at a time.

On his summer vacation, Bert collected souvenirs for his scrapbook.

Trip Timing

Families who make the same trip many times usually get a pretty good sense of how long it takes to get to one point or another along the way. If you are accustomed to trips like this, you could help your child's sense of time by bringing along an alarm clock (one with a buzzy sort of ring that won't startle the driver out of his seat). Set the clock for ten minutes before you expect to arrive at a landmark, stop for gas, or eat lunch. Point out the hour hand, and show your child where it will be when the alarm goes off. (If you are using a discarded alarm clock rather than one you value, the clock face might be more readable to your child with the minute hand removed.) For short trips—and very impatient children—try a kitchen timer rather than a clock.

4 Creative Materials

IF WE WERE never to give a child clay he would—or perhaps already does—use mashed potatoes instead. Which is to say that children will use whatever is at hand to express their interest in the texture of stuff, the possibilities of form and pattern, and the making of "things."

We emphasize this about children to try to expand the idea of what a creative material is. We include sand, dough, paint, crayons, trash, fabric, wood, paper, and boxes in this chapter; but we might have included as well grass, mud, or any other substance that yields to the touch of a human hand. With that in mind, you need not feel overwhelmed by a need to rush right out to buy clay and paints and easels. There are plenty of creative materials available to you around your own home and the nearby outdoors.

One of our suggestions is that you collect and *keep* a number of potentially useful things for future activities you'll introduce to your child. Most of these things are junk—wood and fabric scraps, bottle caps, empty spools, paper cups, filler from packing boxes—and every conceivable sort and size of box. There may be times when you ask yourself, "Why am I saving all this trash?" The answer is: to inspire creativity.

Some insist that creativity can't be taught, but the family that encourages the use of a single object in a dozen ways is demonstrating it, encouraging it. Just as you now say to yourself, "There must be another way to think about this box," so perhaps your child will one day be able to say to himself, "There must be another way to use this stuff, get this done, solve this problem, achieve this goal."

A note to those who are particularly intrigued by the paint suggestions here: There is a way to buy art materials economically. School art-supply houses sell economical sizes and quantities of materials to schools. If your child is in a preschool program, the director may help you place an order through the school. It is also possible to get together with other parents for the relatively modest minimum order required.

Some readers may wonder at the lack of actual finished art projects in this chapter. The reason has to do with the way in which children approach creative materials during the preschool years. They are attempting less to find out *what* to make than *how* to make.

For example, they explore the squishing of dough, the smearing of paint, the lifting, pouring, and pushing of sand long before they are interested in sculpture, paintings, or constructions. "Creative Materials" concentrates mainly on what children concentrate on: process, not product.

This raises the question of what your role as adult is toward the development of your child's skill with materials. If you are not supervising steps toward a recognizable finished product, what are you doing? You are demonstrating techniques. The greater a child's vocabulary of techniques with a material, the more he is able to plan and carry through to the results he will envision as he grows. You are the supplier of the materials themselves, of course, but also of tools your child might not have thought of using; of accessories that will help him to elaborate on what he is doing; and of words.

Words are important to creativity. The child who can think "pink" and "puffy" might invent something a bit wonderful in the way of clouds. Where words are very basic to a child's understanding of what his hands are shaping or his eyes choosing (like *thin* snakes and *bright* fabrics) we have suggested the vocabulary to you. But don't let a few examples prevent you from using your own images to describe to a child how you see his work.

The vocabulary of color is one of the basics we do talk about later in this chapter, page 163, but a note here might be helpful, too. Color, as you probably know from trying to describe the color of a new shirt or wall paint, is an elusive quality. It can't be learned from a single kind of experience—a color puzzle, say, or a set of primary color paints. Rather, color vocabulary and concepts (and a good sense of color, as well) are learned from talking about the color names on crayon wrappers, experimenting with mixing tempera paints, and by many other conversations and activities such as dripping vegetable dyes into ice trays (page 73), choosing clothes (page 230), and sorting socks (page 39).

There is a bonus to the use of creative materials that may make you feel good as you clean up the dough crumbs. Children do a great deal of learning through their hands. If they can see a letter, hear the name of the letter, and then also

shape the letter with dough or inscribe it in sand—the letter is theirs. In the same way, they catch onto the idea of long and short when they construct in wood, to the idea of balance when they make a mobile, and to the concept of orange when they smear red and yellow fingerpaints. It isn't necessary to sit down and teach these things; they just come from allowing children to put all their senses to work to assimilate new information.

A word for the very neat: Don't make yourself suffer over the messier activities. Ignore them, or take them outdoors. There are plenty of cleaner suggestions here to keep your child's imagination going. The messier activities are only for those who are comfortable with them.

SAND

Sand is the easiest and—if you stretch the word to include dirt as well—the most universal of creative materials. It is a favorite of the youngest children because of its yielding quality. The merest swoop of the hand or drag of the foot leaves a mark, a hole, a bump, a smoothness. Although some suggestions that follow include you in a game or project, most of your child's time in the sand will—and should—be spent creating, wiping out and re-creating forms and patterns, or enjoying over and over again the sheer sensation of sand as it trickles through the fingers or packs beneath the palm.

Again, think of yourself mainly as the supplier: you supply the tools, the accessories, and occasionally the words that allow your child to pursue his own experiments. In other words, relax. Playing in the sand is an idle pastime, and you can be idle, too.

Sand Substitutes

Sand isn't an absolute necessity in a child's life. If you haven't access to a sandbox and have no place to keep a sandpile of your own, it's not the end of the world. City dwellers can substitute a large bowl or roasting pan filled with about four cups of salt, grits, or cornmeal. All three substances are granular; they can be sifted, heaped up, and smoothed down. They can also be used for writing or drawing in with a fingertip. Many of the activities suggested below will work as well with these substances as with sand.

Sand Drawing

Because he doesn't have to struggle with a tool of any sort, your child may be able to practice drawing and writing better with his finger in a granular substance than with a pencil and paper. A thin layer of sand, grits, salt or cornmeal in a shallow pan is all you need. Sprinkle a layer of the grains over the bottom of a roasting pan; then show your child the possibilities by drawing your finger through the grains so that the bottom of the pan shows through clearly. Lines, letters or drawings can be "erased" by shaking the pan back and forth a couple of times.

Offering your child this simple activity is one example of something you can do that television can't. The more senses through which a child can experience information, the more easily he can assimilate it. Television lets a child see and hear the name of a letter of the alphabet. You can help your child "feel" the letter as well.

For still another way a child can feel the shape of letters and numerals, see page 105.

Comparisons

No matter whether your child is making sand cakes, mountains, roads, or holes, you can also play a game that involves comparison words. If he makes a mountain, can he build it bigger? If he makes a cake, can he make one smaller? If he digs a hole, can he dig it deeper? And if he builds a road, can he make it longer, wider, narrower, curvier, straighter?

SESAME STREET COMPARISON WORDS			
Big	Small	Near	Far
Bigger	Biggest	Between	Next to
Same	Different	First	Last
Empty	Full	Hot	Cold
Under	Over	Wet	Dry
Up	Down	Beginning	End

How to Build a Sandbox

If you do have space for your own sandpile, here are three different, simple ways to contain the sand:

1. Dig a hole 1 foot deep and about 3 feet in diameter. Fill it with construction sand (available at lumber yards and some hardware stores) to within 4 inches of the top. Some dirt from the sides of the hole will get mixed into the sand, but only a little sand will escape from the hole.

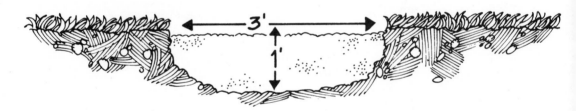

2. Use a worn-out car tire to contain the sand. Dig a 6-inch-deep hole the same diameter as the tire. Lower the tire into the hole, and fill it with sand up to the inside rim.

3. Nail together a wooden box frame from four 3-foot pieces of 10-inch shelving lumber. Or, for a sturdier frame, connect the boards at each of the inside corners with small angle irons screwed into the wood. Paint the frame with creosote or other wood preservative so it doesn't rot. Dig a 4-

to 6-inch hole the same size as the frame. Lower the frame into it and fill it with 8 inches of sand.

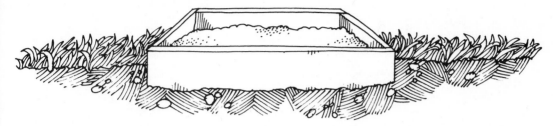

What if the neighborhood cats use your sandpile as a toilet? First, dispose of the smelly sand. Get new sand. From now on, nuisance though it is, whenever the sandbox is not in use, cover it with a cloth or plastic tarpaulin weighted with rocks at the corners, or protect it with a piece of plywood cut to fit.

Dry Sand, Wet Sand

One of the pleasures of sand is the magical change it undergoes when it is moistened. While only a moment ago it trickled through your fingers, now it packs to the shape of your hands. If the sand is fine enough, it oozes through your fingers to form drip castles below. If you can't get to a beach to let your child explore these properties as they occur naturally, try to provide a nearby sandpile with water by hose or bucket. Or remember to go to the sandbox one day after a heavy rainstorm.

Beach Sand Experiments

If you can visit a beach, you can assist your child in relaxed experiments.

Cover each other's feet with sand; wiggle your toes and watch what happens. Show your child how he can unmix a mixture: Mix together sand, pebbles and shells, sift the mixture through a coarse sieve to unmix it again.

Try drawing a picture in dry sand, then in damp sand.

Using wet and dry sand, see which is better for making a really high mountain.

When a damp mountain is finished and packed down hard, both of you dig through it until your fingers meet inside.

Pour a cupful of water into dry sand, and wonder where it has gone to. Then move toward the water, and dig down until you find water.

Sand Tools

After your child has had time to explore the nature of sand using just his own hands, offer him sand tools for more experiments. A child doesn't need store-bought sandbox tools or molding sets to explore sand. Kitchen tools like sieves, colanders, forks, large spoons, and spatulas are wonderful tools. (If you have none

to spare and don't want to share, try thrift shops and garage sales for the cheapest possible tools.)

You can use all sorts of discarded containers for molding damp sand. Good ones are the various shapes and sizes of plastic containers that food comes in. Paper cups, though temporary, work well too. An old set of rounded plastic measuring cups allows a child to mold mountains in graduated sizes. Pieces of board are excellent tools for smoothing large areas of sand and for shaping flat roads.

Old combs or hair picks with widely spaced teeth are good sand tools, too. For the parent who really likes to make things, an even more effective tool can be made. Basically, this homemade "sand comb" is a rectangle cut from either heavy cardboard (such as cigar boxes are made from) or ⅛- or ³⁄₁₆-inch plywood. One edge of the rectangle is cut into either zigzag teeth, like a saw, or straight ones like a comb. Use a matte knife (artist utility knife) to cut teeth in cardboard, page 116, and a jigsaw to cut them in plywood.

When a child pulls the toothed edge through damp sand, the teeth leave a ridged pattern. By moving the comb in arcs and zigzags, the designs are pleasing even though the child has had to use little skill or effort to achieve them.

Accessories

Sand-play accessories to serve as buildings, vehicles, trees and fences become important as a child's skills advance—but they need not be store-bought toys. Twigs, Popsicle sticks, stones, marbles, flowers, grass stalks all serve a child's imagination more flexibly than toys. Small scraps of wood will be used as vehicles, and boxes of various sizes can be buildings.

Buried Memories

Gather a group of small accessories—a toy car, a marble, a shell, or anything close at hand. Mark off a small square or circular area in the sand with your finger. Now you and your child bury each of the objects within the marked area. When everything is buried, ask if he can remember where the car is, or the marble. Let him dig at the spot where he thinks it will be, and see if he can find it.

To make the game easier, bury only three objects in a row within a narrow rectangular area. Your child will have less difficulty remembering position in an area that has a beginning, middle, and end.

You could also play the burying game as a way to practice relational concepts. Build a mountain. Then bury objects *in* the mountain, *under* the mountain, *behind* the mountain, *in front of* the mountain, *beside* the mountain. Use the words as you dig the objects out again. If small objects become lost, rake the sand to find them.

Caution:
• *Don't give small swallowable objects to very young children.*

Sand Stories

Using the flat of your hand or a piece of board, help your child to make roads to form a simple map. Use rocks, boxes, or paper cups for buildings along the road. Decide together what the buildings are. A friend's home? The firehouse, school, or store? Using small toys or pretending with twigs and stones, play out a story you make up as you go along. The story needn't be clever: A little dog is lost and wants to go home. A child hurt her hand and needs a bandage. As the play goes on, use direction words: *Stop at the corner! Here comes a truck. Oh, it's turning right, the girl can cross now.*

A favorite story game that many children invent for themselves is "Bulldozer." The child takes the part of the machine and, accompanied by appropriate "RRRRRR's" and "VROOM-VROOM's," uses the heels of his hands to bulldoze the sand. He can play "Crane," or "Steam shovel" also. Stones can be used for boulders, and twigs for trees.

Sand Map

Some children of four or older may be able—with your physical help and some verbal suggestions—to map in sand the actual streets in their immediate neighborhood. The skill is difficult and develops slowly, but the sandpile is a good place to begin. Start by positioning your own home and the street or road that runs past it. Then pretend to leave the house (with a nearby destination in mind) and "walk" or "drive" along the road. Talk about the corner, crossing, or landmark you would come to next in real life; then add some prop to stand for the landmark. Or mark out the next road in its correct relationship to your own. Don't try to fill in anything but the actual routes and landmarks your child is familiar with.

Good mud is hard to find.

You can say that again!

DOUGH

Most of what follows in this section applies equally to any plastic substance such as grease clay, water clay, commercial play dough preparations, and even good old sticky mud. But we emphasize homemade dough for practical reasons.

Grease clay is very hard to clean from surfaces, under fingernails and out of tools. It is also rather stiff for a child to work with, is expensive, and must be kept moist all the time. Commercial doughs aren't cheap, and are not nearly as malleable as the homemade variety. Alas, *good mud is hard to come by*, and messy besides.

Homemade Dough

Mix together with your hands:

    4 cups flour
    1 cup salt
    2 cups water

The finished texture should be soft and malleable but should not stick to hands. If too dry, add a bit of water. If too sticky, add flour. This mixture can be stored in a plastic bag in the refrigerator for several days.

Color isn't important for most dough activities, but children who are intent on making little cakes for pretend tea parties might enjoy some color. Color can be added to homemade dough by kneading a few drops of food coloring into the dough as you make it. The color won't be as strong as commercial play dough preparations, but you can get pastels such as pale pink, yellow, blue and green.

Measuring

Making dough provides your child with a good opportunity to measure ingredients. If his measurements are inaccurate, you can always add more flour, salt,

The Mudman makes his weekly delivery to Oscar-the-Grouch.

or water to correct the texture. Use individual cup-type measuring cups rather than a measuring pitcher so your child doesn't have to cope with reading the lines on the glass. If you don't want him to mess with the flour, let him add the salt and the water.

Tell him what the recipe says: *One cup of salt*. Hand him the cup and the saltbox. Tell him "one cup" means when the cup is filled right to the top. Let him pour the salt until the cup is full. Say, *Now the cup is full. That's one cup of salt*. You may think this is a lot of verbiage for so simple a task, but the idea that the measuring cup is "one cup" only if it is filled level with the top is not an automatic concept at all. Children, when asked to put three cups of sugar into a bowl, may count the number of times they dump sugar from the cup, without regard to how full or empty the cupfuls are.

Halving and Doubling

One day, just for experience's sake, announce that you are going to double the amount of dough. (Or, you are going to make twice as much dough, or two times as much.) Let your child in on the measuring so he can see what you mean by doubling. When you are done, remark on the amount of dough. *It makes two big lumps instead of one*; or: *It makes twice as much or two times as much dough*; or: *There is enough now for two people instead of only one.*

The idea of cutting a recipe in half may be far more difficult, but there is certainly no harm in using the term and demonstrating the results, even if it is several more years before your child really grasps what "half" means. At first children theorize that cutting something in half can mean cutting something into two unequal pieces—thereby arriving at the perfectly logical conclusion that they might get the "bigger half." Or, more surprising, halving and doubling may appear to them identical. When they make one thing into two pieces they may think they have "doubled" it.

Compliments

When children first begin to handle dough or clay, they don't try to make anything with it. Rather, they poke it, squeeze it, twist it, pound it, pinch it, roll it, bend it. They are busy discovering what the stuff is like, how it is shaped, and what the relationship is between the actions of their hands and fingers and the resulting shape of the dough. To compliment a child on the pretty cake he has made, when actually he is only seeing what happens when he bangs dough with the flat of his hand, may demean his work. Why? Because his pride is in the effort he is putting forth, and in the changes he is producing. Compliment only what you are actually observing: *You are banging the dough so hard! Oh, look how many holes you are poking in it! You are rolling it thinner and thinner!*

Notice the shapes your child is exploring, and comment on them: a *long* roll, a *thin* one, a *fat* one; a *big* lump, a *lot of little* lumps, a *bumpy* ball, a *smooth* one. This is not an exercise in teaching any particular new vocabulary, but only a way of communicating that there are words to describe what his hands have formed.

Tools for Dough

Although hands themselves are a sufficient tool for months of exploration, if your child has ever seen you rolling dough with a rolling pin or using a cookie cutter, he will probably want to experiment with these reliable dough tools. Other tools may include common ones such as dull table knives or tongue depressors and forks for pricking holes; bottle caps, spoons, or other shapes for impressing patterns.

Less common kitchen tools that are particularly rewarding are ravioli cutters (the wheeled cutters that leave a serrated edge) and garlic presses (which squeeze out bunches of tiny worm shapes).

1. The shapes children discover with any plastic substance are pretty standard. Before the first day is out, most children will learn to flatten dough by pounding it into a pancake shape.

2. Before long, they will learn to make round cake shapes by rolling dough between their palms, and sausage shapes by rolling it between palm and table top.

3. Children soon elaborate on their work by poking and pinching dough into more complicated shapes and by adding on other bits of dough.

4. Finally, these various shaping skills are put together to form the items you may yourself nostalgically recall from childhood: coiled snakes, nests with palm-rolled eggs inside, faces with finger-punched eyes, and lumpy turtles formed of stuck-together balls. At this point, the child may become greatly excited by the ability to form recognizable objects.

Decorations for Dough

After your child has explored the nature of dough for a month or so, you may notice that he is beginning to make "cakes" (or whatever he calls them). Now is the time to look around the kitchen for small things he can use as stick-in decorations. Look for toothpicks, plastic straws (cut them into 1- or 2-inch lengths), dried beans, bottle caps, macaroni. Usually these stick-ins will give a child a hoard of new ideas to try, including that old standby, the birthday cake.

Caution:
• *Don't give small swallowable objects to very young children.*

Baked Dough

Small dough objects that you want to keep can be preserved by baking until hard. They will last all through the dry seasons, but will eventually get mushy during humid weather. Preheat the oven to 300°. Lay the pieces to be baked on ungreased cookie sheets as soon as they are finished, and get them into the oven within a few minutes to prevent cracking. Bake them for an hour or until they turn a toasty brown.

These are some things your child might want to make and bake:

1. *Cookie Monster's alphabet letters:* Form the letters from strips or rolls of dough. Stick parts together by working both surfaces, and pressure together.

2. *Name plaque:* The baked letters are glued to cardboard for hanging on the wall.

3. *Miniature breads for doll and stuffed animal play:* After the loaves are shaped and baked, they can be spread with white glue and sprinkled with poppy, caraway or sesame seeds.

4. *Beads for stringing:* Holes are punched through the raw beads with a plastic straw.

Painting and Preserving Baked Dough

Any baked-dough item can be painted with tempera or acrylic paints. When some item you have baked turns out to be so terrific that your child wants to keep it forever and ever, you can spray it after it cools (and after painting, if you wish) with clear varnish to keep it from absorbing moisture.

Lay out a large area of newspaper on the floor and lay pieces of waxed paper on top of the newspaper. Put the object to be sprayed on the waxed paper so it won't stick. Spray it with varnish on one side and let it dry. Then spray the other side. Be sure all surfaces are covered. Repeat the process twice more to give three protective coats. Varnish can be applied with an artist's brush if you don't like using aerosol products.

Caution:
• *Varnish can be harmful. Follow instructions on container and supervise your child.*

Birthday Cake Math

There are many ways to use dough birthday cakes to teach your child some simple mathematics. Math is a cake for each person, and so is a "candle" (toothpick or bit of straw) for each year. Math is cutting a cake in half, or into thirds or quarters (even if you prefer at this point to say "four pieces" instead of quarters). Math is also the effort to make several cakes all the same size, or to make the biggest for Daddy, the smallest for the baby.

FINGERPAINT

Fingerpaint can be offered to children as young as two years old, long before they can handle the more difficult medium of tempera paint. See below for fingerpainting on counter tops and tile surfaces—a good way to start the youngest children out in the joys of fingerpainting.

Homemade Fingerpaint

Mix together to form a smooth paste:

    3 tablespoons cornstarch
    3 tablespoons cold water

Then boil 1 cup of water and add to cornstarch paste, stirring constantly.

Add a few drops of liquid detergent to make the fingerpaint easier to clean up.

Color the fingerpaint with a small amount of tempera paint in any color you prefer. Too much paint will harm the smooth texture and translucence of the fingerpaint.

This fingerpaint will keep for a few days in a closed jar in the refrigerator.

Commercial Fingerpaint

Commercial fingerpaint, it must be admitted, is a better formula than home-made fingerpaint. But the usual set of four or five small jars of different colors is somewhat expensive. Each jar holds enough paint for a couple of active sessions only.

Use of several different colors at once may be instructive for children who are either very good at controlling where the colors go, or for color-mixing experiments. But use of more than one color usually results in a muddy mixture. These sets do come with a small roll of glazed fingerpainting paper and tongue depressors for scooping paint from the jars.

Fingerpainting Surfaces

Fingerpaints are effective on any smooth, light-colored, nonabsorbent surface. Shelf paper used to be the old standby. You can also make a permanent finger-painting board by covering a piece of cardboard with self-adhesive white plastic-coated paper. You can even let a child fingerpaint on the bottom of the bathtub, on glazed tile or plastic walls surrounding a tub or shower, or on plastic counter tops. (Make it clear that this doesn't mean he may paint or write on walls.)

Setting Up for Fingerpainting

To set up for fingerpainting, choose any area that can be wiped clean with a damp sponge. If you feel it might be difficult to clean the working surface, cover it with newspaper first. Your child should have plenty of elbow room, so clear the area of obstructions. Roll your child's sleeves way up (or let him work bare to the waist) so he can get his forearms into his work if he wants to. Put a glob of paint in a shallow dish. Fill a mixing bowl or saucepan with water, and keep it next to the paint. If you are using paper, wet it first under running water.

As he works, your child adds paint by scooping it up with his fingers, and he adds water by dipping his hands in the bowl from time to time. More water gives a more translucent effect, less water a more smeary look.

Fingerpaint Experiments

The best way to understand the delight of fingerpaint is to try it yourself. Below are instructions for using different parts of your hands and different motions to produce dramatic effects. As you try each one, you may find that you no sooner achieve one effect than you are tempted to smear it away and try another. You get caught up in the process; it doesn't seem to matter if an effect ever becomes a picture. This is the spirit of fingerpainting—absorbing, playful, delicious and

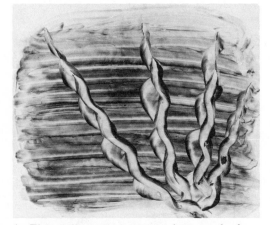

1. This tall waving seaweed is made by "swimming" the side of your hand up through the paint in a fishlike motion.

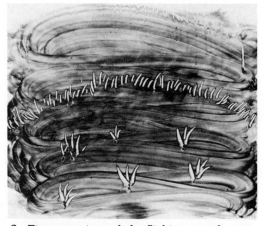

2. Fine grass is made by flicking your fingernails across the paper in a motion similar to flicking crumbs from the table.

3. Feathery effects require your whole hand, fingers spread and moved in a tight zigzag motion.

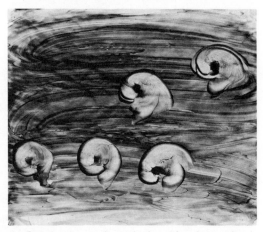

4. Snails are made with the side of your fist, quickly rotated in the paint and then lifted from the paper.

unfinishable. It is not only instant art; it is also disposable art. (If your child *does* want to keep a finished painting, see page 161 for suggestions on how to keep and display tempera paintings.)

5. *To make fuzzy leaves, touch the side of your open hand to the paper; then move it slightly sideways as you lift it from the paint.*

6. *This wonderful ribbon is formed when the whole flat of your closed hand is moved at random about the paper in curves and loops.*

7. *Whirlpools are left when you move your fist in a spiral.*

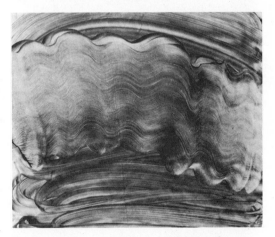

8. *Smoothly undulating backgrounds are done by wiping your whole forearm across the paper.*

Hand Printing

Each of the images on the next page was made by some part of the hand or arm, simply placed on an area of smoothed paint and not moved at all. Try these designs yourself and show your children how you made them. This is a good way to teach the words *fist*, *palm*, *knuckle*, *fingertips*, *fingernail*.

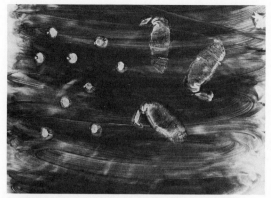

1. *Fingertip prints make polka dots. The side of the hand makes this shape when your hand is held in a fist.*

2. *This fish shape is made with the side of the hand and the whole forearm.*

3. *To make baby "footprints," make a fist print first; then press your fingertips down to print the toes.*

4. *To make dog or cat "paw prints," press with the heel of your hand and then four fingertips.*

Now that you yourself know all these fingerpainting techniques, teach them to your child. Not that he wouldn't eventually work many of them out for himself, but meanwhile he could get stuck in an unexciting scribble technique, using his fingertips as though they were writing instruments. After all, lines of one sort or another may be his only experience in making impressions on paper. Showing him the quite different possibilities in fingerpaint will speed his discovery of new techniques and increase his pleasure in the work.

What if your child doesn't want to fingerpaint? A child may poke a fingertip in the stuff, tentatively make a dot on the paper, and then want his finger washed right away. You can help by showing how easily fingerpaint comes off in water, and let your child wash the paint off his hands as often as he wishes in the bowl you have provided. You can also help by painting with him, on the same piece of paper, so he clearly sees that you feel there is no conflict between being clean and smearing paint. Or you can go on to another activity.

Other Cornstarch Mixtures

Cornstarch is an interesting substance that is fun to fool around with, both by itself and with mixtures other than fingerpaint. Once your child sees you make fingerpaint of it, show him some of its other uses. After his bath, use it as baby powder. It is an absolutely safe, doctor-recommended substitute that leaves the skin satiny soft, and plays the same role as baby powder in avoiding heat rash. Another time, use it to make a pudding. Packaged puddings are basically cornstarch, with flavoring added. (Any basic cookbook has pudding recipes based on cornstarch. So do many cornstarch packages.)

Still another time, make "goop" with cornstarch. Put several tablespoons of cornstarch into a cup or cereal bowl. Add cold water a few drops at a time until the cornstarch has the consistency of thick paste. This stuff has a very peculiar characteristic: when you pick the paste up in your hand, it will ooze out as a liquid between your fingers. But as you squeeze it, it becomes a solid and crumbles into fragments.

There is even a modeling compound that can be made from cornstarch:

> 1 cup cornstarch
> 2 cups baking soda
> 1¼ cups cold water

Mix together in saucepan, heat while stirring until mixture reaches a mashed-potato texture. Turn out on a plate, cover with damp cloth until cool enough to handle. When cool, knead for a minute or so. This compound, when shaped the way you like, can be left to dry and then, if you wish, painted or colored with markers.

PAINT

Besides fingerpaint, the two kinds of paint offered to children are water paint (in dried cakes mounted in a box or on a palette) and tempera (or poster) paint. Water paints are nice to try, but may not be very satisfying to children. The color is thin, the brush too small to cover much surface with, and the dried cakes of paint tend to become muddied up so soon that the child can't tell what color he is getting onto his brush. Tempera paints contain more pigment and are easier to use. They can be used with large brushes to cover big surfaces.

Tempera paint can be bought in art stores, art departments, and often in stationery and toy stores, too. Commercial sets are usually four or more colors in small jars. The paints also come in more convenient large jars, in plastic squirt bottles for squirting into other containers, and in powdered form for mixing in any desired quantity. Though not so widely available as the sets of small jars, these other forms and containers of tempera color are often carried by large art stores.

Big Bird paints a group portrait of his Sesame Street friends.

Although tempera paints are washable, several colors tend to stain. The worst is magenta—a color you can avoid altogether unless your child is wild about shocking pink (which can only be made with magenta and white).

Brushes

"Children's" brushes are poor tools for painting. They hold very little paint, and the bristles soon fall out. Better to buy one good brush that will work well and last a long time. Ask for a ¾-inch square end acrylic brush in an art store or art department. Hardware stores carry small sash brushes which work well, too.

Paper

To many children just starting to paint, a "painting" is a single sprawl on a whole sheet of paper. Needless to say, this can get to be an expensive habit. If you feel you can't support the expense of buying newsprint, use opened sheets of newspaper, instead. Use the plainest part of the paper (classified ads or the financial section) and stack it a dozen or more sheets thick. Each time a painting is finished, take it off the top of the stack and let your child paint the next sheet.

For a bunch of children who wish to paint at the same time, a roll of brown wrapping paper is a treat. Roll out ten feet or so on the floor or outdoors.

If the children begin to make a cooperative picture (this may happen after four years old), it can be kept as a mural. If the children work singly, cut out their individual paintings if they want to save them.

Paint Thicknesses

How thick or thin tempera paint should be depends on the kind of work your child is doing. For brush work (pages 156–157) keep the paint as thick as a milkshake so the color will be strong, and your child can control dripping. For printing (pages 158–160) use paint the same thickness, but add a drop or two of liquid detergent to help the paint stick both to the printer and to the paper. For spattering and blowing activities (pages 157–158) thin the paint to a more watery consistency.

Paint Colors

Young children seem to learn to handle paint more rapidly if they are not distracted by a lot of colors at once. Start with one strong color—bright red, or even black. Let your child dip his brush into the paint and experiment with the lines, drips and dots he can make. As long as he remains interested in these experiments, you don't need to introduce a second color.

When you do offer two colors, choose two that have a dramatic effect on each other. For instance, white with black, or yellow with red.

Your child can use a single brush for all the colors, or a separate brush for each color. If you use a single brush, you can: (a) Let the colors get mixed up as your child dips his red brush into yellow paint (mixed up colors aren't a tragedy), or (b) Show your child how to clean his brush before he changes colors, and hope for the best. A coffee can about half full of water makes a sturdy container for brush-washing between colors, but the fact is that most children get too absorbed in their work to bother with it. Painting, at this age, is not a fastidious art.

PAINTING AT HOME—THE EASY WAY

Practical Suggestions

There is no foolproof way to keep painting neat or easy to clean up after. But these suggestions will help to make painting at home as convenient for you as possible.

Choosing a work area: Crayoning and drawing require small wrist and finger movements and, therefore, a desk or small tabletop. But painting requires large, free arm motion. Children can move their arms freely if they stand to paint on a vertical surface (wall or easel) or if they kneel to paint on a horizontal surface (floor). If you have a low stool or chair for him to stand on, your child might also be able to paint on a counter or worktable. Consider a tile wall over a bathtub as one possibility. Your child can stand in the tub and paint on paper taped to the tile wall. A wall or a room may be set up for painting by taping newspaper several feet across and five feet up the wall, all the way down to the floor. The safest tape to use is freezer tape or masking tape, but even these might mar the wall.

You may find it easier to cover a door with either paper (newspaper or brown wrapping paper) or with coated paper for a permanent painting area. A bulletin board, hung on two hooks to prevent it from slipping to either side, will make a good surface for tacking the paper to be painted.

If you have low shelves in a child's area, you can improvise an easel from either a bulletin board or a piece of plywood. The board is propped on the shelf and kept from slipping by a small strip of wood glued or tacked to the shelf in front of the board.

Protecting surfaces: Spread several layers of newspaper below and to both sides of where your child will be working. Or cover the area with a fabric paint cloth or a heavy plastic tablecloth (plastic paint cloths are hard to handle). If you are using a shelf easel, drape newspaper, cloth, or plastic down over the front of the shelves, as well as over the floor.

Setting up the paints: If your child is standing to paint, a small table set to one side of the work area is the most convenient place to keep paints, brushes and water. If your child is painting on the floor or a counter, the paints can be kept beside him. As an additional precaution against spills, keep all the equipment on a tray with sides, or in a roasting pan. If something spills, at least the puddle will be contained.

The small jars in which many paints come spill easily, and are too narrow for a child to dip his brush into. Instead, pour small quantities of paint into wide cans, saucers, or muffin tins. Coffee cans are deep enough to allow the child to rest his brush in when he is not using it.

If your child is using one brush for several colors of paint, you will also have to supply a pot or coffee can full of water for washing the brush.

Making a smock: Use a man's worn-out shirt. Cut the sleeves the length of your child's arms. Cut the collar off. Put the shirt on your child backwards, buttoning one or two buttons in back to hold the smock on.

Storing paints: If your child will be painting again within a day or two, his containers can be covered with plastic wrap to keep the paint from drying. When paint does get too thick, add a few drops of water to each container and stir with the wooden tip of the brush.

If no one plans to paint until next week, pour as much of the paint as you can back into its original container and seal tightly. Dried-up paints can be restored to a liquid by adding water and letting it soak into the pigment for about a week, then stirring.

Cleaning up: Children usually don't mind helping to clean up after painting if your expectations match their capabilities. Use a floor sponge and a pail half-filled with warm water (for comfort). Ask your child to do only the preliminary work—wiping any large spills or drips with the floor sponge. You do the wringing and cleaning of the sponge, and all the finish work. If cleanup is done before the paint has dried, the job is easy and fast. If paint has dried, squeeze water onto it and let it soften for fifteen minutes before you wipe it up.

Brush Experiments

Painting effectively is a learned art. It is not true that all it takes is "talent," just as it is not true that the untalented can't find gratification in painting. Art is for everyone, but everyone has something to learn. For a young child, using a brush is a not-so-easy experience. Try these experiments yourself to discover the nature of the tool:

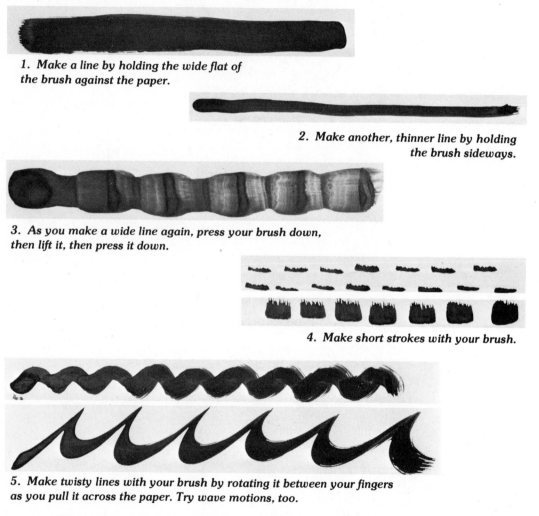

1. Make a line by holding the wide flat of the brush against the paper.

2. Make another, thinner line by holding the brush sideways.

3. As you make a wide line again, press your brush down, then lift it, then press it down.

4. Make short strokes with your brush.

5. Make twisty lines with your brush by rotating it between your fingers as you pull it across the paper. Try wave motions, too.

Now as you watch your child experimenting with the things this new tool can do, perhaps you can even show him a thing or two.

Color Mixing

A muffin tin makes a good container for color-mixing experiments. Using only every other hole, pour a little blue, green, red and yellow into the separate compartments. Let your child mix different colors into the empty compartments with his brush to see what happens. Comment on his work, using the names of new colors he is making: *Look at that! The red made the yellow into orange!* Another time, use the same colors plus white for new effects and make comments using the words *light* and *dark*.

Tempera colors may disappoint you by not mixing nicely. Blue mixed with yellow is greenish, but not a clear green. The same is true of the purple and orange you get by mixing blue with red and red with yellow. Red and white make only a sickly sort of pink (magenta and white make a bright pink). For clearer color experiments, using food coloring, see page 73. A way to talk about colors, with crayons, is suggested on page 163.

Paint Experiments

Now forget for the moment about painting pictures and think of paint simply as a colored liquid. How does it behave? What can it do? The following experiments are quite intriguing. Try them yourself; then introduce them to your child one at a time.

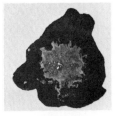

Thin the paint a little, and let some drops drip from the end of the paintbrush a foot or so above paper on the floor. Now stand up (or even stand on a chair) and drip drops again. Drip a drop of a different color into a puddle of paint on the paper. The result is called "bleeding."

With a very wet brush, make a flat line across the paper. Hold the paper upright and let the paint drip down. Now make two wet lines of two different colors of paint. Hold the paper up and let the paints bleed into one another. (Try a rainbow, too.) Drip one drop of paint on a small piece of paper. Tilt it this way and then that way in your hands to make the drip go where you want it. Wet a piece of construction paper in the sink. Paint on the wet paper and watch what happens. For a really dramatic technique that never fails to make an impressive painting, paint with thinned white paint on wet black paper.

Straw-Blowing

Use a plastic straw, an eyedropper, small pieces of smooth paper and diluted paint for this technique. With the eyedropper, make a puddle of paint in the middle of the paper. With his head right down to the level of the paper, let your child blow on the paint through the straw. The results are very pretty, especially as a child learns to force the paint to go where he wishes.

Spattering

Spattering, while wonderful fun and gorgeous to look at, is an outdoor activity. On a windless day, spread sheets of paper out in a flat area. Let your child dip his brush in paint, and then use big, fast swoops of his arm to spatter the paint down on the paper. Use several colors for the most decorative effect. Don't try this with

Spattering was the technique used to make this leaf design.

more than one child. Several will inevitably try spattering one another.

Another spattering method involves some preparation by you, but is a technique that could possibly be used indoors. Bend a piece of metal window screening over a shoebox to make a lid. Put a piece of paper inside the box. On top of the paper, place a leaf, some grass stalks, twigs or any other flat shapes. Cover the box with the screen lid. Then dip an old toothbrush in paint, and brush it over the screen surface. The spattering will outline the shape of the leaves on the paper—a very effective result!

Printing

To print with tempera colors, put several layers of paper towel into a plate or a disposable foil pie pan. Pour a puddle of thick paint onto the toweling, and mix two or three drops of detergent with it. Spread the paint on the toweling, and let it soak in to make a sort of stamp pad. To print, press the printer onto the paint-soaked towel, then onto paper.

There are many kinds of printers you can use, and many sorts of paper. Here are some suggestions. Print with: jar tops of various sizes; fork tines; the edges of pieces of cardboard; the end of a carrot from which the tip has been cut; cotton-tipped swabs; pieces of sponge; corks; plastic foam meat trays that have a raised pattern in the bottom; half a raw baking potato, with any pattern cut into it; the ends of paper-towel and toilet-paper tubes; grease clay molded into any shape you like; a round lump of clay flattened at the bottom with a pattern made by adding little balls or thin rolls of clay to the flat part.

Try printing on different papers for different effects: aluminum foil, foil wrapping papers, paper bags, newspaper, waxed paper, cardboard boxes, paper-towel tubes, paper towels and napkins. The detergent in the paint helps it stick to slick papers.

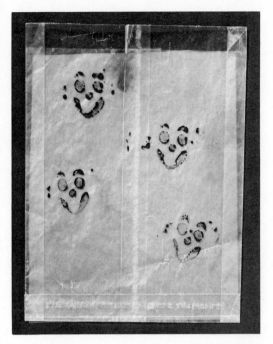

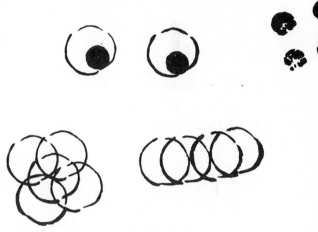

A cork and the end of a paper-towel tube were used to print these patterns.

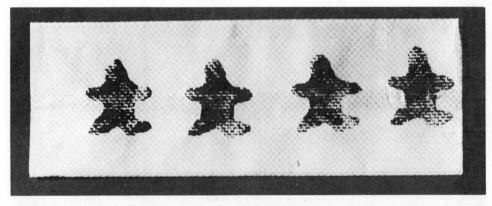

potato printing

Print Puzzles

If you have time one day, you can make a family guessing game out of prints. Use a lot of small pieces of paper, and print each one with a different implement. Match the design on the paper with the implement used to make it. Let young children guess by looking at the paper while examining the implements you used. Older children would have more fun guessing without these obvious clues.

String Printing

String can be used to make both prints and "pulls." Use soft, white string, cut in 10-inch or shorter lengths. Run water over the string first to soak out any sizing that would prevent it from absorbing paint. Pour a puddle of paint in a plate or pie pan. Dip the string into the paint; then holding on to one end, let it fall in squiggles onto the paper. Lift it up again, carefully, to get a clear print, or for a terrific effect, pull the string sideways off the paper. If you are using several colors, they will look cleaner if you wait for one to dry before dipping another piece of string into the second color and printing again.

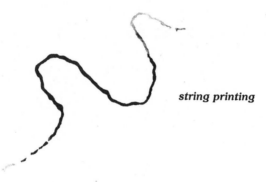

string printing

Uses for Printed Papers

Brightly printed newspaper or brown paper makes swell gift wrapping. The paper can be printed ahead of time, or you can actually wrap the package and then print the paper. Even small grocery store bags can be printed and used for odd-shaped gifts.

You can make very inexpensive greeting cards by using the size of writing paper that, when folded in half, fits in an envelope. Fold the paper first, and then print the outside of the card. You could print the inside too, or leave it plain for a message.

Outdoor Painting

Buy one jar of tempera paint (white is the easiest to clean) and one brush. When you get a chance to be outdoors for an afternoon, bring the paint, brush and a jar of water with you. Let your child paint sticks or rocks you find lying around. All the white paint will wash off with the next rain (or you can speed it along with a hose if it's in your own backyard). If you haven't far to go, you could even carry along an egg carton, a cardboard box, a shopping bag, or piece of board to paint. Silly as these suggestions may sound, they are delightful to children, and a perfectly good way to learn to use a brush and paint.

Finish the Picture?

Should you prevent a child from "spoiling" his picture by continuing to work on it when you think it is perfect? If he wants to work on it some more, apparently it is not finished in his eyes—and he is the artist, after all. This doesn't mean you have to stop yourself from expressing your point of view: *Oh, I love that painting just the way it is now!* But in the end, he must be the judge of his own work.

Should you save all your child's works of art? Should each new piece be displayed? Since these are the child's products, done for his own satisfaction and not necessarily for yours, consult your child. Each time your child shows you a picture, ask him if he would like to save it. Saving may mean no more than putting the painting in storage on a high shelf. It may never be looked at, but it is there. Now ask if he would like it hung up where he can see it for a few days before it is put away. He may like that; he may not. The point is that whether to throw out, save or display is the child's decision. If your child makes you a painting as a gift, that is another story. Of course, you must keep it. And if you fall in love with a particular painting, by all means ask if you may have it. Perhaps grandparents would like to receive some paintings, too!

Display Areas

A practical method for displaying art is a kind of laundry line strung up in the part of the home where your child spends most of his time. Stretch heavy string the length of the room along one wall, and four inches below the ceiling. (Wood homes will have wood studs beneath the plasterboard in the corners, so that nails will hold the string in place.) In city-type homes or apartments you may need to drill holes into plaster and insert plastic Rawl plugs for receiving screw eyes, rather than nails. Use spring-type clothespins to hold the paintings or other works of art on the string. When you run out of space in this display area, let your child choose what he wants to discard or put away to make room for new work.

Small magnets, available in hardware stores and dime stores, will hold smallish works onto the front of a metal refrigerator. A cork or composition tack board is good for smaller work, too. Use thumbtacks or pushpins.

Any of these display methods can be used for displaying art that is given to you, too. When you run out of room in your own display area, choose what to keep and what to throw away. It is not an insult to a child to learn that your taste differs from his own.

What if your child makes only messy, muddy paintings? It's discouraging to

Bob admires his friend's artwork.

parents, especially when a fuss is made about the natural creativity of children. People who have worked a lot with children are seldom so romantic. They have observed that many, if not most, children's first approach to paint is not to draw with it, but to mess with it. In the first year or so, children apply paints liberally, one atop the other—and if the colors turn brown or blackish, they like it fine. Then they smear the paint about with a brush, often all over the paper and several inches beyond, as well. And then they march proudly home and present you with this "work of art." What are you to say? "*Oh, that certainly is a lot of brown! And you spread it over the whole paper!*"

Once in a while, a child may continue to use muddy or dull colors, or refuse to paint at all. He could be discouraged. Read through the many art activities suggested here, and choose one or two of the simplest, most glamorous, instant-success projects such as clay printing (page 158), spattering (page 157), or rock painting (page 161). Give him only one bright color to work with (red, yellow, or pink). Compliment his work, keep it, and encourage him to continue developing his skills along these less challenging, more encouraging lines.

CRAYONS

Crayons will be used by the youngest children for scribbling, and then gradually for drawing, and finally for both drawing and coloring in spaces between the lines. For more learning activities than the ones suggested here, see pages 107–112. Any of the pencil-and-paper games suggested there can be done using crayons and large sheets of paper.

Not all crayons are good crayons. Before you buy the least expensive brands, try a few crayons out. If the color is weak, if you have to press hard to get a clear line, don't buy them. Children can't feel satisfied with their work when, after energetic scribbling, they can barely see the color they have worked so hard for.

Good crayons have a high proportion of pigment in the wax and leave an intense color on the paper, even with little effort.

All brands of crayons break easily—even instantly—under the unskilled fist pressure used by young children. For starters, buy jumbo crayons if you can. We say "if you can" because jumbo-size crayons in good quality are hard to find. Try art stores or art departments rather than toy or stationery stores.

Use a rough-textured paper for crayoning. Either manila or less expensive newsprint paper are good surfaces.

Colors

There's probably no easier way to teach children the names of the subtler colors than with crayons themselves. Soak crayons of different color in cool water so you can remove the papers (the papers don't always correspond to the colors of the crayon). Then as your child is working, suggest he try a purple this, a pink that, a light blue, dark green, and so on. On scrap paper, try out all the greens you have to see which is darkest, lightest, brightest. By five or six some children can even deal with yellowish green, greenish blue, pinkish or orangy reds. In the process, you'll get an idea of what colors or groups of colors confuse your child, and what he might be able to learn next.

What about coloring books? Do they stunt a child's imagination and squelch his creativity? Presumably, if a child were to get the impression that coloring is true art, or that accuracy is more important than his own impressions and efforts, coloring books might be damaging. But it is perfectly legitimate for a child to want to improve his control over a crayon, and coloring in a coloring book is a convenient, innocuous way for him to practice. Parents have power to influence their children. Coloring books don't.

You may be tempted to correct your child's use of color. (Whoever heard of a purple tree, or a pink dog?) But this is often seen as criticism by the child. If you want to use similar remarks to be sure your child knows his colors, try it this way: *Wow! A purple tree. Wouldn't it be fun if we really had a purple tree.* Then don't be surprised if he has noticed a purple beech somewhere!

Scribble Patterns

When your child has made any loose sort of scribble—one that has holes of various shapes between the lines—suggest he color-in the holes. It may be a new experience to him to see that there are all sorts of shapes formed by his random lines, and the effect of coloring-in can be very pleasing. This is also good practice for the time when your child will want to color in the shapes he has learned to draw.

What if your child won't use broken crayons? This sudden fastidiousness in even the messiest of children is common. What's more, you can't argue them out of it. If you haven't already, soak broken crayons in cool water until you can remove the papers easily. Keep broken crayons in a special box. Sympathize with your child and explain that, naturally, you don't expect him to use *broken* crayons for drawing! But see if he will use the broken ones for scribbling or for filling large areas. (Lay the broken crayon on its side and demonstrate how well it works for making broad bands of color.) The following are other suggestions for using broken crayons.

Light Pictures

Scrape shavings off broken crayons from the broken crayon box with a paring knife, or grate them on a grater. (Clean either tool by pouring boiling water over it to melt off the wax residue.) Sprinkle shavings of different colors onto the waxed side of a square of waxed paper. Cover it with another piece of waxed paper (wax side down) and iron it with a warm iron. The warmth melts the crayon wax, and spreads it. When the finished square is held up to the light, the colors glow like colored glass.

Crayon Scratching

Digging again into the broken crayon box, show your child how to cover an area of paper with solid, thick areas of color. Then rub black crayon thickly over the design until you can't see it anymore. Your child can use a ball-point pen that has run out of ink, a toothpick, or the flat of the blade of a table knife (with supervision) to scratch and scrape a picture through the black crayon. The colors underneath will show up intensely where the black has been scratched away.

Crayon Resist

In the technique called crayon resist, crayon is applied to paper first, then paint is brushed over it. The wax in the crayon lines "resists" the paint (the paint won't stick to the wax), so the crayon lines show through the paint. Undiluted tempera paint is too thick; thin it first.

To introduce the technique to your child, ask him to scribble with a white crayon on white paper. He can hardly see his work. Now brush thinned tempera paint over the paper. The invisible crayon scribbles will instantly appear as a pattern against the paint background.

Try black scribbles on black paper, and paint with white paint. For a lovely snowy effect, wet the paper after the crayon scribbling is done by dipping it in shallow water in the sink; then paint the white paint onto the wet paper.

For stained glass effects, let your child scribble with crayon in areas and lines of many bright colors on white paper and then paint in black over the whole design.

TRASHCRAFT

In a child's hands almost anything can become a creative material. That fact is the essence of trashcraft. The only rule to this game is: *If it looks interesting, don't throw it away.* And the only techniques to learn are how to stick one thing onto another.

Trash to Save

All the following items are often thrown away, but they can instead be saved for trashcraft:

• Packaging materials such as plastic and Styrofoam meat trays; plastic bubble packing; Styrofoam packing, both the block shape and the "macaroni" shape; plastic ice cream and other food containers; plastic or composition egg cartons; shirt cardboards; the backs of paper pads; corrugated carton dividers; paper-towel and toilet-paper rolls.

• Scrap materials like leftover fabric, foil, tinsel, string, yarn, ribbon, cotton or polyester stuffing, wrapping paper, sandpaper, greeting cards, cellophane grass, postcards, damaged but unused paper bowls, cups, and plates. And corks, bottle caps (but not the sharp-edged aluminum ones), and plastic straws (wash used ones in hot water and detergent); and used, washed Popsicle sticks, toothpicks, tongue depressors, cotton swabs (remove the cotton).

• Assorted hardware and notions like nuts, washers, bolts, knobs, wire (if you have a telephone installed or repaired, be sure to ask the repairman if he can spare any lengths of telephone cable, which contains dozens of multicolored wires). Bent hairpins, coat hangers, paperclips, unused buttons, and even used pipe cleaners with the dirty end snipped off with scissors.

• Any other trash that your child notices, or any other stuff that with any stretch of the imagination could be used to make something interesting.

Caution:
• *Don't give small swallowable objects to very young children.*

Junk Storage

All this junk is a pain to store, but it can be done. Next time you get something that comes in a good sturdy box, save the box. A dress-size box will hold bulkier trash such as egg and other food containers. A shoe box will hold cards, ribbons, strings and fabric scraps. An even smaller box might be fine for buttons, bottle tops and assorted hardware.

With enough boxes (and enough storage space to hold them), even ill-assorted trash can be mildly organized. Label boxes with categories like PAPER; CLOTH; PLASTICS; STRING AND YARN; HARDWARE (or SMALL STUFF). Really cumbersome trash like lumber scraps and coat hangers may have to be stored separately in a big carton.

If after some experience with saving trash you find that only a limited number of things really appeals to your child, keep only that trash, and use more specific labeling. Using shoe boxes, for instance, glue a sample of fabric on the one that holds fabrics, and a bottle cap or button on the one that holds small items. With this sort of labeling, your child will be able to find what he wants without rummaging through everything.

What if you have neither the space nor the inclination to store any trash at all? That's fine, too. But before you discard an intriguing bit of trash, ask your child if he can use it. After he's done with it, he may well be ready to throw it out anyway. The learning value in most of these projects is in the process, not the product. Unless particular pride is attached to the product, you may consider it as disposable as the trash it was made from.

Glue

The best glue for every type of trashcraft is white glue. White glue is a nontoxic product that produces no fumes. It is washable, easy to use, and bonds well with a variety of materials. White glue can be purchased economically in sixteen-ounce containers, but the relatively large opening and heavy bottle hamper a child's efforts. We suggest you also buy a two-ounce container, and remove the dispenser top to refill it from the larger bottle as necessary.

Children can use glue straight from the bottle, squeezing it out in either drops or thin lines from the dispenser top. For spreading glue over larger surfaces, screw the dispenser top off the bottle and pour a puddle of glue into a saucer or other shallow container. Thin the glue slightly with water, and spread it with a paintbrush.

To glue constructions in which the glue must hold pieces together against the force of gravity, as in stabiles, use only tiny drops of glue to cut down on drying time. Pieces may have to be held together for a few minutes until the glue sets and bonds.

What if your child messes around in glue? If you can stand it, let him smear the glue around with his fingers instead of with a brush or the dispenser top (keep a damp washcloth or sponge nearby for occasional wipes). If you can't stand it (especially if he is wiping his gluey fingers on furniture and clothing), offer finger-paint or dough to mess with instead.

Don't worry about excess glue on a child's work. Though white when wet, the glue dries clear and doesn't distract from the design. If the glue gets on furniture or clothes, try to wipe it up while it is wet. Glue that has already dried can be soaked for fifteen minutes or more to soften it before wiping, or it can sometimes be gently pried from the surface with a dull table knife. Glue on fingers both washes and peels off.

Collage

Collage is any construction that consists of a surface to which a variety of other materials has been glued. The surface can be a shirt cardboard, a scrap of wood, a paper plate, a cardboard tube, or a box. Materials to be glued can be anything from beans to cotton balls.

The advantage of collage work is that a child can make a terrific-looking product quickly and with little skill. Because so many different kinds of materials can be used, concepts of color, texture, shape, and pattern can be learned from the work. Below are a few suggestions for collages children especially enjoy making. (Remember that the bean and pasta collages are foodstuffs, and may attract insects and vermin.)

Bean Collage

Cut shirt cardboards (or postcards, old greeting cards, cut-up cardboard boxes) into four pieces to use for these and any other collages that require manipulation of small items. Or substitute similarly sized pieces of other cardboard or lumber scraps.

In a muffin tin or several small dishes, set out two or more varieties of dried beans. Choose beans that contrast with one another in color or size; for instance, kidney beans and yellow split peas, or black beans and navy (pea) beans.

There are two methods your child can use to decorate his cardboard with beans. Teach him both. The first is to put a drop of glue on the cardboard, and place a bean on it; or a line of glue, and place a line of beans on it. The other way is to brush a layer of glue over an area of the cardboard, sprinkle beans over it, and tip the cardboard to spill off the excess loose beans. The first method is good for larger beans and for children who enjoy planning and executing a design in detail. The second method is good for smaller beans and for children who need quick results. With either method, you don't have to wait until the glue is dry to go on to the next portion of the design.

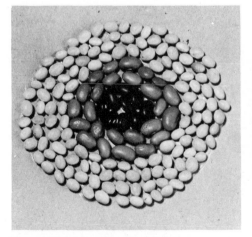

The child who made this bean collage started with a round shape in the middle and then added the rest of the design, one ring at a time.

This collage is by a younger child and has less pattern.

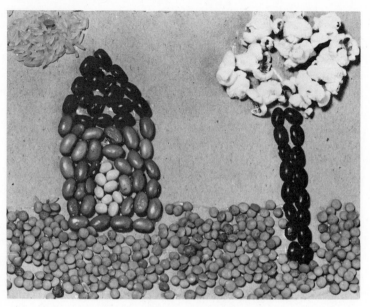

Older children can plan well enough to create a bean "picture." The larger white pieces are popped popcorn, and rice has been used, too.

Caution:
• *Don't give small swallowable objects to very young children.*

Pasta Collage

Use the same process suggested for bean collage to make ones of macaroni, noodles, or any other kind of pasta. It can include wheels, bowties, shells, elbows, broken spaghettis, as well as tiny shapes such as pastina for backgrounds. Suggestions for using small pasta collages as holiday decorations are on page 250.

Alphabets

Your child could use alphabet noodles (or alphabet cereal) to spell out his name on a collage, or he could construct letters of the alphabet using straight and elbow macaronis.

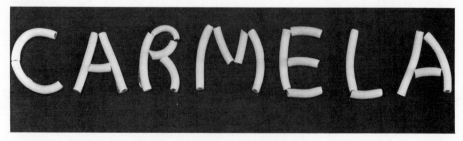

Another way to form letters for alphabet collages is with short bits of string. Cut thick string into pieces that range from two to four inches long. Your child can dip the bits of string into glue and arrange them on paper or cardboard to form letters. Although the excess glue will look messy at first, it dries clear.

If you have the time, an adult-made string alphabet on separate cardboard cards may come in handy for teaching your child letters. He can run his fingers over the raised shapes to help himself memorize the forms. The best way to do a good job is to draw a letter first, cover the lines with a thin stream of glue, then lay the string down on the glue. Cut any excess string with sharp scissors while the glue is still wet.

Nature Collage

When you take a walk together in the country or the park in the fall, or if you go to the beach, or even if you can wander no farther than a weed-filled vacant lot, take along a paper bag and collect for collage. Fall, with its beautifully colored leaves and strangely shaped seeds and pods is a natural. So is the beach with its sun-dried seaweed, pebbles, shells—and don't foget a little sand. But even that vacant lot may offer the seed heads of a variety of grasses, ailanthus leaves and cockleburs. Store fresh leaves in a plastic bag in the refrigerator until you are ready to make a collage. When you are ready, get out a piece of thin cardboard,

glue and the collected treasures. Ask your child to make a collage that looks like the woods, or beach, or vacant lot. As he works, notice the things he is using, name them if you can, and remember together your collecting walk.

Fabric Collage

This suggestion is especially for those who sew their own clothing and, therefore, have a variety of scraps at hand. Save scraps in a scrap bag and add to it bits of yarn, ribbon or items like cotton balls or torn knitted mittens that have a fabric feel to them. When you have an interesting variety collected, go through the scraps and cut them small enough (one to three inches, any shape) for collage work. Let your child glue scraps of this and that on a shirt cardboard or a piece of heavy paper. Since fabric is easy to handle and covers an area quickly, this might be an opportunity to see if your child is interested in trying collage on a cylindrical cereal box or a small carton. Even a rather crude result makes an attractive storage container.

Collage Concepts

As your child works on collage, your comments and ideas can direct his attention to various attributes of the materials he is using. If you notice that he is selecting the brightest colors of fabric, offer to sort out the *dull* from the *bright* pieces to make his task easier. If you notice he is running his fingers over the surface of his work, remark that the cotton balls feel *soft*, the sandpaper *rough*, the foil *smooth*. If he is using scraps of gift wrapping and ribbon, see if you have some tinsel left, or some glitter he could use to make his collage *sparkle* and *shine*.

The trick to this sort of teaching is not to develop a "lesson plan" in advance, but to be alert to any trend in your child's work. Then, by commenting or by supplying new materials that fit his scheme, to articulate and emphasize what he is already dimly aware of.

Another way to focus a child's ideas is to limit the types of material he is working with. For instance, cellophane grass, bits of polyester stuffing, pastel colored crepe paper or fabric will make a springtime look inevitable. If the conversation turns that way—and he remains interested—you might try crumpling crepe paper to look like flowers, or you might give him some beans to use as bird's eggs, or you might remember that the pussy willows are out and snip some for him to add to his collage. In the process, your child would be learning many of the themes we identify with spring.

Other limiting combinations are glitter, ribbons, bits of evergreen trees, red and green or gift paper for holiday collages; the insides of an old wind-up clock, plus assorted pieces of hardware and some string for a "machine" collage; and twigs, bits of cotton, aluminum foil and a background of blue or gray paper for a winter collage.

Caution:
• *Don't give small swallowable objects to very young children.*

What if you plan a springtime collage and your child uses the cotton for "explosions" instead of clouds? Go along with him. He may have something on his mind that he wants to deal with. He may be concerned with what he has heard or seen about bombs or guns or war. Through your willingness to turn to his concerns in spite of your own plans, your child will learn that he is free to pursue what he himself feels the need to know. There will be another spring.

Stabiles

A stabile is a three-dimensional construction that doesn't move. It can be a bunch of small lumber scraps glued together; or it can be a structure made of

boxes, tubes, paper plates and cups; or it can be a delicate construction of pipe cleaners, straws, corks, feathers, and macaronis. Stabiles are more difficult to make than collages because pieces must be either balanced or held in place until the glue dries enough to hold them.

Help your child start out well by building a firm base with him. In our illustration, for instance, an adult has helped to form a solid base of large shell macaronis and thick tubes to support the more delicate structure above. As the design progresses, you may also have to help your child to balance his pieces, or do his holding for him while the glue dries. White glue bonds within five minutes if used sparingly.

Mobiles

Mobiles are constructions that move when they are touched or blown upon. Children's mobiles are usually constructed on a base that can be hung up to increase movement. All mobiles involve balancing the elements attached to the base and, unlike stabiles, which can be glued together, require a variety of attachment methods that may be difficult for many children. Because your child will probably need a good deal of help, we have suggested only the simplest mobile, and concentrated instead on the methods by which one sort of "trash" can be attached to another.

Many of the methods described here are valuable for other activities, even if your child never produces a mobile to move in the breeze.

Coat Hanger Mobile

The easiest children's mobile is a wire coat hanger from which strings of objects are hung. An adult might naturally hang the hanger up before starting to work so as to check the balance as construction progresses. Children might find it easier to work with the hanger on a table or floor and hold it up from time to time to see

how the decorations are balancing. If the construction becomes so complicated that the child could work better with it hung up, turn the coat hanger hook at right angles and hang it from a shelf.

As you work together on the mobile, comment on the idea of balance: *This is hanging way over to one side; I think we need something on the other side to balance it. Let's move this heavy piece into the middle so it will balance.* Use words like *crooked, uneven* and *weight*.

Mobiles are not the easiest things to display. If you have any ceiling light fixtures, they are the most convenient base to hang the hanger mobile from, but you have to be sure no flammable portions touch a bulb. Or try tacking the mobile up on the wood frame over a window. If you live in the country, hang the mobile on a tree limb outside so your child can watch the motion and balance he has achieved.

Attaching

Attaching requires not only a good deal of finger dexterity, but also some tricky problem-solving. It's best to teach each method as it is needed, separately and with patience. For your enlightenment, here are the possibilities:

Poking: A sharp object (toothpick, wire, pipe cleaner) is poked into a soft substance (cork, Styrofoam, grease clay, gumdrops). Or a pointed object is poked into a hole (the shaft of a feather into the hole of a macaroni, the end of a twig into the hole in a plastic straw).

Stringing: An object with a hole in it (spool, doughnut-shaped cereal, paper ring, washer, piece of straw) is strung on a thin shape (spaghetti, pipe cleaner, wire, string, twig).

Twisting: Two bendable materials (wire, pipe cleaner, hairpin) are twisted about each other; or the bendable material is twisted about any other material (wire around a twig, pipe cleaner around a scrap of cloth). Wire and pipe cleaners can also be shaped into hooks from which to hang objects.

Tying: This is an obvious attachment method, but few children can handle it. Help is definitely necessary at first to tie string, yarn, strips of cloth or ribbons.

Stapling, Stitching and Clipping: Staplers, needle and thread, and paper-clips may come in handy when other techniques don't work. And for lightweight materials, there is always glue. (Occasionally, sticky tape is helpful but it is not particularly attractive on a mobile.)

Caution:
• *Don't give young children small, swallowable, or pointed objects without careful supervision.*

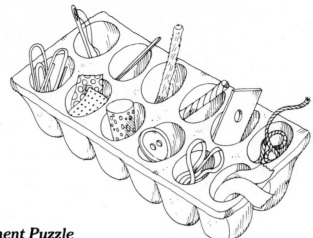

Attachment Puzzle

To experiment with various methods of attachment, or to teach your child specific techniques, or simply as an enjoyable problem-solving game, set up an empty egg carton with the following items in each of the compartments:

1. two paperclips

2. a threaded needle

3. two scraps of cloth

4. a toothpick

5. a cork (or a small ball of grease clay or Styrofoam scrap)

6. a piece of wire (or pipe cleaner)

7. a button

8. a section of plastic straw

9. two rubber bands

10. wood or cardboard scrap with a nail hole punched in it

11. two scraps of paper

12. a six-inch length of string

Now ask your child to connect together in any way he can as many different objects as he can. There is no one answer to this puzzle. A child might string the paper, fabric, rubber bands and piece of straw on the threaded needle. Or he might poke the toothpick through the pieces of paper and impale the cork or clay ball on it as well. Maybe he'll discover how to clip paperclips to one another or how to loop one rubber band through another. If he doesn't, you can always show him. The point is to familiarize your child with many different ways of getting one object to "stick" to another. The more methods that are at his disposal, the more inventive and persistent his work will be.

Stringing

Both boys and girls may love to drape themselves with outlandish necklaces and bracelets. Stringing objects—less tricky by far than constructing mobiles and stabiles—is excellent practice in accuracy. The variety of objects you can find around for stringing is lively and impressive:

SOME STRINGABLES:

paperclips (several shapes if you have them)	paper rings	old beads
	springs from broken flashlights and ball-point pens	plastic Christmas tree balls
colored rubber bands		plastic straw sections
straight macaronis, pasta "wheels," some alphabet noodles	large buttons	punched bottle caps (punch with a hammer and large nail)
	spools	
	shells that have erosion holes in them	
doughnut-shaped cereals		nuts and washers
	jingle bells	

Caution:
• *Don't give small swallowable objects to very young children.*

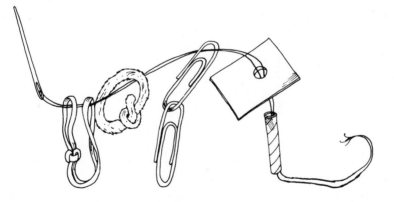

A long shoelace is a good string for a younger child because the plastic-wrapped end is easy to handle. String can also be used. Prepare "points" on lengths of string by dipping the last inch of one end in white glue, twisting it tight, and leaving it to dry hard on a piece of waxed paper. Or, for the older child, thread string double on a large plastic needle. If you suspect your child has patience enough only to string a couple of objects, use narrow ribbon threaded through the plastic needle. Even with a single bead, the necklace will still be pretty. Any sort of string should be at least two feet long for a necklace. Anklets and bracelets strung on one-foot-long hat elastic can be slipped on and off easily, and the elastic is usually stiff enough to push through beads.

Before your child begins stringing, tie some sticklike object (a twig, a Popsicle stick, a toothpick) to the end of the string to prevent objects from falling off as they are strung.

When your child has finished stringing, cut the stick off and tie the necklace so that it is large enough to fit easily over your child's head. For elastic anklets and bracelets, tie the ends together to fit around wrist or ankle.

Copycat Necklace

One of the many skills necessary for learning to read and write (and do arithmetic too, for that matter) is the ability to recognize and reproduce sequences—for instance the sequence D–O–G in dog. The skill can be practiced with beads. Accumulate a group of each of several kinds of beads. They can be identical washers, plus identical macaronis, buttons, paperclips and so on. Prepare two necklace strings—one for you and one for your child. Lay your string out on a table next to your child's string and start a pattern—for instance, one washer, two macaronis. Ask your child to copy your pattern. Now repeat the pattern as you string (say it out loud: *one washer, one–two macaronis; one washer, one–two macaronis*). As your child catches on to this idea of patterns, vary both the complexity and the length of the sequences.

Homemade Beads

There are several kinds of beads you can make yourself. Instructions for baked dough beads are on page 146. But you can also bake bits of raw vegetables and even chicken neck vertebrae. To make vegetable beads, cut slices or chunks of carrots, beets or potatoes. Gouge a hole in the center of each with the point of a potato peeler. Let the beads dry at room temperature for a few hours, then spread them on a cookie sheet and dry them in the oven at 250° for several hours or until they are brown and leathery. The chunky wrinkled look of these beads is pleasingly natural.

For bone beads, boil chicken necks until the meat comes off easily. Clean the meat off, and dry the bones in the oven at 300° for about an hour. The central hole in each vertebra is large enough for stringing.

Baked beads, macaronis, beach shells—even cereals—can be painted with tempera or acrylic (plastic) paints if you wish. Necklaces can also be elaborated upon with bits of feather, fabric, ribbon, tinsel, or glitter. After the necklace is strung, use white glue to add these fancy decorations to the objects used as beads.

Jingle Bell Anklet

Your child will need help with this one, but he'll love the result. Help him string a jingle bell on a twelve-inch length of hat elastic. Knot it in place about three inches from the end of the elastic. Now have him string on another bell and knot it about an inch from the first. Continue until there are three or four bells on the elastic. Hold the elastic around your child's ankle or wrist, and tie it so it is snug but not tight. When your child stamps or dances, the bells will emphasize his rhythm. Children can get these bracelets and anklets on and off easily by themselves, and they last a long time.

FABRIC

If you sew—especially if you actually construct garments from whole cloth—your children are going to beg to sew, too. It looks easy to them; the sharp little needle appeals to them; and the ability to produce a garment fairly gleams of magic. Few childish ambitions, however, are quite so frustrating. First of all, you probably should say "no" to using the sewing machine if you have one. Even if your child fails to pierce his finger, he will tangle the mechanism for sure. And as for hand sewing, your child will not be able to make the wonderful toys and clothes he can so easily imagine. Nevertheless, the suggestions below are ones that have worked well with children as young as three.

Needle and Thread

A child should use carpet thread, as it tangles less easily than lighter threads. If you keep paraffin or beeswax in the house, pulling the thread across the wax before starting to sew will help, too. Use the thread double, with a large knot at the end. Children's stitches can be measured in inches, so you will have to rethread the needle frequently. A large embroidery needle with its long eye will be easiest for you to thread and for your child to hold.

Scrap Strings

Rather than start right out to teach stitching, start with something your child may already know—stringing. Prepare a batch of small fabric scraps, each no bigger than a matchbook. Thread a needle with about two feet of thread, doubled to end up a foot long. Show your child how to put his needle through the middle of a scrap. Then show him how to hold the scrap in one hand while he pulls the thread through it with the other. Show him that he should pull until the knot of the thread touches the scrap. Supervise him through the next few scraps, each time making sure he is holding the fabric and pulling the thread all the way through. This is the first important step in stitching. (When he feels he is finished, you can either cut the knot and take the scraps off and start over again or cut off the thread at the needle, and tie the ends together for a necklace.)

Caution:
• *Young children need supervision when using a needle.*

Stitched Strips

Cut a two-inch strip of fabric about a foot long. The fabric will be easier to work with if it is thick and firm, not flimsy. Thread the needle with a double thread at least eight inches longer than the fabric strip. Lay out a modest number of large buttons, other bits of fabric, or items like rubber bands and paperclips. Help your child insert the needle close to the end of the strip (and from the wrong side) and pull the thread through to the knot just as he did when stringing scraps. Show him that he can put his needle through one of the objects you have laid out, and then stick his needle back down through the cloth strip and pull the thread through to attach the object. Now—and this is the hard part—help him to understand that before he attaches the next object, he has to stick his needle up through the back of the strip and pull the thread to the front again. You will have to supervise his next few attempts to be sure he understands the concept of back and front.

Though at this point your child makes two separate motions instead of one to take each stitch, he is nevertheless stitching. (When he is finished, secure the end of the thread by taking several small stitches in the fabric yourself. With the addition of a safety pin, the finished strip could be used as a doll's belt or a stuffed animal's collar.)

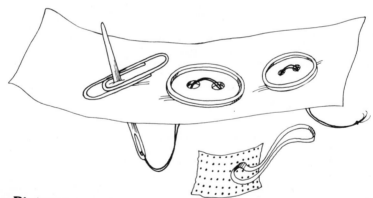

Yarn Pictures

Use burlap, needlepoint canvas, or other very coarse fabric for this stitching project. Cut a piece of fabric about eight or ten inches square. Thread a large tapestry needle (a blunt needle sold for needlepoint work) with any bright-colored knitting worsted-weight yarn. Use the yarn single rather than double this time. Start the yarn yourself by taking several small stitches near the center of the

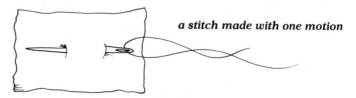

a stitch made with one motion

fabric square, or make a large knot. Demonstrate a one-stroke stitch to your child, explaining that the needle goes into the fabric, then comes up out again before he pulls the thread through. Let him try it. When he gets the knack of making a one-stroke stitch, let him just keep stitching with stitches of any length he likes. The brightness of the yarn will be pleasing no matter how crude his work.

Note:
- Younger children may not have the patience or dexterity for sewing activities. If your child isn't interested or ready, try again later.

Troubles

These are the troubles young stitchers get into, and suggestions for how to avoid or cure them.

1. Using up all the thread so there isn't enough left to secure the end. (Keep your eye on your child's work. Stop him before he has used all the thread up. If you are using light-colored thread, try marking it six inches away from the needle with a marking pen. Tell him to stop sewing when he gets to that mark.)

2. Tangling the thread. (Keep thread no more than two feet long. Other than this—and using heavy thread, waxed if possible—there isn't any way to avoid tangles. When it happens, cut the thread between the fabric and the tangle, rethread the needle, and pull out enough thread from the work to tie the end to the new thread.)

3. Pulling the thread too tight so the work is all bunched up. (Have your child work at a table, and show him how to pull the cloth flat after each stitch.)

4. Losing a single thread from the needle. (Use a single thread only when you have to, as with yarn.) Show your child how to hold both the needle and the yarn when he is pulling it through so that the needle stays threaded.

5. Cutting the thread before you have had a chance to secure the end. (Demonstrate what happens: the thread pulls right out. Next time, he must tell you before he cuts the thread.)

What if nothing we have suggested works and your child loses his temper or gives up? Reassure him that there are other ways to get pieces of cloth together such as using white glue. Let him decorate a piece of cloth with glued-on scraps, buttons, ribbons, yarn. Occasionally, firmly state your conviction that sewing certainly is a hard thing to do.

What if your child is determined to make doll's or animal's clothes? Below are a few simple ideas that don't require the impossible skills of garment construction. All of them can be made with felt to avoid frayed edges.

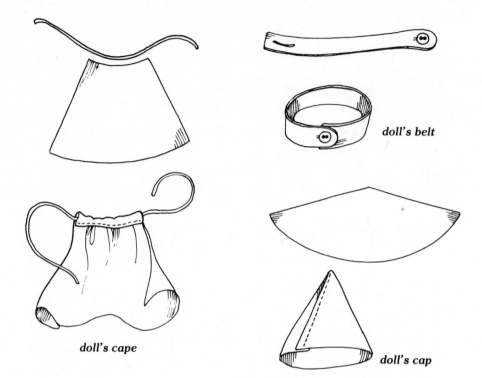

doll's belt

doll's cape

doll's cap

WOOD

Wood is the most difficult of the creative materials suggested in this chapter simply because, literally, it is hard. On the other hand, its very solidness is what makes even the simplest wood product so satisfying to children. We have kept the ideas below as easy as possible—some suggestions require no tools at all—so that even the child who is not interested in real woodworking might still derive some pleasure from the material.

One warning: Children may be discouraged by any project that requires a lot of steps.

One reason that children in preschools may turn out more impressive products than children at home is that projects requiring many steps are spread out over several days of short work intervals. The children aren't necessarily confronted with a number of steps at once. One day, they have fun sawing wood up. Another day, it is suggested that the children glue their cut-up pieces together. Another day, they may be offered paint. And by the end of the week, perhaps some decorative bits like strings, nails, and bottle caps are made available.

whittling to make a stool leg

Although the child brings home an impressive product, it has happened as a result of rather disconnected episodes. So if your imagination can envision a complicated end product, try to present each step as a separate episode. The technique does ultimately teach step-by-step planning toward a goal without intimidating a child with what would seem to him an interminable process. What's more, the child is both surprised and pleased with a final product he may not have been able to envision while he was only sawing wood.

One more warning: Your child may hurt himself when he tries woodworking. But hammered fingers and mild saw scrapes, though painful, are not serious. Assure your child that even experienced carpenters have such accidents. He should not be accused of carelessness or clumsiness. Get a bandage, give a kiss, and get him back to work.

Where to Get Wood Scraps

People who do even small amounts of home carpentry have only to remember to save their scraps in a carton instead of throwing them away with the trash. But those who don't work with wood themselves will have to find scraps elsewhere. Lumberyards may keep a bin for free or cheap scraps of their own. And if someone is constructing a house near you, by all means ask if you can pick up the smaller, smoother scraps that would be dumped with their rubbish anyway.

No-Tools Toys

To make the simplest boat, use white glue to stick a smaller rectangle on top of a larger one. Use spools (though they are, alas, no longer made of wood) or dowel sections for smokestacks.

To make the simplest airplane, glue a thin rectangle across a slightly fatter rectangle.

To make the simplest car or truck, choose two pieces of wood that are the same width, but of different lengths. Glue the shorter piece above one end of the longer piece. (Wheels aren't necessary for two-year-olds, and many three-year-olds won't complain either.)

To make little wooden people, look for scraps that have a blocklike shape and stand upright. Or use sections of thick dowel or wood turnings. Let your child draw eyes, noses, and mouths with a marker. The merest resemblance to human faces is most convincing and, in only minutes, gives your child a host of little people to play with.

As you can see, these wooden toys require no carpentry tools and only the crudest skills. Nevertheless, their forms are evocative enough of the real thing to allow imaginative play. They can be painted with tempera paints, of course.

Tools

Tempting as sets of toy tools are, they usually do not really work. The only way that children can work effectively with wood is by using sharp, heavy, well-made adult tools. Of course, the saw will be cumbersome, the hammer heavy. But the blade will cut with far less effort than a child's saw, and the weight of the hammer is what gets the nail through the wood.

Besides hammer and saw, an older child who really enjoys woodworking will need a drill, a vise, and some clamps. The clamps can be used to hold a plywood working surface to an existing table as a substitute for a workbench.

Caution:
- *Supervise children's work with carpentry tools, and explain that they are not to experiment with tools on their own.*

Nailboards and "Porcupines"

Children tend to be very repetitive when learning a new skill. Nailing is an example: Let a child hammer in a single nail, and he will want to hammer dozens more. It's a good way to learn, and easier than trying to nail one piece of wood onto another.

Buy a half pound of three- or four-inch spikes (lumberyards call them tenpenny nails) or use any similarly large nails (with heads) that you may have around. Give your child a real hammer to work with, though it can be a lightweight one. Use any scrap of board that is at least three-quarters of an inch thick. If your child can't work outdoors, or over a concrete floor, better safeguard your floor with a larger piece of wood underneath his work. Either start a few nails for your child,

or show him how to hold the nail while he takes the first few taps to secure it. Then let him pound away.

If this seems unproductive to you, call the bristling product a porcupine and give it some marking-pen eyes. Or, once a scrap of board is covered with nails, supply your child with a bunch of colored rubber bands to stretch between the nails for decoration.

Sand Blocks and Rhythm Sticks

Sand blocks and rhythm sticks are simple noise-making toys that can give your child practice in sawing. Use an old mop handle or broomstick for rhythm sticks. Fasten it securely in the vise, and let your child saw off two pieces, each about a foot long. They are banged together to make noise.

For sand blocks, use a scrap of narrow shelving board. Fasten the scrap into the vise and let your child saw off two pieces about three inches long. Glue sandpaper on one face of each piece with white glue. When brushed together like cymbals, the sand blocks make a pleasing chuf-chuf noise.

Peek Boards

For practice in drilling holes, let your child drill to his heart's content in a scrap of wood large enough for him to hold in place with one knee as he works. Be sure you have a large scrap of lumber under the board he is drilling. Even if he works outdoors or on a concrete floor, the extra wood surface is needed to protect the end of the drill and to achieve a clean hole in the board. Call the result of your child's work a peek board, since it will probably occur to him to peek through the holes anyway. A nice addition would be pieces of colored cellophane glued over the holes on the back of the board.

Fancying Up

As your child learns the basic carpentry skills of nailing, sawing, and drilling, his own ability will give him new ideas of what to make. To stimulate his imagination further, suggest the following ways to elaborate his products with string,

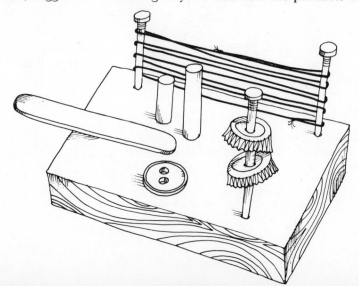

paint, crayons, felt, bottle tops, dowels, and other items you can find around.

String wrapped around nails makes a "railing." Two bottle caps, nailed into wood with a longish nail, clink when the toy is shaken. Crayons, markers or paint, no matter how haphazardly applied, jazz up plain wood. And anything that can be added with white glue—buttons, bits of dowel, Popsicle sticks, parts of broken toys, felt hinges, small paper cups—adds the drama of complexity to the simplest product. The ease with which children imagine these add-ons to be machinery, or inventions, or "secrets," makes up for functional accessories they can't yet handle.

PAPER CONSTRUCTIONS

Scrap-paper constructions can be formed by cutting, tearing, folding and bending. Each of the constructions that follow is simple to make, takes only a minute, and uses a minimum of material. But best of all, each will absolutely amaze your child. The magical change the paper seems to undergo comes as a revelation to most kids.

Try a construction that appeals to you first, demonstrate it slowly to your child, and then let him have a try. Slick magazine paper is excellent for most paper work, but you can also use notebook paper, construction paper, and—last but least—junk mail!

Fringes

Fringing is an excellent project to give a child his first experience of cutting with scissors (see page 116 for remarks on good scissors for children). Let him fringe junk mail and magazine pages. Just for fun, you can curl his fringes for him by rolling them around a pencil (see Paper Curls, following). Or roll up opened-out sheets of newspaper, let your child fringe the edge, then roll up again and pull the roll upwards from the inside—extending the roll to make a "beanstalk" or "palm tree."

To make a newspaper palm tree:

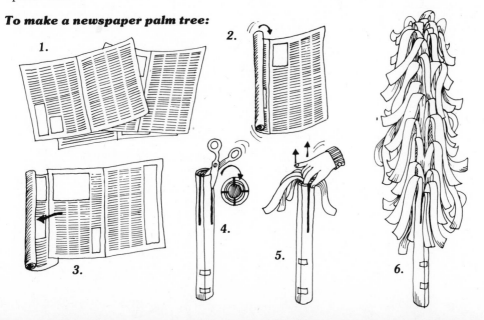

Paper Curls

Cut heavy paper like construction or magazine paper into one-inch-wide strips. Lay a strip down flat on a table, lay a pencil across it at one end, and roll the pencil up tightly inside the paper. When the pencil is pulled out, the paper will stay curled.

Paper Springs

Beginning at a corner, cut a piece of magazine construction or other heavy paper in a spiral pattern until you reach the center. When the spiral is held up by its center, it extends into a three-dimensional spring that bounces as you move it.

paper spring

Pinwheels

Make a pinwheel, again using firm paper like brown wrapping paper or a magazine cover. Cut a perfect square first. Then cut and bend the square, as shown.

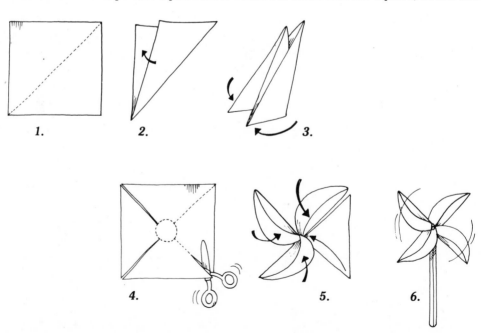

1.   2.   3.

4.   5.   6.

Push a pin through the center and into the side of the eraser on a pencil. Blow on the pinwheel to make it twirl.

Caution:

- *Preschool-age children shouldn't make or play with a pinwheel without adult supervision.*

Twirlers

Cut a rectangle out of firm paper. The rectangle should be about two by six inches, but you don't need to be exact. Tear or cut one end of the rectangle as shown to form the "propellers," then fold the propellers in opposite directions. Fold the bottom of the twirler into a point. To fly the twirler, just hold it up by its body and let go. It will spin as it falls.

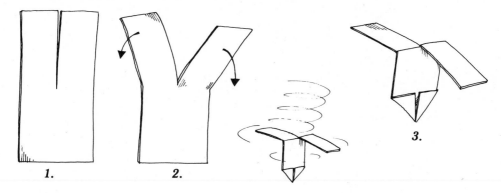

1. 2. 3.

Gliders

Most people know how to make this glider already, but we include it here just in case it wasn't part of your childhood, or in the unlikely event that you have forgotten the folds. Use letter-sized sheets of paper saved from junk mail. Paper-

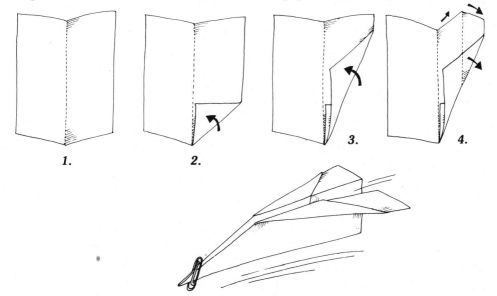

1. 2. 3. 4.

clip the bottom creases together. The clip will help your child keep his glider together and the extra weight will make it fly more steadily.

You may have to show your child how to launch a glider. Children tend to throw it like a ball at first.

Floaters

Children can amuse themselves for quite a while by simply letting an unfolded sheet of paper float downwards from a height. A stairway offers a good height, but if you don't have one, let your child stand on a counter or a chair. Pages from small magazines float nicely; so do opened sheets of facial tissue.

Caution:
- *Don't let young children stand near stairwells or on counters or high chairs without supervision.*

Fans

Pleating is not all that easy, but even an unevenly pleated piece of paper makes a functional fan. Hold the bottom together by wrapping tape around it.

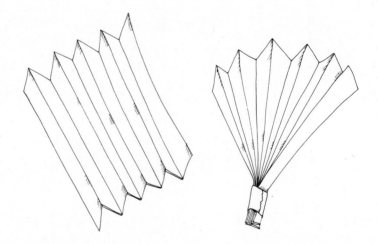

Accordions

Crisp paper like brown wrapping paper makes the best accordions. Cut two strips an inch wide and at least twelve inches long. (Even longer is better.) Lay the two strips at right angles to one another as shown, and glue the top strip to the bottom one. Now fold one across the other repeatedly, as shown, until both strips are used up. Cut the uneven ends of the strip, and glue them together so the accordion doesn't come apart. The springiness of this object is enjoyable in itself, but it may also be used to mount cut-out pictures so they wave and bounce above the background paper.

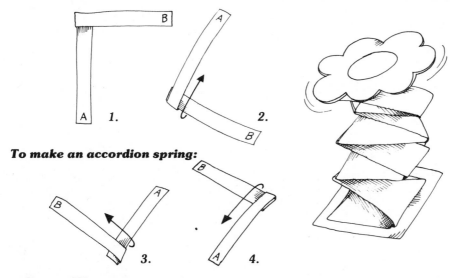

Paper Weaving

Use the two covers of a magazine for this project. Cut one cover crosswise into strips one inch wide. Cut the other cover lengthwise into strips one inch wide. Glue an end of the short strips onto one of the long strips as shown. Then weave the other long strips in and out of the short ones. Tack the edges down with spots of glue as you go along so the weaving doesn't "unravel."

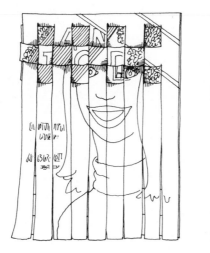

Paper Chains

This old favorite still gives great satisfaction to children. Cut used gift paper, colorful magazine papers, or other scraps into inch-wide strips. They should be about six inches long. Use either glue or staples to hold the ends of the rings together.

Paper Tricks

Both these tricks are guaranteed to delight kids. The first is too hard for a child to duplicate; it's just for fun. Take an ordinary postcard. Say, "I bet I can step right through this postcard!" Now cut the postcard as illustrated, using sharp-pointed scissors. When all the cuts are finished, the card will open out large enough for you to step right through it.

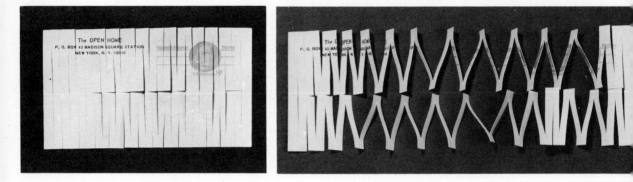

The second trick might be one your child can learn to do. It requires the type of soda-fountain straw that is wrapped in thin paper. Tear the paper open at one end. Push the paper wrapping down around the straw until it is scrunched to within an inch of the bottom of the straw. Now pull the scrunched-up wrapping off of the straw and lay it on the table. Say, "This is a worm! Want to see him wiggle?" Drip a drop of water onto the "worm." Believe it or not, he'll wiggle!

BOX CONSTRUCTION

There's an often-repeated story one hears about the family who carefully plans wonderful presents for a child, only to find that the child ignores the gifts and plays with the boxes they came in. The fact that the story seems to have happened so often should tell us something about boxes—and children.

A box is a wonderful thing—light, strong, openable and closable, shaped this way or that, big or little, plain or gorgeous. And a child is a wonderful thing—made with the potential to imagine dazzling possibilities for a box. Collect and save boxes: cigar boxes; shoe boxes; egg, milk, ice cream and oatmeal cartons; compartmented liquor cartons and Styrofoam-stuffed packing cartons; slide-open matchboxes; collapsible cake boxes; metal bandage boxes; hinged jewelry boxes and foil or patterned gift boxes; *any* box.

Shoe Box Vehicles

The simplest of all uses for a shoe box, other than to hold something, is as a vehicle. Toddlers can just push shoe boxes around, or with a string tied to one

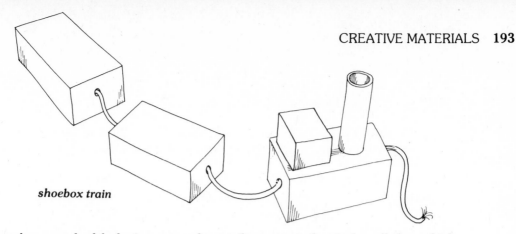

shoebox train

through a punched hole (use an awl, a nail or a pencil point), pull the vehicle behind them. Several shoe boxes tied to each other with loops of string make a train. (The engine has another box glued on top to make a cab and a toilet-paper tube for a smokestack.)

Milk Carton Boats

Waxed milk cartons are not only sturdy, but are waterproof as well. The illustrations below show several ways to cut milk cartons into bathtub boats.

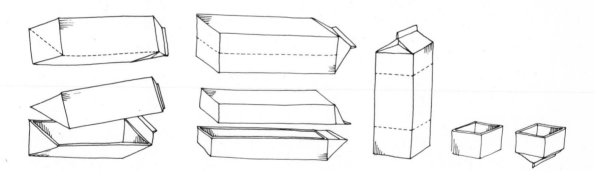

Egg Carton Toys

Egg cartons, torn or cut up in various ways, make a multitude of temporary toys. The drawings below show a few of them you might suggest to your child. There are others he might invent by himself. Use both plastic foam and molded cardboard egg cartons.

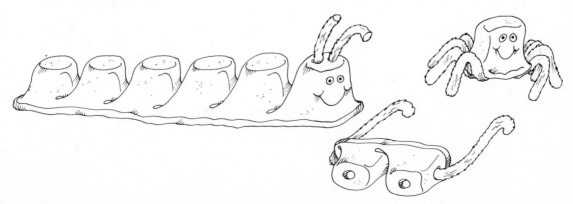

Oatmeal Box Drums and Shakers

Cylindrical boxes (cornmeal, grits, and oatmeal still come in them) can easily be made into drums or shakers. For a drum, glue the top back on an empty box and let your child beat it with his hands like a tom-tom. Or cut two ten-inch lengths of one-half-inch dowel to use as drumsticks. A wooden spoon also makes a good drumstick. To make a cereal box into a shaker, a small amount of rice, dried beans, or a few pebbles are put into the cereal box before the top is glued on. Each thing makes a different sound when the box is shaken.

Cigar Box Banjo

Make a cigar box banjo by cutting the lid off an empty cigar box, using a sharp knife, and putting rubber bands around the whole box in several places. The instrument will be most interesting if the rubber bands vary in width (they will all have to be four inches long or more to fit around the box without snapping.) The edges of the box can be notched with a sharp knife to hold the bands in place. An old-fashioned wooden cigar box produces the most noise, but children seem perfectly happy with the quieter cardboard versions.

Sound is produced by plucking at the rubber bands. Looser or wider bands make a lower sound, tighter and narrower ones make a higher sound. Show your child how he can tighten a rubber band by pulling on one side of it to stretch it over the open top of the box. Let him listen to the result.

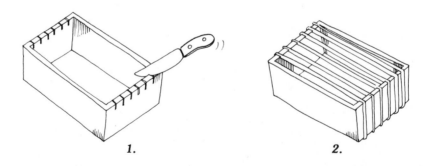

1.   2.

Box Blocks

Shoe boxes, with their lids glued in place and taped with the widest freezer tape you can find for further security, make lightweight, easy-to-handle blocks for younger children. Although they aren't big enough for building a playhouse-size house, if your child starts in a corner of the room he need only build a wall in front of him to create the cozy feeling of a little home.

Liquor or grocery cartons make more substantial blocks than shoe boxes. Ask for ones with lids (often the lids are slit on three sides to form a hinged top).

Leave corrugated divider systems inside the cartons to give them structural strength. Spread white glue along the corrugated edge where the lid was slit, and hold the lid closed until the glue bonds. The edge will be more secure if freezer tape is folded along it after the glue is dry.

A dozen such boxes could make a substantial "home" for a child. A dozen such boxes also take up an awful lot of space. Luckily, they can be stacked up quite high when not in use. Even if the stack should fall, the empty boxes shouldn't injure anyone.

Box Towns

Save a large piece of corrugated cardboard or a piece of scrap plywood as the base for a box town. Collect small boxes for houses. Grit, oatmeal and cornmeal boxes make circular houses or silos. Glue small- to medium-sized boxes, bottoms down, to the cardboard. Keep the lids for removable roofs, and cut doors or windows in the houses if you wish. Add a toilet- or paper-towel tube here and there for interest, or use tubes as tunnels from one house to another.

Keep your eyes open for the pieces of folded or notched cardboard used to pack fragile items. Often they have interesting shapes that your child can find a good use for in his box town. Many, for instance, are ramp-shaped so toy cars can roll down them, or are bent to form a clever roof shape, or die-cut in a way that suggests a pond or pool. Formed plastic cookie box trays are useful, too; the thin corrugated layer dividers make good roofs.

The less you try to be strictly realistic, the more ideas your child will have about how to play with his town. For children who love to steer vehicles about, use a marker to indicate streets and roads in the town.

Box Dollhouses

There are two ways to make dollhouses from cartons. The first, a cross-section house, is the familiar dollhouse with the front or back wall missing. The second, a mapped house, is like a block house with only one story and the roof missing. Try both because together they represent the two major ways a child must learn to conceive space—looking at a configuration horizontally (as in many do-it-yourself construction plans), and looking down upon it (as a map).

Both types of dollhouses can be put together simply out of assorted boxes held together with white glue. Except for door and window openings, no particular attempt is made to make these houses look like cottages, castles or anything else. The rooms formed by the boxes are enough stimulus to a child's imagination.

Cross-Section Dollhouses

Collect any group of three or more boxes that are at least as deep as shoe boxes. The depths of the boxes can vary by several inches, as long as the sides are deep enough to provide "floor" space in the rooms. If cartons don't seem to come your way when you want them, ask at a liquor store. Liquor cartons are among the strongest available, and, though very deep, the sides can always be cut down somewhat to save space. Choose the deeper boxes for the downstairs rooms, the shallower for the upstairs rooms. Glue the two downstairs rooms together by their short sides. Glue one or two upstairs rooms on top; the long sides are floors, the short ones are walls.

Variations: a group of squarish boxes connected in a row make a garage for several vehicles, or a barn with stables. A group of large boxes stacked and con-

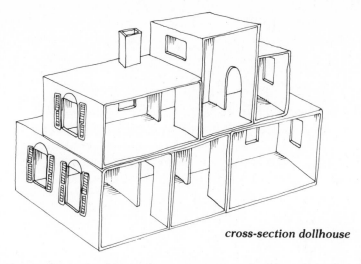

cross-section dollhouse

nected on top of one another make an apartment building. Smaller rooms can be added to large buildings by glueing shoe boxes or other smaller boxes *inside* the larger cartons. If any house is wobbly, glue it to a larger base of corrugated cardboard.

With a sharp knife, cut any windows or doors your child would like. Doors between rooms are especially fun. If you have time to do a careful job—and if your knife is sharp enough—you can cut the windows with shutters and the doors so they open and close.

Mapped Dollhouses

Accumulate approximately shoe-box-sized boxes for a mapped dollhouse. Glue them together in any arrangement that looks intriguing, openings facing up. Boxes can stick out in any way to make the pattern more interesting. The more boxes, of course, the more rooms your child will have in his dollhouse.

Cut doors between rooms with a sharp knife. It's easiest to make doors by cutting both sides straight down from the box edges, bending the door over, and

mapped dollhouse

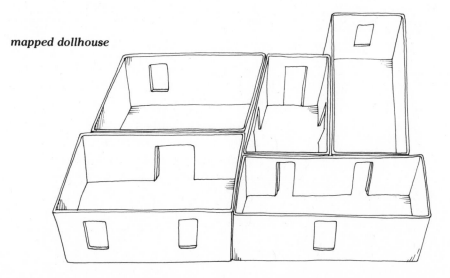

cutting it completely off at the bottom. Since your child will be looking downwards on this house while playing with it, you may be able to get away without cutting windows.

What if your child wants a fancy dollhouse? We haven't suggested that parents go to the trouble of decorating these houses with paint and curtains because, after so much trouble, it is upsetting when the house proves only temporary. Carton houses will last for months perhaps, but not for years. There's no reason, however, to prevent your child from decorating his house to his heart's content according to the suggestions that follow.

Decorating a Dollhouse

Tempera paints can be used for the outside and inside of these carton houses, and so can crayons and markers.

Boxes can be used for beds, cupboards (glue them to the wall), tables or stools. Spools make good stools, too. Scraps of fabric will serve as rugs, curtains and bedding. Curtains can be cut to size and glued above the window with white glue. Heavy materials like burlap, velveteen, and wool make good carpets. Save screw caps, like those on ketchup bottles, to be used as pots. Shallower ones make serving dishes. Tiny bottle caps and toothpaste caps can be cups and bowls.

Tiny bottles can be used for vases and pitchers or to hold supplies of "food" such as small pasta (pastina), sprinkles, beads, or spices.

Little dolls can be made by simply drawing a face with a marking pen on old-fashioned nonspring-type clothespins, short lengths of dowel stick, or wooden pegs from an old toddler toy. See woodworking, page 184.

Caution:
• *Don't give small, swallowable items to very young children.*

5 Dramatic Play

ALL THE PLAYING in this chapter—dressing-up, playing house, puppet and doll play, block-building—is "pretend" play. The dolls and animals come alive, the puppets speak, the block world hums with activity. And the child becomes what he wishes to be. A great part of every day in every child's life is spent in pretend. Why do children pretend so much?

Imagining seems to be the way the human mind does a great deal of its thinking. Children pretend much the same as adults fantasize. But unlike adults, who can keep their thoughts inside their heads, children behave as if their imaginings were real. They act upon them; they pretend.

A child as young as eighteen months can already pretend. He pretends when he offers you an apple from the page of a magazine. As he becomes adept at pretending, he learns to enact more complicated fantasies. No longer a baby, he can behave as if he were. Not yet an adult, he can pretend to be one. He becomes capable of dramatic play, the subject of this chapter.

In dramatic play a child may not only pretend that his doll is a real baby, but also that he is a parent. The baby has spilled its milk, and he is very angry. Object, role, situation, and emotion are all pretended.

But what is the good of it? One value of dramatic play is that it gives a child perspective.

He dresses himself to fit a fantasy, steps back from the mirror, and looks at the idea he is trying on. He fantasizes a world in blocks, builds it, and stands up to view the result. Or he enacts a fantasy with puppets—at arm's length. Such literal perspectives substitute for the way an adult can examine a fantasy from another kind of distance called "point of view." In fact, dramatic play is one way in which different points of view—the mother's, the baby's, the doctor's, the patient's—are learned by children.

As time goes on, you will notice that an individual child's dramatic play may become repetitive: the same costume for weeks at a time, the same episode between puppets, the same sort of miniature block world. The play is often very intense as well. It looks like work—and it may be work. When children enact by pretending, they are often paradoxically trying to accept reality.

As a child crashes cars into his block-building, spanks his baby doll, plays doctor with a friend, he may be trying to master a real experience in his life: an accident, a punishment, an operation. Each time he plays, he might take one more peek at the situation—try out a little part of it, perhaps vent some emotions, and get more used to it. Eventually he could look at the whole event with the new awareness of, "Yes, it happened, it was not pretend, it was one of life's experiences. This is how I feel about it, this is how I can deal with it."

In other words, through pretending, a child may be helped to distinguish reality and to accept it. But this may not happen without some adult help. Use the words "pretend" and "imagine" to describe the playing of roles and the expression of wishes. Use the words "real" and "true" to describe reality as you know it. It is true that a child sometimes wishes to be a baby again. It is fun to pretend that. But, really, he is able to do many things babies can't do.

Because all of dramatic play is highly personal, this chapter does not suggest any actual play situations for you to set up for your child. To encourage dramatic play, think of yourself as the propman. You see to costuming, stage settings, and props. Your child will imagine the play.

DRESS-UP PLAY

When a child tries on dress-up clothes, he is trying on adulthood. He is fitting himself out in his view of the adults he sees around him. You can notice by the roles he chooses and the getups he thinks appropriate that his idea of being a grownup is different from your own. He may copy obvious work, powerful feats and wear striking clothing.

Some of a child's acting out may seem stereotypical, such as that of a boy who plays at spraying big hoses, driving trucks, and shooting everything in sight. But some acting out may not be stereotypical at all. The same boy may stuff a pillow under his shirt to "try on" pregnancy. Either way, the child is exploring for a working definition of what sex he is and how that sex behaves. Once a boy is quite sure pregnancy is one thing men can't do, he may take care of his baby doll to practice being a father, not a mother. Girls may "try on" roles that seem male to them in the same way.

We may know that male and female roles are not so simple or defined. We may know that being an adult is not so exciting, so powerful, so colorful as children think. But we can let children have it their way by supplying a variety of "dress-

On Sesame Street, Anything Muppets are developed into characters when they are given features and costumes. Children "try on" roles by dressing up.

Little Grover Monster becomes Super-Grover in the costume his mother made for him.

ups" until they are secure in their gender identity, and sure of their ability to become as big as we are.

Neither adults nor children save their fantasies only for dress-up time and costume balls. We all use clothing to express how we feel about ourselves, and how we wish others to see us. Perhaps green is "just not you." Perhaps you have had a favorite hat for twenty years. Perhaps you can't face a job interview unless you are wearing a particular suit. So don't be surprised if your child thinks he can't go anywhere without his cowboy hat; or won't ever, ever wear that polka-dotted shirt; or has to wear a party dress for the first day of school.

All clothes are costumes. For children, belts, hats, boots, leotards, big zippers and many pockets may be crucial details of everyday clothing. Often textures—furry or velvety ones that make a child feel cuddly, or slick fabrics that outline his body—may be important, too. To some extent, dress-up is all the time.

Keep your eyes open for extra "dress-up" clothes. Favorites are often fancy shoes and boots, pocketbooks and briefcases, sashes and shawls, fake flowers, jewelry, party dresses, neckties, and hats of every sort. Always think about whether something you are about to throw out or give away would make a good dress-up costume before you dispose of it. Stop in at flea markets, browse in thrift shops and church bazaars.

Homemade Dress-Ups

These are dress-ups that are reasonably easy to make at home:

Tail: A length of clothesline or string, either tucked into the waistline of your child's pants or attached with a safety pin.

Crown: Cut a five-inch strip of yellow poster board (available in art departments) or yellow construction paper. Wrap it around your child's head, overlapping it about two inches. Mark the right length and cut it off to fit. Cut points with scissors. Staple and glue the ends together, trying it on again first.

Wings: Cut paper wings to the wing shape below. Twelve inches is probably long enough. Attach to shirt shoulders with safety pins. More permanent wings can be cut from felt or other material stiffened with starch. A more flappable pair of wings can be sewn permanently under the arms and along the sides of a worn-out shirt. Lay the shirt out flat, with the arms raised above the shoulders, over a doubled piece of fabric. Outline the angle formed by the shirt sleeve and the shirt body on the fabric. Draw a scalloped line between wrist and hip. (The finished wing shape is roughly triangular.) Cut through both layers of fabric to make two wings. Sew them each onto the shirt along the inside seam of the sleeve and along the side seam of the shirt body. When a child flaps his arms down, the wings fall in folds along his sides.

Capes: Any large square of soft fabric—a scarf, flat diaper—can be loosely tied around a child's neck to form a cape. Towels can be used, too, but have to be fastened around the child's neck with a diaper safety pin as they are too bulky to tie. Old curtains—the kind that slip over a rod—can be cut to the right length for capes. To make a drawstring, tie a string to the end of a safety pin or paperclip and work the pin through the fold at the top of the curtain until it emerges at the other end. Pull the string through, and tie it to hold the cape around your child's neck. Or make a similar cape from any soft fabric by sewing a fold at the top to hold a drawstring.

Animal "Fur": For the ambitious parent (or for a special gift) the following illustration shows how to make an animal fur cape—an idea with appeal for many children. Use patterned corduroy or other fabrics in tiger stripes or leopard spots patterns. The lining fabric can be any light cotton or polyester. When a child

1. To make animal "fur," cut two pieces of fabric to this pattern. (One piece will be used as lining.) Stitch right sides of both pieces together, leaving an opening. Turn right sides out and sew up opening.

animal "fur" costume

2. Following the same steps, make a tail and sew onto the fur body.

crawls along the floor with this cape on, the tail and rear paws hang down in their proper places. When he walks, the cape billows in princely fashion.

Helmets: Plastic bleach bottles make perfect helmets. Before you make anything out of a bleach bottle, wash it out *very well!* Then cut it with a sharp, pointed knife in any of the ways illustrated below.

football helmet   *martian helmet*   *astronaut helmet*

Badges: Badges of all sorts can be made with construction paper, decorated with markers or crayons, and attached to your child's clothing with a piece of tape curled into a ring, sticky side out so it will stick to both badge and clothes. Consider a star-shaped badge if your child wants to be a sheriff, the initial letter of his name (make it large) if he wants to be a superhero, a shield shape for a fireman, a fat red cross for a nurse or doctor.

Mirrors are good for children to use to help them see themselves literally and figuratively. A mirror is indispensable for dress-up time. With a mirror, a child can "try on" the various roles and characters he has observed in the adult world. A hand mirror is fine for close-up views, but a full-length mirror is better for getting a total look. Unfortunately, mirrors are expensive. Fortunately, adults rather enjoy looking at themselves, too.

"Dress-ups" can be kept in a carton, but each time your child wants something, he will dump the entire contents out on the floor to find it. Hooks to hang them on are better, if you have the room.

For children who like to really parade around in their costumes, suggestions for homemade rhythm instruments are on page 186. They can all be played to march music (you can borrow marching records from many public libraries) or to accompanying singing.

Grover points to himself in the mirror.

Another favorite instrument for parades is a kazoo. One can be made by folding crisp tissue paper over the toothed edge of a comb. A kazoo is played by barely touching the lips to the paper, and humming to get a buzzing tone.

PLAYING HOUSE

Dressing-up and playing house often go together. Not that the house is always a home, nor the activity always housekeeping. The house may be a store, an office, a cave, secret headquarters, or a spaceship. The following ideas for "houses" range from simply transforming an existing room by substituting colored lightbulbs, to the whole panoply of possibilities for old-fashioned "let's play house" games.

Blanket Houses

Many imaginative structures for dress-up and pretend play can be made from existing furniture, blankets, and C-clamps. The structures are temporary; the materials take up no extra storage space. The crudest blanket house is made by pulling a chair over forward so that it rests on its front, and draping a blanket over it. An armchair works best, but two armless chairs tilted over with their backs toward each other work, too. So does setting up a card table if the blanket is large enough to cover it and hang down the sides. Bedspreads or sheets may work better than blankets here. Use books as weights where necessary. Windows and other details can be drawn on an old, discarded sheet with marking pens.

More interesting to children who like to invent things is a house made of blankets clamped to furniture. Use C-clamps, available in many sizes in hardware stores. Before you buy the clamps, measure the thicknesses of pieces of furniture you feel you can allow your child to use. The clamps should open up to ¼ inch wider than the thickest furniture leg or top it will be used on.

To make the house, a child folds an edge or corner of the blanket around a tabletop, furniture leg, or bed board; then secures it by putting the C-clamp over the cloth and tightening the clamp into place. Since the blanket protects the furniture, the clamp can't scratch finishes.

By securing other edges and corners to other pieces of furniture, your child can make quite a large house; even larger if you have more blankets, old sheets, or bedspreads he can use as well.

A-Frame Playhouses

A temporary but quickly constructed playhouse can be made with any larger pieces of corrugated cardboard. Mattress boxes, slit open along one long edge, are perfect. Open the box out—stand it up tentwise—and there's your house. If no mattress box appears, use instead any two large pieces of cardboard taped together with freezer tape along one edge. This sort of house, while large enough to play inside, can be folded flat and leaned against a wall or slipped under a bed when not in use.

Carton Playhouses

You may have to do some trekking to find a single carton large enough for a playhouse. The best ones are the cartons large appliances such as refrigerators come in. Naturally, anytime you know a neighbor who just happened to get a new refrigerator, save the carton. If that isn't about to happen, ask around at appliance stores. They may have the cartons from new display models available, or they may bring back a carton for disposal after delivery of a new appliance. When you get the box, orient it in any way that gives you a houselike shape tall enough to allow your child to stand in. Repair any tears or openings with white glue and freezer tape.

With your child as your consultant, plan, mark with a marker, and cut windows and a door. Keep openings small to preserve the strength of the carton. Cut the door at the top, bottom and one side only so it will open and close. Cut out the windows altogether, or cut down the center and across the top and bottom to form closable shutters.

You may paint a cardboard playhouse with tempera paints or, more practically, with any leftover latex wall paints you may have around. Or you can leave the painting of the house to your children as an outdoor project. Another alternative (besides doing nothing, which is perfectly all right) is to let your child decorate the house as he wishes with crayons and marking pens. Since there is so much surface, this kind of project may keep him busy from time to time for many weeks.

The Comforts of Home

Some children use these playhouses to play in with friends and siblings in a social way. Others may wish to retire into them as little creatures into dens for private, snuggling comfort. Provide the snuggler with all the comforts of home: an old blanket, whatever pillows you can spare, a snack, and perhaps a flashlight. Let him take into his den good company: favorite books, favorite dolls or animals. And help keep away sisters and brothers—the company he may be trying to escape for a while.

Homemade Housekeeping

Children who play house a good deal may nag you to buy them tea sets, play stoves, and other expensive household accessories. Here are some ways to make these items at home, or provide junk-shop substitutes.

Stove: Use a strong cardboard box, such as a liquor carton, with the top glued back in place. Cut the oven as shown. The wooden knob is bought at a hardware store and glued in place. See the detail for how to make the oven latch. Paint the burners on, or draw them with markers. Thick labeling markers are the easiest to use for this job. Other knobs could be glued on for burner controls if you wish. They cost only a few cents each.

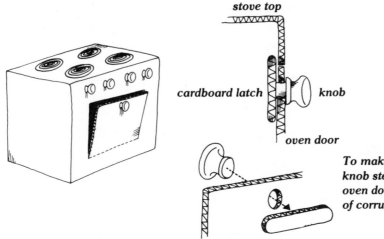

stove top

cardboard latch   *knob*

oven door

To make the oven latch, put the knob stem through a hole in the oven door and glue to a small piece of corrugated cardboard.

A less complete stove, but one that takes up far less space, can be made from a two-foot length of ten-inch shelving. Sand the edges smooth. Heat an electric stove burner to medium. Dampen the board on one side with a moist sponge. Place one end of the damp side briefly on top of the burner to scorch its pattern into the board. Repeat on the other end of the board for the second burner. Draw or glue on two control knobs. This stove can be set on any surface for playing house. Make it clear that your child is to "cook" on this stove only—not on the real one in the kitchen.

Sink: Any rectangular or square plastic dishpan can be used for laundering doll's clothes or washing play dishes. The large ones meant for adult dishwashing will spill less easily than small ones. Bubble bath solutions give more suds with less soapiness than other detergents. Fill the container with only two inches of water, add only a little bubble solution, and let your child whip up suds with an eggbeater or wire whisk.

Housewares: You may be able to find a variety of other accessories in thrift shops and at garage sales. Things to look for include: broken travel irons (small enough for pretend play. Pull out the wire and throw it away), plastic measuring cups, eggbeaters, small pie plates, and other unbreakable kitchen equipment.

Foodstuffs: For foodstuffs, save small empty food containers: milk cartons; cylindrical grit, cornmeal, or oatmeal boxes; frozen orange juice cans, pudding boxes, single-serving cereal boxes, and small vegetable cans with the labels still on. Fake foods are quite expensive to buy, but see page 145 for the basic method of making things out of baked dough. Easy shapes to fake, bake, and paint are carrots, small apples and potatoes, cookies, pretzels, doughnuts, whole fish, and chicken drumsticks. (Large shapes may crack in baking.) All can be painted and varnished as suggested on page 146.

Colored Lights: An inexpensive and simple, but very effective, substitute for an enclosed playhouse is different-color lightbulbs to occasionally replace the existing bulbs in a room where your child plays. These are not available in most supermarkets, but stores that specialize in lighting and electrical accessories are sure to have them. The change in color seems to turn the room into an altogether different place. Try blue bulbs for a ghostly or nighttime environment, red for a snug, underground feel. Surprise your child with the new light some dark winter afternoon—especially if he has a friend over and is already playing an adventurous dress-up game.

DOLLS AND STUFFED ANIMALS

Whether it is the one beloved doll or animal that has accompanied your child from infancy, or a host of characters who people his playtimes, dolls and stuffed animals are an essential to almost every child. But some have also become very costly toys. We can't suggest, of course, any homemade substitute for a good washable, bendable, dressable baby doll; but there are quite a few simpler dolls and toy animals you can make at home.

Most of the ideas in this section are too difficult for a child to execute by himself. On the other hand, they aren't as demanding as similar projects in family magazines. They are a compromise: work meant to be shared between adult and child. Do the harder parts yourself; let your child do the easier parts. None of them requires such exquisite workmanship that you will feel irritated with your child for making the mouth smeary or the eyes crossed.

When you are making dolls or animals with your child, don't assume he wants each one to be sweet, cute and smiling. Ask first. Sometimes it is necessary for a child's play that a character be mad (turn that smile upside down), or sad (make the mouth a straight line and add some tears), or a baby, a man, a woman. More variety in expression provides more situations and feelings for the child to try out.

A good assortment of accessories will help your child set up the situations he is interested in exploring with his dolls and animals. Some are suggested on pages 212–216, but a little observation of your child's play may suggest many others to you.

Handkerchief Doll

Lay a handkerchief out flat. Place two or three cotton balls or a smallish wad of cotton or shredded facial tissue in the center. Gather up the handkerchief around the ball of stuffing and wrap a rubber band around beneath it to form a neck. Arrange the cloth smoothly around the face by pulling the folds of handkerchief under the rubber band toward the back of the head. Make a face with washable markers if your child wishes.

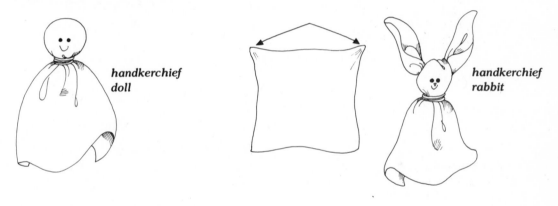

handkerchief doll

handkerchief rabbit

Handkerchief Rabbit

Hold up two corners of a handkerchief; tie them once, the way you begin to tie a shoelace. The two corners are the rabbit's two ears. Arrange the cloth between the ears so that it lies flat and smooth. You'll see that it falls into place naturally on one side—the bunny's face—and stays somewhat creased on the rear side. Wrap a rubber band around beneath the face to make a neck for the rabbit. You can draw a face with markers if your child feels it's necessary. Faceless handkerchiefs are more reusable.

Pillow Baby, Pillow Bear

The following two patterns, one for a pillow baby, the other for a bear, are about the simplest stuffed shapes that are convincing enough to be dolls. Draw the body shape to any size you want on paper. Cut it out, fold it in half lengthwise, and trim the two edges even with each other so the pattern is symmetrical.

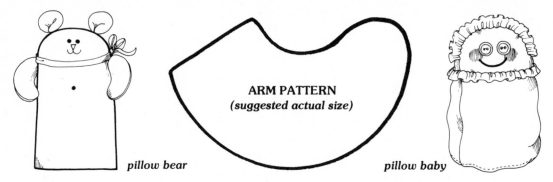

ARM PATTERN
(*suggested actual size*)

pillow bear   *pillow baby*

Cotton, polyester, flannel or felt are the easiest fabrics to work with. Fold the cloth double and trace the outline of your pattern with pencil on the top layer of cloth. Cut both layers of cloth, leaving a ¼-inch margin all around your pencil line. Stitch up the seam, joining the two pieces with right sides facing, and leaving the bottom open. Turn right-side out.

Stuff loosely with polyester or cotton batting. Old stockings, cut in shreds crosswise, also make a soft, even stuffing. Turn the bottom edges to the inside, pin in place and stitch together. For the bear, add ears cut from felt. For either the bear or the baby, you can also make small arms by following this pattern. Attach arms up quite high to get a babyish look.

Faces can be made with a marking pen, with embroidery, or by sewing on button eyes and making the mouth and nose with plain small stitches. We have shown very simple faces to demonstrate how little you have to do to make these dolls appealing.

The line that separates the head from the body can be drawn in marker or made by stitching on a bit of lace or ribbon at the "neck."

Beanbag Animals

Beanbag animals are satisfying to children because, unlike stuffed toys, which may be rather rigid in construction, beanbags can be plunked down even on their heads without falling over. A beanbag shape with legs can sit realistically in a little chair, with legs hanging down properly!

Felt, sold in bright-colored squares in fabric departments, is the easiest cloth to work with to make beanbags. Since the cloth doesn't fray, you don't have to turn in edges. Make a pattern in any shape you want, remembering that the pattern, especially if it includes small projections for arms or legs, must be about an inch fatter than you want it to look when stuffed with beans. For starters, try a turtle or a fish.

Draw the pattern on paper, cut it out, and trace around it with a marker on the top of two pieces of felt. Pin the pieces of felt together, and stitch along your marked line with a running stitch until you have only a two-inch space left to sew. Leave the needle and thread in place. Trim the excess felt away from edges, leaving ⅛- to ¼-inch margin beyond your stitch line. Stuff the beanbag loosely with small beans. Soybeans, black (turtle) beans, pea (navy) beans, and whole

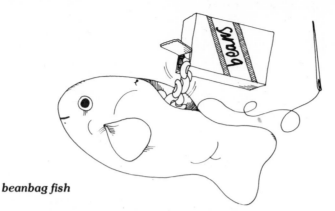

beanbag fish

dried peas all work well. A funnel may help to channel the beans into the opening. Pick up the needle again and finish stitching across the opening.

If you want to decorate the beanbag animal, you can sew or glue other felt scraps wherever you wish.

Sock Stick Horses

Heavy knit socks or thick gym-type cotton socks make firmer stick-horse heads than thin or stretch socks. Though any size is possible, a small man's or a woman's size makes a generous head. Your best bet would be a sock that has lost its mate rather than a worn-out sock you will have to patch before you begin.

Stuff the sock with old stockings shredded crosswise, cotton batting, or polyester stuffing. As you get to the heel of the sock, start forming a central hole in the stuffing with your fingers as you work so you won't have trouble later pushing the stick up through the stuffing. Stuff quite firmly to within two inches of the top.

Push an old broom handle or ¾-inch dowel stick up into the horse's neck as far as you can. It should reach the heel of the sock. Jam more stuffing around the stick to keep it in place, but leave those last two inches of the sock unstuffed so you can tie the sock end to the stick.

Squeeze white glue all around the stick at the point where you will tie the sock.

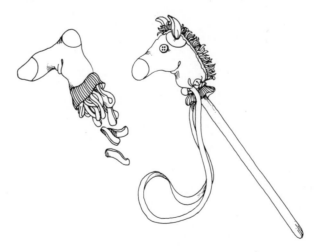

Then hold the sock gathered around the stick and wind string tightly about it four or five times before you tie the string in a knot. Leave the horse to dry before doing any more work.

When the horse is dry, let your child "ride" it for a minute so you can see how short to cut the stick. Two and a half feet is about average. Saw it to the right length with a hand saw. Decorate the horse with felt ears, folded in half with the fold faced backwards to look like horse's ears, and with any of the following: button or felt eyes, a curtain-fringe mane, a string or ribbon bridle, and jingle bells.

Doll and Animal Clothes

Some clothing can be made without sewing at all. Use an old handkerchief to tie around a doll's or animal's neck for a cape; or use it for a kerchief or a diaper. An old sock may fit over the head as a stocking cap; cut off the foot of a large sock and discard it, pull the remaining part of the sock over a doll's body, and cut holes for arms to stick through—an acceptable sleeveless shirt. With a ribbon tied at the waist, a sock top can also be used as a skirt on a smallish doll.

For those who wish to sew, here are simple but effective felt hats and belts:

Make doll belts and animal collars from strips of felt. Close them with a button and a snipped buttonhole, or with snaps, or a hook and eye. Since pockets are such fun, see the illustration for how to make a pocket that hangs on a belt. By

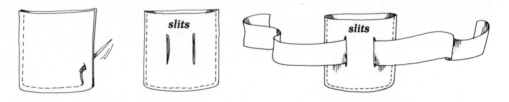

To make a pocket: *Cut two matching squares of felt and sew around three sides.*

pocket on waist belt

cutting the slits in the back of the pocket horizontally instead of vertically, the same pockets could be used as saddle bags on a belt that goes around the belly of an animal that stands on four legs.

To make a hat, wrap felt around a doll's or animal's head in some position that feels firm. Pin it closed. With more pins, make the hat the shape you prefer. Take the hat off, substitute pencil lines for the pins, then pin or baste along your lines

felt hat

and try the hat on again before you stitch it up. Such simple shapes can be decorated with ribbon, other scraps of felt (they could be cut like flowers or feathers), or with buttons, tassels, yarn.

Doll Beds

Shoeboxes or other elongated cartons can be used as beds. Cut one-third of the lid off and glue the rest of the lid upright against one end of the box for a headboard. Fold rags neatly for a mattress, or use layers of cotton batting. A folded disposable diaper could make a mattress, too. Use worn-out receiving blankets or other soft materials to cut into blankets. Wool fabrics can be fringed along the edges by carefully unraveling the threads for about a quarter of an inch.

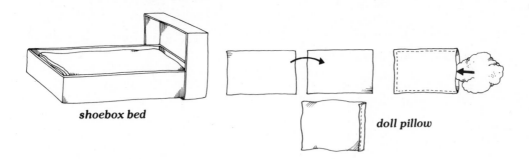

shoebox bed   *doll pillow*

Make pillows by cutting two rectangles from cloth. With right sides together, stitch three sides, turn, stuff, turn bottom edges under and stitch up the remaining side.

PLAYING DOCTOR

Sickness and injury are themes often and intensely played out by children. This is one of the major ways children reassure themselves that hurts can be fixed.

For a treat, buy a bargain brand of adhesive bandages and dole them out a few at a time when your child plays doll games that require them. Gauze and sticky tape are helpful, too. Slings can be improvised with a triangular piece of cloth. So can diapers. A couple of tongue depressors—a clinic or doctor's office usually won't mind parting with a few—come in handy. And a red washable marking pen is swell for making chicken pox.

Of course, children will want to give their dolls and animals "shots," too. Suggest that they pretend to inoculate with a finger rather than give them anything resembling a hypodermic needle.

When an injury actually does occur to a doll or animal, it may be important to repair the damage. To a child, teddy bears can see; a teddy bear who loses an eye is blind. To a child, a teddy bear can also feel. Don't be surprised if your child is

"Dr. Ernie" gives Bert a checkup.

tortured to see you put a needle through the bear's skin to sew the eye back on. It would not be crazy of you to give a bear a pretend shot of anesthesia before operating on him. A torn body, especially if stuffing is falling from the hole, can be terrifying to a child. Since you can't explain to him yet exactly how his body really works, you must at least convince him that adults know how to fix cuts.

A broken arm on a doll is just as bad. How is a child to know that "broken" in humans does not mean broken off? So fixing a broken doll limb is important, unless it is totally beyond repair.

PUPPET PLAY

The major purpose of puppet play is to allow a child to express, absorb and work at various feelings and roles he is trying out.

For Sesame Street, Jim Henson created puppet characters—Muppets—that children could identify with and be amused by, such as Ernie and Bert. Other Muppets, such as The Count, were designed with specific educational goals in mind. But all of them—Kermit the Frog, Big Bird, Grover, all the monsters and grumpy Oscar-the-Grouch—have personality characteristics meaningful to children.

The puppeteer has as much to do with conveying these characteristics as does the puppet's lovable appearance, of course. But even though your best efforts at puppet creation can't compare with the real Sesame Street Muppets, your child will probably find your homemade puppets just as intriguing to play with. Watching Sesame Street should give your child many ideas and inspire him to try puppet play.

You will look in vain for the one character that your child uses as "himself" in

*Jim Henson and
his Muppet, Ernie.*

his puppet play. In fact, each puppet may portray a different aspect of the child
himself. One of the values of puppet play is that it allows children to integrate the
angry, fearful, selfish, babyish or other "unlovable" sides of himself into a whole
personality.

As a child mediates between his various puppets—scolding, blaming, soothing,

**Kermit the Frog is a reporter on
Sesame Street News.**

forgiving—he is experimenting with ways to accept all these different parts of himself. You may notice that he uses an almost parental voice with his puppets on occasion. The parental voice is no accident. You, in accepting your child in his many moods and actions, give him the model for integrating all the apparently different people who inhabit his personality. The Muppets of Sesame Street have a range of facial expressions to represent various emotions and aspects of personality and character. The puppeteers alter eyebrows, mouths, eyes, or add hair, teeth, and tongues to make "Anything Muppets" appear to be everything from fierce to pathetic.

FINGER PUPPETS

Finger puppets are intimate friends, a child's very own "little people." They stay close, they act lively. And judging from the delight with which children learn that fingers have names, it seems it is natural to them to think of their fingers as individuals. Following are several ways to animate fingers so they can be used as puppets.

Ink Faces

With marking pen, make eyes, nose and mouth on the plump tip of one of your child's fingers. Make a face on a finger of the opposite hand, too. When you are in the mood, add a face to one of your own fingers so you can talk with your child's.

If you have felt scraps around, it only takes a minute to stitch up a few finger hats just for your child's amusement. A triangular hat is easiest, either a shallow one or a tall dunce-cap shape. The hats will not stay on very well, but they certainly animate a finger.

Ordinary sewing scissors or shears may be too clumsy for cutting out tiny bits of felt. The best tool is sharp, pointed embroidery scissors. On page 209 are instructions for making a handkerchief doll. If you stuff the head only loosely, your child can poke one finger up through the rubber band and into the doll's head to use it as a finger puppet.

Glove Finger Puppets

Worn-out gloves, especially ones that don't fray, make cute, permanent puppets. Cut the fingers off at about two inches from their tips or to fit short of your child's second finger joint. If the fabric frays or runs, stitch over and over along the edge of the opening to hold the threads in place. You can make a face with a marking pen if the fabric is light-colored and smooth. For dark or rough fabrics, glue on tiny buttons, bits of felt, or even dots and slivers of colored paper to make the faces. Hair can be added by glueing on a few strands of yarn, thread, or string. You can even add tiny bowties or hair ribbons, belts, collars, or capes. Such intricate touches would turn these puppets from an everyday item to a fine present.

Mitten Puppets

The easiest hand puppet of all is made from your child's everyday mittens, adapted to the new role by the addition of eyes. Their eyes can be paper circles. Round black pupils—cockeyed, centered, or peeking to one side—are ridiculously effective. Glue them on or stick them on temporarily with a piece of sticky tape folded in a ring, sticky side out. Sewn-on button eyes don't make mittens unwearable. Families with several children and many mismatched mittens might enjoy making a crew of permanent mitten puppets.

Attach the eyes to the mitten about halfway between the tip of the mitten and wrist.

Hand Puppets

Follow the basic pattern below to construct a puppet with a movable mouth. Young children will find these easier to manipulate than puppets with hands. The

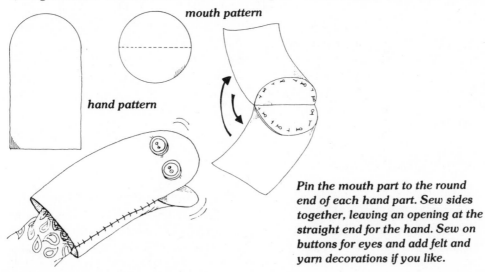

mouth pattern

hand pattern

Pin the mouth part to the round end of each hand part. Sew sides together, leaving an opening at the straight end for the hand. Sew on buttons for eyes and add felt and yarn decorations if you like.

fact that the mouth moves so naturally will encourage children to talk through their puppets. They may also feed them—and yes, they will make them "bite." Since the biting is so obviously in play and doesn't hurt, these puppets are helpful in playing out aggressive emotions. If you dislike being the bitten object, make two puppets who can happily attack each other.

Paper Bag Puppets

Small paper bags make good puppets, too. The crease where the bottom folds forms a mouth. The child holds his hand flat inside the bag and flaps the bottom to make his puppet talk. Use markers for making the face.

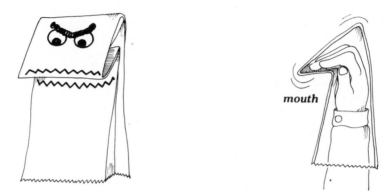

mouth

If you allow yourself to converse quite frequently with your child through puppets, you may learn unexpected things about how he thinks and feels. For some reason—perhaps because while speaking through puppets one does not have to be responsible for "silly" ideas or "pretend" emotions—children may spontaneously confide thoughts they would not otherwise speak of.

Although there is no way to *make* this happen, you can encourage it by taking a naive puppet role in which you can ask questions such as, *I wonder what makes the wind* or *What would happen if someone ate all the candy in the store?* or *What does God look like?* or *Where does the moon go in the daytime?* If you find the answers your child gives to these questions wrong, bewildering or scary (as they often are), you can, still sticking with your role, innocently disagree: *Oh, I didn't know leaves make wind when they move. I thought the wind blows the leaves.* Keep what you think to yourself.

PUPPET STAGES

Up to the age of six, most children play with puppets much as they play with stuffed animals. They remain face-to-face with them, the puppets speaking in one voice and they in another. Or they put a puppet on each hand and face them toward each other. But occasionally a child will want to actually stage a show, most likely still with himself as both actor and audience, but possibly even for others to watch.

Impromptu stages abound in any home. Show your child that he can duck behind a table or chair, or hide behind a doorway so only his puppet shows. Let him stand to one side of a mirror so he can't see himself, but hold his puppet hand out to watch its image in the mirror. Or at bedtime, sit on the floor beside your child's bed, duck your head, perch a puppet on your hand and speak through the puppet awhile.

For finger-puppet stages, cut holes in a shoe box or even in a paper bag. Your child can put his hand inside and make his fingers speak through "windows." He might enjoy seeing his finger puppets performing in front of a little hand mirror, too.

The inside of a stage can be decorated and furnished in any of the ways suggested for dollhouses (page 198), though the scale will be larger. To decorate the rear of the stage, your child can crayon or paint whatever pictures he likes, and tape the appropriate one temporarily to the rear wall. That way he can change scenes as he wishes.

PUPPET STAGE. *Cut out one side of a large packing box. This opening becomes the proscenium of the stage, and the inside back wall becomes the backdrop which the child can decorate. Smaller "doors" cut out on the other two sides of the stage are the openings through which the performer sticks his arm and puppets. Using this stage, the child can watch his puppets perform.*

What if you don't want to make puppets or stages or don't like pretending? Relax. First of all, your child will probably manage to do the equivalent of puppet playing all by himself with whatever dolls or animals he has around. Pretending in this way does not require parents' help.

PLAYING WITH BLOCKS

The difference between play-acting in real-life size, as in dressing-up and playing house, and play-acting on a miniature scale, as in playing with blocks, is more than a difference in scale.

When children build whole miniature worlds, they are reversing their true situation in life. Now, they are the boss. It is they who steer the cars, plan the buildings, tell people what to do and where to go. And they are very serious about it. This is, after all, real practice for the real probability that they will one day have to "run the show" themselves.

Although blocks are emphasized here, almost identical dramatic play can be enacted in sandboxes (see page 140), in box towns (page 195), and in dollhouses (pages 196–198).

Nevertheless, there are special reasons for discussing blocks separately, and for recommending that you consider buying or making blocks.

There is probably no single more useful toy for children than a good set of unit blocks. The child who is already able to play with blocks at two may still be building with them at ten. They can be played with by one child alone, or by a group of children. They interest girls as much as boys. They last for generations, can be stored in a small space, and can be bought a few at a time. Further, they are among the most versatile of toys, used one day for roads, another for a barn or garage, and again as a setting for a battle or nursery tale.

There is even a largely unsuspected bonus to children's blocks: they are a math-learning toy. Unit blocks, the unpainted ones most often seen in schools, are based on exact numerical relationships. The pictures below will give you an idea of the "arithmetic" children soak up automatically as they construct with unit blocks.

arithmetic with unit blocks

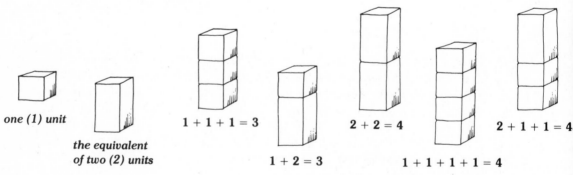

one (1) unit

*the equivalent
of two (2) units*

$1 + 1 + 1 = 3$

$1 + 2 = 3$

$2 + 2 = 4$

$1 + 1 + 1 + 1 = 4$

$2 + 1 + 1 = 4$

Commercial blocks come in both hardwood (birch or maple) and in softwood (pine). Schools usually buy the hardwood blocks because they are more durable and because their weight makes for steadier construction. But hardwood blocks are expensive, and softwood unit blocks are fine for home use.

Block Accessories

Besides the special shapes sold to extend unit block sets, there are a number of good accessories that you can find around your own home. Shoe boxes and other small boxes make ready-made houses for young children who are only at the stage of making roads and walls that can connect one house to another. Lengths of clothesline or heavy string can be laid out in parallel lines to form roads. Any decorative odds and ends like spools, cylindrical and square wooden beads, small wood scraps, empty juice cans and so on can be used to make a building look more elaborate. Large pieces of corrugated cardboard make sturdy roofs. And, of course, all sorts of miniatures—vehicles, animals, people, furniture—encourage a child's dramatic play.

Caution:
- *Be sure very small children aren't given small, swallowable items, and that "accessories" of metal don't have sharp edges.*

Block Storage

There are several ways to store blocks, even if your storage facilities are minimal. Schools usually prefer shelf storage because blocks can be kept sorted neatly by length and shape. The system helps children become aware of block sizes as they stack them, and also helps them to find exactly the block they need when they need it. If you have shelf room, good. But if not, a cardboard carton or even a laundry bag will do. Both have the advantage of being portable so your child can get his blocks back into their container without lugging them, a few at a time, across the room. Both have the disadvantage of being disorganized; but that is not a serious problem.

Learning to Build

No matter when a child is introduced to block shapes—at two or at ten—he will follow a certain sequence in learning to build. Most children begin by placing blocks down flat, end to end. A two-year-old might play with blocks this way for weeks or even months, elaborating only by pushing his "train" along the floor. A six-year-old would probably play this way for only minutes before experimenting with stacking blocks on top of one another, or setting them on edge to form walls. Sooner or later, walls will be turned at right angles to one another to form "houses"; a block will be placed across two other blocks to form a bridge, a roof, a tunnel; and the child will attempt to build some of his constructions several layers tall. Unknown to you, your child may already have passed through the first stages of block-building before he has played with blocks. How can that be? Because sugar cubes, square wooden beads, or empty milk cartons may have been his first real block set.

box blocks

As you watch your child experimenting with his construction methods—and often failing—should you help him? The answer is yes and no. If a roof block falls down continually because the walls it is to span are too far apart, it wouldn't hurt to show your child the solution to his problem. But to get in there and build a terrific castle that is way beyond your child's capabilities isn't "help"; it's taking over. And that's discouraging. If you want so badly to build with blocks (they are very tempting), do it after your child is in bed for the night.

One excellent construction method that may not be discovered by children is the one illustrated below. When your child has discovered on his own how to stack blocks and how to build walls, and when you can see that he is trying to

build up tall, by all means teach this method to him. Given enough blocks, a child can use this to build a building taller than himself.

Block Puzzles

After a child has been building relatively complicated structures for some time (for instance, roads that interconnect, buildings with doorways and rooms, buildings connected to one another by roads), you can challenge him to thought-provoking problems. Build a series of closed rectangles that share walls in common like the rooms of a house. Ask him to make openings in the walls so you can get from one room to another. Stack four blocks flat, on top of one another. See if he can figure out a way to make steps that go up to the top of the stack. Can he make windows in a wall? A table, a chair, or a bed? A tunnel over a road? Can he build a house the same as a simple plan you have drawn on paper?

Each of these problems, once solved, will add to the methods your child can use to create the scenes and props he needs for playing out his ideas in miniature.

Pickup Time

Block pickup time often poses a problem. Sometimes a child doesn't want to take down his building at all. He seldom has sympathy with your passion for vacuuming the floor. And always, putting away is more tedious than building. Fairness demands that a particularly enjoyable landscape building or scene be allowed to stay around a while if it's at all possible. Perhaps he will go back to it tomorrow morning; that might be a pleasure for you, too.

As for picking up, the task may be too complicated and long for a child to do all by himself. If so, do it together. You pick up the cars, he picks up the long blocks. Then you pick up the shortest blocks while he finds all the medium-sized ones. Try to make this a matter of good-humored routine.

6 Special Times

WHEN YOU REMEMBER back to childhood, are there memories so strong that you can almost touch them? A birthday. The taste of Thanksgiving. The swirl of the first snowfall of the year. The feel and smell of a new jacket for school. And the day you shucked that jacket to race the wind of spring.

This chapter is about those times—seasons and holidays, outings, birthdays, little celebrations of all kinds. These are times that may become nostalgic recollections to your children when they are grown, times that are in the making now. Special times.

Of course the threads that will weave the memory of childhood into your child's future are made of all sorts of ordinary stuff. The songs you sing in the car and the pattern of the dishes you eat from will all be part of childhood remembered. But there are brighter threads you can spin on purpose for your children and for the whole family. As a family grows older year by year, a history grows behind it. "Remember when we ate the giant turkey?" "Remember when you took me on the train and the conductor let me wear his hat?" Those two words, "Remember when," become a strong bond between the people who live together as a family. Your effort, your love, your sense of humor and your good ideas now are contributing to the history of your family and the future of your children.

TRIPS

A special trip can be a simple thing. To you and to your child, a half hour's lingering at a particular statue in the park may be enough to relieve the sameness of the day or enough to talk about at suppertime. So if the word "trip" has so far summoned up images of limp lunches, tiresome bus rides, and cranky children, think anew. To a three-year-old, a pet shop may be as fascinating as a zoo, and a construction site more enticing than a museum. For the most part, this section is about short, local, simple trips.

Neighborhood Trips

Look around your own neighborhood carefully. Is there a library, a firehouse, an open-air market, a pet store, a post office, a fish store? Each of these neighborhood locales can be the goal of an interesting trip. Just going to watch animals in a pet store is a trip. Asking a fireman to let you walk close to a fire truck—and climb up onto it if rules allow—is very exciting. Choosing a fat piece of fruit for lunch or a gorgeous picture book at the library makes a trip to an open market or a library special.

Point out to your child such processes as weighing fruit, stamping mail, and marking the due date in a library book. Questions are in order, too: *Where do you get these apples? How many books are in the library? How will this letter get to where it's going?* You may have to start the conversation, but the information might catch your child's interest.

Around the Corner

Once you become aware of what to look for, you will find resources for short trips within walking distance of your home. A construction site is most interesting to a child during the excavation phase when powerful machines seem to gobble up dirt. Even a street repair is fascinating, both when the pneumatic hammer is breaking up the pavement and when the underside of the city is revealed beneath a manhole cover. If you are lucky enough to be near a waterfront, watching the activities of ships and boats is terrific.

Caution:
  • *Construction and waterfront sites may be dangerous. Supervise your child.*

Take minitrip opportunities as they come. Look along the street or road for climbable landscape: in the city, areas of low walls and steps; in the country, a rock outcropping or a fallen tree. The joys of window-shopping are discussed on page 44, and nature walks are on page 232. Simply riding up in the elevator of a tall building and finding a window from which to look over a city is as good a spur-of-the-moment trip as any.

Mr. MacIntosh sells fruit and vegetables on Sesame Street.

Short Rides

Taking a bus, subway, ferry, or even a one-stop train ride just-for-the-ride can be delightful. Check local routes and see if you find something particularly interesting. For instance, there may be a subway route that emerges onto a bridge across a river. Or a short bus ride may take you to a store where you could get an escalator ride in the bargain. Standing at the front window of any train is a thrill. Many of the things you see together on these trips have a bearing on your child's life. The water that spurts into the sink comes through the pipes in that street-repair hole. The library is there to provide him with the books he likes. The apples he eats for lunch grow on trees like this one. No young child can appreciate his environment in sweeping terms; but each remark you make about his own relationship to something you notice together expands his sense of the interconnectedness and the meaning of all that he observes.

People are also involved in one way or another. A bus can't drive itself, a book can't check itself out of the library, an apple doesn't get itself from tree to market. Children are intensely interested in what adults do. Answer your child's questions (and don't be afraid to ask for answers if you don't know them). Point out special dress, such as hardhats and tool aprons, and explain what they are for. Notice details: The buttons on a train conductor's uniform usually have the insignia of his railroad; Gas station attendants may have their own names embroidered on their shirts. Remember that what no longer interests you—ticket punchers, labeling guns, protective goggles—may be exactly what intrigues a child about an adult activity he may long to replicate in his play.

When a trip has captured your child's imagination in some way (he talks about it a good deal, he seemed absorbed while he was there, he pretends the trip over again at home), you can encourage the enthusiasm by suggesting drawing a picture of what he saw; building the site with blocks or in the sandpile (pages 220 and 140); dressing-up as an adult who has interested him (page 201); finding library books on the subject. Did he taste a new food you could cook together? Did he see an animal you could keep as a pet? (Page 261.)

Bigger Trips

Check into local newspapers regularly and look at local maps to see what is available for more complicated trips. These are possibilities, depending on your child's interests: airports, dock areas, zoos, nature centers, museums, old house or ship restorations.

Newspapers announce special exhibits and entertainment—and sometimes they are free. Even poultry farms, orchards, pigeon coops, dairy farms, or truck gardens might be located surprisingly close to city dwellers. Give a call to the 4-H Club or to a county agent (under U.S. Dept of Agriculture in the phone book) to discover what's nearby.

If you do wish to take one of these more ambitious trips, plan it well. How long will the entire trip take? Will you need to bring a snack along (see page 127 for suggestions)? Are there entrance fees? Waiting lines? Are children allowed (there are some restored houses and museums that do not encourage children as visitors)? Are you sure you know how to get there? Disappointment—and whining—may be avoided by asking in advance what you will be able to see and do. Not every "farm" raises cows and chickens; and a child who expects to climb aboard a sailing ship will not be pleased to simply observe it from a distance. Airports and waterfronts may be windy and cooler than home, so bring extra clothing.

Big Bird visits the airport.

What if your child tires easily, bores easily, or whines constantly on longer trips? There are children who whine, "When are we getting there?" and then turn around and whine, "When are we going home?" The interval between may be about thirty seconds. Naturally, your trips will have to be less long, less ambitious, and should certainly include a snack. Be very specific about what you will see and do: *We will go to the museum to see a dinosaur skeleton, have a hot dog, and go home.*

Don't be disappointed if your child fails to appreciate your efforts. You may go to the trouble to take a child to see tigers and crocodiles, and all he's interested in is chasing pigeons. This sort of thing may happen; it does not mean that you have failed or that your child is an ingrate. His interests simply don't correspond with yours, and there's no reason why they should.

Forget the reptile house, sit on a bench and leave him to his pigeons. When you talk about the trip on the way home or at supper that night, talk about the pigeons, too. *Any* interest is important. Any subject is a learning experience. And all curiosity is to be encouraged.

Shopping Trips

Shopping is one kind of trip that is inevitable—especially when a child must try on clothes. Compromises you make between your child's taste in clothes and your own, decisions you allow your child, and guidance you give him (what fits, what looks nice on him, what styles become him, what colors go with his hair and eyes) all help a child to "find" himself. He, Paul, wears "slims," looks swell in red, and is a person who prefers turtlenecks. He is that much more *the* unique Paul Smith than he was before he knew these things about himself.

Catalog Shopping

A mail-order catalog, even if you don't actually shop from it, is a wonderful device for planning a shopping trip. Use it the following ways: first, just wish aloud together. You wish you could have that whole basement tool shop. He wishes he could have that electric car. (Too bad they are both so expensive; neither of you will be able to have that wish come true this time.) Compare your points of view: you love that simple old-fashioned school dress, she loves those crazy T-shirts. (Grownups and children often have different ideas.) Compare these wishes and preferences to what is practical: *The jacket with the furry collar is too expensive, but how about a zippered jacket with big pockets?* Occasionally, compromise: *We could get a dress something like this one for school, but maybe we could get a crazy T-shirt, too.*

SHOPPING LISTS

Lists are another way to help a child go about the process of shopping with a minimum of fuss and realistic expectations. For instance, he can know in advance that he is limited to one pair of sneakers, two pairs of pants, and three T-shirts for the season. When he wants both sneakers and desert boots, you can pull out the list and remind him of what was discussed between you in advance.

It is even more helpful if the list is made in the context of the child's wardrobe. Lay out and count underpants, socks, shirts, and so on. Examine the clothes for damage and discard those that are too far gone to be mended. See what hand-me-downs now fit him. If you come upon a shirt you realize he has not been wearing, ask why. His answer will give you a clue to patterns, fabrics, or styles to avoid in the future. (Note his dislikes right on the list.) Recite aloud the formula you use for determining how many of each item he needs (*Let's see. We do laundry every other day, but sometimes you need two pairs of pants in one day, so we'd better have three pairs of pants altogether*). By letting your child in on this sort of inventorying (which you would have to do in some form, anyway), you are helping him learn good shopping sense.

Clothes Sense

A three- or four-year-old would not, of course, be sensible enough in his choice of clothing to allow him an entirely free hand. But allowing some decisions now will help him learn to choose responsibly later, and to develop a taste in clothing that's uniquely his. This is how to begin: *Both of these shirts look nice with the blue pants. Which one would you like to have?* And perhaps the next season: *Let's carry this brown jumper over to the blouse department and see if you can find a blouse that goes with it.* And by the time the child is five or six: *This brand of jeans* (show the label) *fits you well. Why don't you choose the colors you like best?* And finally: *We can buy you three pairs of pants and two shirts. You choose them while I help out your younger brother.*

Sizes

The size of clothing he wears is one item in his list of facts that helps a child identify himself as an individual. If you buy by mail order, the process of measuring your child to determine size may interest him very much. When sorting clothes, the job of finding his own size 4 underwear may be fun, too. If sizes aren't clearly marked on clothes, mark large numerals inside garments with a laundry pen to help him identify his own belongings. If you like, you could write his name next to the numeral as well. As he grows, make a bit of a fuss over his graduation to the next size!

Getting Lost

If you shop in department stores, sooner or later your child will probably get lost. It may be helpful to understand why this happens so easily. A child's sense of space is not at all secure. You carry in your head at least a rough plan of the store—the location of stairs or elevators, the front, the back, several routes you can use to get from linens, through housewares, to children's clothes. You know the concepts of "aisle," "counter," and "department." Your child is equipped with none of these concepts. Unless you are in sight, he is "lost in space," even if he is no more than a dozen steps from your side. Furthermore, he has no strategies for finding the spot where he last saw you. He can't describe you or the department you were in. He may not be able to retrace his steps. He may not even be able to put together the words to ask for help. You can't hold hands every minute, and you probably can't expect your child not to wander to the next object or location that catches his eye. Do check his whereabouts with your own eyes very frequently.

Getting Found

It is wise to prepare your child for the eventuality of becoming lost. First: Explain that lost means "not able to see me." Lost, in this case, does not mean gone forever, as with a sneaker lost at the beach. Second: Find out from the stores you shop in what method they use to reunite parents and children. Explain the methods to your child. Third: Tell your child to call you out loud if he can't see you and feels frightened. If you don't answer, he should go to a person who works the cash register or a person behind the counter and say, "Please find my

Mommy or Daddy." Fourth: For a toddler, write his name on a piece of paper and pin it to his clothes or put it in his pocket. Tell him to show the piece of paper when he is asked his name.

SPRING AND SUMMER

Warm weather creates opportunity for special activities in step with the season. This section suggests springtime activities such as nature walks and planting seeds, as well as simplified versions of traditional summertime sidewalk games and rainy-day games. For good beach activities, see pages 137–140; and for crafts that could be done outdoors in warm weather, see Chapter Four.

When you step out of the house on a balmy spring morning, you notice the warm air, the "smell of spring." Knowing what to expect, you look to the branches to check for swollen buds or the first green leaves or blossoms. These are expectations your child will pick up from you quite naturally.

To sharpen the perceptions of both of you, and to enjoy the day even more, find a quiet spot to sit down. Then close your eyes. Listen very carefully. You may hear the buzzing of a fly. It has just recently hatched from an egg laid long ago last fall. You may hear a bird. It has possibly just returned from hundreds or even thousands of miles away. You may hear the croak or peep of frogs and toads. Stare at the ground. You may see other creatures—tiny enough, but a sign of spring still.

Even if no glorious blossom has caught your eye, look again. Every tree blooms, though the blossoms may be small and green. The pussy willow is a blossom. So is the red or green blush on the smooth branches of a maple tree before the leaves are out. And so are the long catkins that hang down from a birch tree. Kick aside last fall's leaves and examine the earth beneath. Acorns that fell there last fall have lost their caps. A strong root has poked down toward the ground. A sprout is growing toward the light; it's a baby oak tree. Young leaves of grass and other plants will also be hidden under the leaves.

All this is not to make you go into raptures over spring, but only to strengthen in your child those powers of observation that bring him information about spring—or anything else.

Bird-Watching

As birds begin to return from their southern homes in the spring, you can attract them within sight of a window by keeping available birdseed (cracked corn, sunflower seeds), peanut butter, suet (solid animal-fat scraps), or a mixture of birdseed and hardened bacon fat. Even bread crusts will attract some varieties. Look in the library for books on

Little Bird

Bert watches his favorite birds.

how to make bird feeders, or buy one, or simply scatter the feed on the ground or on a wall, ledge, roof, or fire escape.

If you find a bird's nest in the spring, peek inside to see if there are eggs or baby birds. (But keep hands off!) If eggs have been laid, one or both parents will be close by and you may be able to watch them bringing food to hatched baby birds. When the babies are grown, the nest is no longer occupied and it's fine to take it and examine with your child the clever way it is constructed. For many children, the care and wisdom with which birds prepare a nest and care for their young until they can fly away on their own stands for the whole process of parenting and growing up.

Field Guides

As an experience in classification for your child, try using a wildflower or a bird guide. Say you find a blue wildflower on your nature walk. You turn to "blue flowers" in the guide. (At the same time, of course, this teaches the concept "blue.") In the blue section, you will find the groups further classified by flower size and shape. If your blue flower has many petals, you will find it on a page with other many-petaled flowers in the blue section. Then compare the leaves of your specimen with those in the several pictures. If the two of you are still undecided, the text accompanying the pictures will point out even minor differences that you can compare. Needless to say, this is an extremely coherent exercise in visual discrimination and in classification. Surprisingly, children are often better than adults at noting details.

As you are using any guide, make comparisons and build vocabulary: *Is the bird bigger than the robin we saw yesterday? Does it have a crest? A short or a long beak? A white patch on its throat?*

Fast Sproutings

Because we feel excitement as spring approaches and the world greens into life again, we may want to share our feelings with our children by planting seeds and watching them grow. The trouble is that most seeds are slow to sprout. We plant the seeds, water them—and the child stares at the surface awaiting the magical sprouting. Nothing happens in the next hour or the next day. The child may lose interest.

For results that are fast enough to maintain a child's interest, cut a branch of forsythia when its buds are full, but not yet opened. Put it in water in the house. The flowers should burst open by the following morning. Put a twig of pussy willow in water. The little stalks on which the yellow pollen forms will grow

rapidly. Leaf buds will open into leaves within a couple of days. In a week, tiny rootlets may appear on the lower part of the stem.

Place a sprouting onion or garlic bulb half buried in a dish of damp soil or sand. The sprout will grow visibly from one day to the next.

Soak dried, whole beans intended as food (such as kidney beans, pinto beans, black or white beans) in water overnight. Drain them and put them in a jar covered with a piece of cheesecloth held in place with a rubber band. Run water through the cheesecloth once a day to rinse the beans, then pour the water out again. The beans will sprout within a day in warm weather, a couple of days at cooler temperatures. The sprouts themselves are edible.

Caution:
* *Beans bought from the garden section of stores or seed catalogs are intended for planting rather than eating, and may be treated with chemicals. Do not use them for this experiment.*

Interesting Plants

All of the plants listed below are of particular interest to children because of the speed with which they grow, their color, scent, taste—and in one case, movement. All except aromatic geraniums are available as seeds in packets or as baby plants at hardware or garden stores and all are particularly easy to grow. Aromatic geraniums are sold at nurseries that specialize in herbs and at some plant stores.

Coleus: A leafy plant, colored in blotches and streaks of bright red, purple, green and white. Seeds or plants.

Basil: A fast-growing plant, very aromatic. Can be used to flavor pizza, egg salad and other dishes. Seeds or plants.

Scarlet runner bean: Extraordinarily fast-growing bean vine. Produces scarlet flowers and edible beans. Train the vine up strings in the window, or on stakes outdoors. Seeds.

Mimosa sensitive: Lacy pretty plant whose leaves recoil and fold down when touched. The movement is instant and dramatic. Seeds and plants.

Aromatic geranium: Comes smelling like a rose, a lemon, an apple, or other scents. The smell is strongest when a leaf is crushed. Plants only.

Cress: Tiny seeds that sprout very rapidly. Can be harvested for cress and butter sandwiches in a few weeks. Seeds only.

Grass: Lawn seed will sprout within days in a warm spot. Grass can be cut with scissors to maintain it as a tiny lawn. Seeds only.

Sidewalk Games

While grown-ups may sit and enjoy the weather, the warm seasons bring children out of the relative confinement of winter into a surge of activity.

Most childhood versions of hopscotch, penny-pitching and jumprope are too difficult for preschoolers. But there are sidewalk games a younger child can enjoy. Chalk, a length of clothesline and a beanbag (page 210 tells you how to make one) are all you need for the following games:

Frog in the Puddle: Pretend the beanbag is a frog. Draw a circle on the sidewalk. Pretend it is the puddle. Standing two inches or two feet away from the puddle (whatever is relatively easy), the child tries to toss the frog into his puddle.

simplified hopscotch

frog hop   *rope walk*

rope jump

Frog Hop: This time your child pretends he is a frog. He himself jumps into and out of his puddle. Or draw a series of small circles (about foot size) on the pavement. Using one or both feet, let him hop from one circle to another.

Rope Jump: If he likes to jump, tie one end of a rope to a bench or tree, and hold the other end so your child can practice jumping over the rope. Hold it loosely so that if he jumps into the rope, it will pull out of your hand rather than trip him up.

Rope Walk: Lay the rope out along the ground. He could lay it out in a wavy line like a snake, straight as a street, or in a circle. Then he can try to walk along his rope walk. The same lines could also be drawn in chalk, either as a single line or doubled to form a wider path.

Sidewalk Cracks: Use the seams and cracks in sidewalks or manhole-cover circles for the jumping, tossing and walking games above.

Beanbags and Balls

The beanbag games suggested here can also be played indoors on rainy days. Use a wastebasket or a carton as the target. If there are two children, let them play beanbag toss together. If one fails to catch the beanbag when it is tossed to him, there is much less danger of something getting broken or of neighbors complaining of noise than there is with playing ball. In fact, it is much easier for a child to learn to throw and catch with a beanbag than with a ball. Beanbags are easier to grasp, don't bounce away, and their weight makes them easier to control. The only drawback is that a beanbag thrown really hard can hurt if it hits someone. Show your child how to lob it gently underhand.

If your child is adept with a beanbag, he can try the same games with a ball. Let your child graduate from larger to smaller balls when he has gained some control over larger ones. A large ball is best for toddlers just learning to roll a ball back and forth to a parent. A basketball size is better for games of catch and for bouncing off walls or floor. A six-inch rubber ball is a good size for a young child to practice accuracy games that involve targets.

beanbag toss

All of the simple games above have to do with the skill of eye-motor coordination. Examples of activities that require a coordination between what your eye sees and what your muscles do are hitting a target, walking along a narrow path, jumping into or over a space. Eye-motor coordination is basic to pencil-and-paper skills such as writing, circling, underlining, and connecting—skills that your child will need in school. Accuracy games that use muscles in arms and legs will help develop finer skills—although, of course, your child should have a chance to aim pencils accurately, too.

What if your child can't hop, skip, or jump, walk along a narrow line, or get a beanbag to hit a target? There are enormous variations in how quickly and how well children develop the eye-motor accuracy required to catch and to throw, the smooth muscle control necessary for hopping and jumping, or the sense of rhythm required for skipping.

If you are concerned about your child's own development, suggest the easiest pencil-and-paper games (pages 107–112), and the rhythm activities on pages 96, 179, 186 and 194. You can also encourage him by changing these and other games to make them easy.

By easy, we mean absurdly easy. Here are two examples of how to start easy and get harder: Have your child stand right next to a wastebasket and drop in a beanbag. Then try it from two inches away. Have your child walk along a two-foot chalk line. Then make it a foot longer. Have him draw a line between two six-inch circles a couple of inches apart. Then make the circles smaller, and the distance greater. What you want is for your child to say, "Gee, that's easy!"

FALL AND WINTER

This section offers fall nature activities, some good ideas on what to do with snow, and suggestions for keeping track of the busy fall and winter events with calendars specially made for children. Of course as the weather becomes cold or nasty and you must stay indoors a lot, you may want to look at the chapter "Creative Materials" for good ideas. As the fall and winter holidays arrive, check pages 245–256 for appropriate things to make and do.

Short Calendar

September, for most people, heralds a flurry of activities that will continue on into the New Year. First there's getting older children ready for school, then there's Halloween, Thanksgiving dinner, holiday shopping and cooking, perhaps visits to relatives. Weeks (sometimes months) before each event, children begin to ask, "How long until . . . ?" Even if they haven't the slightest idea of what a "week," a "month," or "four days" means, the questions persist. This "short calendar" won't ease the problem right away, but it will slowly help your child develop a better sense of time.

Cut a long strip of brown paper from a grocery bag, or use a long cash-register

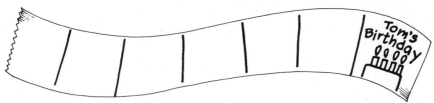

Cut off one square every day.

tape. Mark it in squares as shown, one for each day remaining until the big event he's waiting for. On the last square draw some mark to symbolize the event. Leave the squares blank. The point is for your child to get a feel for "how long" a unit of time is. For a young child, cut off a square at the end of each day, so he can see the "time" getting shorter and shorter.

Solomon Grundy

The only way children learn the names of the days of the week and the months of the year is by memorizing them. They can just be recited in order, or taught with any verses you chanted as a child, nursery rhymes such as "Solomon Grundy. . . ," "Monday's Child . . . " and "Thirty Days Hath September . . ."

Thirty Days Hath September

Thirty days hath September,
April, June, and November;
February has twenty-eight alone.
All the rest have thirty-one,
Excepting leap year, that's the time
When February's days are twenty-nine.

Poor Solomon Grundy (Sesame Street Style):

Poor Solomon Grundy
Washed the left side of his head on Monday,
Washed the left side of his neck on Tuesday,
Washed his left arm on Wednesday,
Washed his left hand on Thursday,
Washed his left side on Friday,
Washed his left leg on Saturday,
Washed his left foot on Sunday.

Poor Solomon Grundy.
He's still half dirty!

What if your child can't keep yesterday, today, and tomorrow straight? Don't worry. It's doubtful that anybody else's child can at an early age, either. The trouble is that these simple words stand for a relative concept. Yesterday is only yesterday in relation to today. If you use the words often enough, however, it will eventually get through to your child that today will be yesterday tomorrow, when tomorrow is today. (You can see that it isn't easy.)

What to Wear?

Because temperatures vary so much during the fall, you will have a natural opportunity for helping your child learn to plan his own outdoor clothing realis-

tically. Before he goes outside, open a window wide and let him feel the air against his skin. Ask him what he thinks he should wear (never mind for now what you think). You may even wish to allow him to go outside wearing exactly what he thought was appropriate. If you're sure he's wrong and will need a sweater after all, bring one along without contradicting him or making a fuss. Let him come to his own conclusions about whether his choice was a comfortable one for him.

What if your child refuses to wear his jacket, button up, put on boots, cover his head? First, analyze the disagreement. Think hard about the problem before you make a daily hassle out of it. Are your child's movements seriously hampered by heavy or tight clothing? Does he really feel as cold (or hot) as you do under the same temperature conditions? Many children seem to require less clothing than adults. Their bodies burn food at a greater rate and tend to maintain a higher temperature.

Leaf Games

Gathering gorgeous leaves in the fall is an activity few children can pass up but, once gathered, what do you do with the leaves? Here are several ideas:

At home, lay all the leaves out on a table and sort them by shape. If you can, find out what trees they came from (use a Guide to the Trees) so your child can learn the names maple, birch, dogwood, oak, blueberry, sorrel, or whatever trees are in your area. If your child is particularly adept—and interested—you can go further and sort the swamp maples from the Norways and the sugar maples; the scarlet from the chestnut, white and pin oak.

Let your child select his favorite leaves. Get out a large, heavy book; open it out flat somewhere in the middle and place a paper towel over one page. Lay the leaves out flat on the towel. Cover them with another towel and close the book. Put the book flat on the floor or table and pile other books (or a heavy object such as a pail filled with stones) on top of it. The leaves will be dry and pressed flat—with most of their color preserved—in a week.

Choose smallish, thin leaves of pretty colors. Tear off two pieces of waxed paper. Place one sheet, waxed side up, on an ironing board and arrange a group of leaves on it. (Allow some space between leaves, and about two inches of clear space around the edges of the paper.) Lay the other sheet, waxed side down, on top of the arrangement, and iron the surface with a warm iron. As you iron, the wax coating on the paper will melt temporarily and the two sheets will stick together. The result can be taped against the window so light can shine through the bright leaf colors.

Fall Findings

Fall wanderings provide all sorts of gathering possibilities beyond the usual colored leaves. Just a few of the finds that are beautiful or interesting are:

Bittersweet (Can be hung to dry and used as decoration.)

Pinecones (Can be made into little "creatures" with the help of toothpick or pipe-cleaner legs.)

Strawflower tansy, *Everlasting* and *Sea Lavender* (These can be hung to dry for use as decorations, and do not require expensive gels needed for drying other flowers.)

Burrs (Can be stuck together to form small pieces of furniture, animals or necklaces. See that they don't get into your child's hair.)

Cattails (Dip in shellac when fresh to prevent them fuzzing all over the house.)

Interesting *seed pods* from plants like Honesty, Mimosa, ailanthus, Rose of Sharon, Teasel, Millet and Mullein. (Fun just to save.)

Horse chestnuts (Kids just collect these because they're shiny and beautiful.)

Acorns (Sometimes children like to make faces on them with marking pens. The "caps" may come off.)

Fall Planting

If your fall wanderings take you to a wooded area, the soil under the leaves may contain many seeds—often too small to notice—that have accumulated over the summer.

Gather a plastic bag full of soil from any woodlot. Put it in a pot. Place it in a warm window where there is some sun or good light. Water it as often as you would an average houseplant (once or twice a week, depending on the size of the pot). Within a few weeks some of the seeds should sprout.

Seed Experiment

This is a genuine scientific experiment to discover what seeds need in order to grow. Use the same kind of woodland soil you used above, but divide it into four pots. Wonder aloud where you should keep the pots: *Well, let's keep one in the refrigerator. This one can go in the closet. These can go on the windowsill.* Water the pots that are going to be kept in the refrigerator and the closet. Water *one* of the two pots on the windowsill. Decide you won't bother to water the other pot. Check the pots every few days over the coming weeks. The seeds in the cold refrigerator pot won't sprout. (It's winter in there!) The seeds in the closet will probably sprout if watered, but the plants will be skinny and pale, with under-developed leaves. (It is always nighttime in the closet.) Of the two pots on the windowsill, the unwatered one won't sprout at all. But the other window pot should sprout and the plants will develop normally, at least for a while. The experiment is a classic way to show even a three-year-old that plants need warmth, water and light in order to grow.

Beachcombing

Fall, when the weather is too cool for swimming and the crowds are gone, is a wonderful time to walk the beach. If you and your child are able to do this, look together for pretty pebbles, shells, the dried backs or legs of crabs, dried sea urchins, bits of seaweed—or whatever you find of interest. These can be used at home for collage work (page 171) or just collected and kept as treasure.

Handling natural materials such as soil, leaves, shells, and seeds may stimulate a child's curiosity. Let this curiosity lead to the library. There are many nature books available in child versions. Nature books for children explain such things as how seeds move, how plants change through the seasons, or how the creatures found on the beach lead their lives. Ask the librarian to suggest books for your child at his age level.

First Snowfall

Here are some ideas for expressing the excitement of the first snowfall: look around for a scrap of dark cloth with a nappy surface. Velveteen, corduroy, flat wools, and felt all work. Hold the cloth outside to catch a snowflake, and look at it quickly under a magnifying glass—as Sherlock Hemlock would—before it melts.

Bert is bundled up for the cold weather.

Gather snow in a bowl. Pour fruit syrup or pancake syrup over it. Mix it up and eat it with a spoon. Messier but more appealing to children: Shape the snow into a small snowball first, pour the syrup over it, and let your child hold the ball in his hands to eat it.

Caution:
• *Snow in big cities may never be clean enough to eat.*

Make a large snowball for your child. Show him how to roll it along in the snow to make it larger. If pushed around long enough in a fairly wet snow, it can grow into a giant snowball.

Make a big pile of snow and pack it together fairly firmly. With a small shovel

or your hands, shape it crudely into an animal. Seals are an easy shape to make, but you could try a horse or a camel. Let your child ride his snow creature.

Winter Birds

Some birds—such as English sparrows, starlings, chickadees, blue jays and others—do not migrate south with the coming of fall, but stay in their own neighborhoods all year. It is easy to attract them with feed in winter—especially in snowy weather when food is scarce. (See "Bird Watching," pages 232–233, for feed ideas.)

Even Big Bird dresses for the weather.

Icebergs

For children who really seem interested in ice (and for families who have a bit of room left in the freezer compartment of the refrigerator), make an iceberg. Half fill a plastic bag with water. Tie the top into a knot. Place it on a plate and put it in the freezer to freeze. When frozen, tear off the bag. The result is a small iceberg that makes an interesting bathtub or sink toy until it melts.

Ice Pops

Mix up homemade lemonade or squeeze some orange juice. Pour the juice into an ice tray. Cover the tray with aluminum foil. Stick a toothpick through the foil into each compartment. Freeze. The resulting ice pops make a good snack, and when you make your own they can be low in sugar.

HOLIDAYS

However *you* celebrate a holiday, you are saying something to your children about your culture and about your own unique family. To one the church or synagogue, to another a feast, to another the visits or the songs or the handed-down-through-the-years ornaments might be the essence of a holiday. Do it your way. Emphasize your culture and your family for all they're worth. Your child will love your ways best. They tell him who he is, to whom he belongs, what his roots are.

Holidays are times for families and friends to get together. Remember this when you plan for visits to relatives during Christmas or Hanukkah; for a gathering of friends on New Year's Day; when you send cards or go out in a group to see

the lights, to hear the songs, to window-shop. This being with one another, enjoying each other's company, is part of what you are passing on to your children, too.

Make children a part of holiday preparations, as well as the socializing. Perhaps your child could make a dip or a snack for New Year's, or have a friend of his own over for the day after Thanksgiving, or have his turn to talk with relatives over the phone. The "givingness" in doing for and being with others helps to minimize the idea that holidays are times when we *get* things *from* others.

Halloween

Although Halloween is considered today the children's "own holiday," young children can be truly frightened by it. They don't understand "pretend" very well yet. How are they to know that scary witches, ghosts, and monsters are not real? In fact, they may frighten themselves merely by putting on a mask. There is too little difference between dressing-up like a monster and becoming one. Ask older children to go easy on the scare acts. If your preschooler wants a mask, go for the bunny or the cute face instead of the horror mask. Prepare your child by explaining about costumes and pretend before Frankenstein with the bloody hands knocks at your door. And, of course, safeguard your child in realistic ways as well. If you want to take him on a "trick or treat," visit friends and relatives only.

Costumes

For three- and four-year-olds, a Halloween "costume" may be no different than any of the dress-ups suggested on pages 201–204. At this age, the idea of dressing-up to disguise one's identity or to scare others is not natural, and not fun. Surprising himself, his family or friends with slight changes can certainly be fun for the child, but that doesn't call for anything elaborate. As your child gets close to five, he might like to paint up his face, wear slouch hats and sunglasses. A few children—but by no means all—are ready for a relatively innocent mask by this age.

Bag Masks

The easiest mask of all is a paper bag with the eyes cut out and the face drawn with Magic Marker pen or a crayon. To get the eyes in the right spots, put the bag over your child's head, press it to his forehead and feel for the bone over each eye. Mark the two eye spots there with a pencil. (They will be quite high and very close together.) Cut out small holes, try the bag on the child again, and then enlarge the holes until your child can see through them clearly. Take the bag off and decorate it together with markers, paints, or with cut-out ears and other additions as illustrated below.

How to make a shopping bag mask:

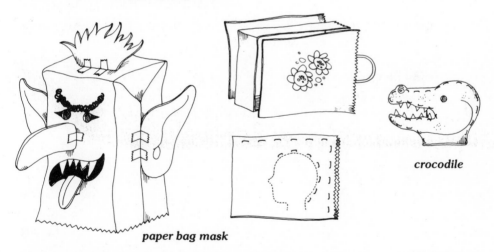

crocodile

paper bag mask

For children who want to dress as animals, above right is a relatively easy method, also using paper bags. Cut out the front and back sides of a large shopping bag. Discard the remaining strip. Turn the printed sides toward each other, and staple them together along the top and one side. Put the construction over your child's head. Now carefully staple in from the edge to get a headshaped contour, as shown, from his forehead to the nape of his neck. Trim off the excess.

Lay the construction flat on the table and draw the profile of the animal he wants to be on the side of the mask. The design shown is a crocodile. Staple all around your design and trim off the excess paper. Try the mask on the child again and locate the eyeholes as suggested for the other paper-bag mask. Paint the animal mask or decorate it with felt markers.

Unsweet Treats

How can you avoid a surfeit of sweets on Halloween? Not easily with older children. But a preschool child need not go to twenty homes to stuff his bag with treats. Confine him to three or four. Tell him in advance that he may not take handfuls of candy, but only what you help him to count out. And when you offer treats for Halloween yourself, you are free to keep the sugar low and perhaps even the nutrition high. Suggestions include: boxes of raisins, popcorn balls, sugar-free chewing gum and lollipops, apples, roasted peanuts in the shell, cubes of cheese, and packaged snacks such as cracker sandwiches.

Bert cooks up his favorite oatmeal treat for special occasions.

A tasty homemade treat can be roasted pumpkin seeds. Wash the seeds from your pumpkin, remove as many shreds as you can, dry the seeds between paper towels, and spread them in a shallow baking pan. Add a few drops of oil or margarine, sprinkle with salt, and roast in a 350° oven, stirring every fifteen minutes, until they are evenly brown and crispy.

Feasts

Thanksgiving, although it is specifically an American holiday, grew from harvest festivals that are celebrated similarly in many countries. The basic idea is always the same: to give thanks for the bounty of the land, and to celebrate the end of summer's labor with a feast. For those who live in or can visit the country, the plucking or picking up of nuts, windfall apples, wild grapes, squashes or watermelons is part of the fun. Any basic cookbook will give you recipes for such things as applesauce, grape jelly, squash pie, and watermelon pickles. None is hard to make, and each is a holiday treat made special because it was done from scratch.

Ask older people what they remember best about holidays when they were children, and the answer is likely to be the cooking. The tastes are memorable, of course, but often the process—rising dough, simmering soups, dripping jellies— is dramatic and exciting. Suggestions for ways children can participate in your cooking are found on pages 71–76.

Salt to Taste

When you are cooking something that requires judgment in flavoring ("salt to taste," "add more spices to suit," "sweeten as desired"), let your child in on the flavoring process. First, let him sniff the herb or spice you are using, or taste a few grains of salt or sugar on his tongue so he knows what flavor you are talking about. Then let him taste what you are mixing up. Ask: "Does it need more cloves? salt? oregano? hot pepper?"

Glitter and Shine

Just as a feast is the essence of a harvest festival, shine and glitter are the essence of a winter festival. Christmas, Hanukkah and the ancient Yule festival fall during the period when the days are at their shortest, the nights longest. In ancient times, it must have been a worrisome thing. Would the sun really come back high in the sky? Would the days get long and warm again? Candles, Yule logs, evergreen trees, and glittering decorations may have been a way of expressing both hope and gratitude that the light and warmth we need would not abandon us.

That idea can be the basis for any holiday decorations. Whether you are cutting cardboard stars to hang in the window, decorating candles, pinecones, or cookies, make them fancy. Use colored sprinkles, store-bought glitter or tinsel, a few sequins to catch the light. Spread white glue on whatever you are decorating, from Styrofoam balls to macaroni; then sprinkle the glitter over it. When the glue is dry, shake off the excess glitter and scoop it up to use on another object.

The joy of thinking this basically about holiday decoration is that your child can't fail. No matter how crude the paper shape or card or collage or stabile that he contributes to the decorations, it will look gorgeous and colorful to him.

Collage Decorations

If you and your child like making collages (pages 168–173) you could try making small ones that can be hung up for holiday decorations. Cut construction paper into interesting shapes: a long triangle for an icicle effect, or hearts, circles, stars and doughnut shapes. Make a pencil mark near one edge to indicate where a hole will be punched for a string loop later. Don't glue over that spot. Cover the rest of the paper shape with pasta or beans, including the area just above the pencil mark.

The ornament will be floppy while wet, but will become rigid when the glue dries.

When the decoration is dry, punch a hole through the pencil mark with the point of a scissors. Tie a loop of string and put it through the hole. For instant glamour, spray or paint these ornaments on both sides with gold or silver paint. You'll be surprised at how impressive golden beans and silver shells can be.

Caution:
• *Spray paints can be dangerous. Follow directions on container and supervise your child.*

Dreidl Games

During the winter holiday season, stores may sell wooden or plastic dreidls, a four-sided top used traditionally in Hanukkah games. The dreidl is marked with Hebrew letters on each side, but if you prefer, cover these symbols with pieces of paper or freezer tape and mark instead with numbers, letters, colors, or shapes.

For a three- or four-year-old, the game can be simple. Each person spins the top by twirling it between thumb and fingers (A two-year-old might not be able to manage this.) As the top falls, one side lands face up. The player calls out *Red!* or *Two!* or *Triangle!* Pointless to adults, perhaps, but sufficiently intriguing to the child—and a good learning game.

Piñatas

To make a *piñata*, buy a really large balloon, and favors or candy small enough to fit down through the neck of the balloon. Gumdrops and jelly beans will fit, and so will small rings, plastic charms and dollhouse miniatures available in variety stores. Put all the sweets and favors into the balloon. Then blow it up nice and big and tie the neck.

Dilute white glue with an equal amount of water in a shallow dish. Tear newspaper into short strips. Pull a strip of newspaper through the glue and stick it onto the blown-up balloon. Cover the entire balloon with one layer; let it harden, then apply a second layer of glued-on newspaper strips.

When it is all dry, this is the basic *piñata*. What you do from here is up to you. The easiest thing to make might be a face, or perhaps a fish, a bird, a pig, or a watermelon. Each is improvised with a combination of tissue paper or crepe paper attachments, or just tempera paint. (If you use enough paper and paint, the *piñata* will be colorful and gay whether anyone can identify the object or not.)

Let the *piñata* dry for a week or so. Then tie a loop of string to the top. When it's time to break open the *piñata*, the tradition is to hang it up and let blindfolded

children take turns beating it with a stick until it breaks open—and the goodies spill out!

Caution:
• *Supervise carefully if the "goodies" include small, swallowable items.*

GIFTS FROM CHILDREN

Though giving presents doesn't come easily to a preschooler—especially to older sisters and brothers—helping a child buy or make a few small gifts is good preparation for later generosity. A handmade present is gratifying to grandparents, other really close relatives, or family friends—as well as the giver. Look through the crafts and art projects in Chapter Four to see what might appeal to your child.

Nonfail presents to buy may be such things as balloons, playing cards, miniatures, costume jewelry, whistles, balls, bubble bath, and colored washable markers.

National Heroes

Many children are curious about national heroes. Here are some ways to celebrate famous birthdays. Read a book together: libraries will have quite simple, illustrated books about famous Americans, even for the level of three-year-olds. Adult photography books make a good jumping-off point for just talking with your children about men and women you admire. You might celebrate a famous person's birthday in a jolly way—a cherry pie for George Washington—or with reverence—a minute of silence in honor of Martin Luther King.

Valentines

Valentine's Day is a great favorite among children and sweethearts for the simplest of reasons. It is a day of love—and of things that mean love, like sweets and lace, hearts and flowers. Although the constant eating of sweets is unhealthful, you may wish to make exceptions for special occasions. For cards, help your child to fold colored paper in four, and cut a pattern. (See page 116 for a discussion of children's scissors.) The cutting, even if crude, will look dramatic when the paper is opened out. See page 168 for basic techniques of glueing.

For valentines, substitute paper doilies, bits of ribbon, and red paper. You will have to cut out the hearts for most small children, but they can do the pasting.

Valentine's Day is a good opportunity for a child to learn something about the process of mailing letters. When he has made a card, put it in an envelope and let him watch while you write out the name and address. Let him lick the stamp and show him where to stick it down. At the same time, make a card for him, put that in an envelope and let him watch you write his name and address on it. Then let him take both letters to the post office or put them in a mailbox. In a couple of days, he will receive his own card through the mail, and you can tell him that Grandma (or whomever he sent his card to) has no doubt received hers, too.

Egg Ideas

The egg from which life comes is basic to both Passover and Easter. Its use as a symbol for both springtime and rebirth is probably older than both holidays. Here is a "natural" way to dye eggs and some child-participation recipes for using up extra hard-boiled eggs.

1. Dye eggs the natural way with onion skins. Try to find a store that still sells onions in bins. Gather up the loose, dry outer skins that accumulate in the bottom of the bin. Hard-boil white eggs. Cut cheesecloth into five-by-five-inch squares. Lay onion skins in the center of each square, place the egg on top, then gather the corners of the cheesecloth about the egg, distributing onion skins to cover the egg. Secure the top with a rubber band. Boil the egg "packages" for another ten minutes; then run under cold water and remove the wrappings. The eggs will be dyed in a marbleized pattern of ambers, yellows, and occasional streaks of green and red.

2. On Passover, hard-boiled eggs are eaten in a bowl with salt water—a dish many children find novel and good. Here are other ways children enjoy leftover hard-boiled eggs (let your child peel eggs, slice them with a table knife, chop them in a bowl, mix ingredients, stuff or spread mixtures to help with preparation):

   Deviled: The hard-boiled egg is sliced in half lengthwise, the yolk removed and mashed up with mayonnaise, lemon juice, salt, pepper, and mustard and then stuffed back into the whites.

   Egg rounds: A slice of hard-boiled egg is put on a round of toast that has been spread with mayonnaise.

   Creamed eggs: Chunks of hard-boiled egg are mixed into a hot cream sauce and served over toast, rice or noodles. For Passover, substitute matzo or other unleavened breads for toast.

Flag Flying

Flying the flag on national holidays is a tradition many families observe and enjoy. If you have no American flag to fly, make one. Or make a family flag of your own design. Paint what you wish directly on a piece of old sheet with acrylic (plastic) paints. Or, using the zigzag stitch on a sewing machine, make a family banner by appliquéing patches of bright cloth onto sheeting. For either flag, stitch or glue it onto a broomstick for waving in the air parade-style, for planting into the ground, or hanging out a window.

Another practice common to many spring and early summer holidays is to use wind toys. These can include anything from banners and whirligigs that wave or spin in the breeze, to flying toys. A perfectly good way to celebrate the Fourth of July—or any breezy spring day—is to go fly a kite, balsa airplane, paper airplane (page 189), or Frisbee.

Noisy Holidays

Noise-making is basic to many holidays, from the fireworks of the Fourth of July and Guy Fawkes Day to the din of horns on New Year's Eve. But ten minutes of sustained noisemaking may be all any adult can take. If you tell your children that a particular moment on a particular holiday they will be allowed to make all the noise they want for ten minutes, you'll find it strikes them as a marvelous celebration. Besides plain old shouting, stomping, and banging on pot lids with wooden spoons, see pages 179, 186, and 194 for homemade drums, rattles, and other noise-makers. Louder rattles than those mentioned can be made by putting small pebbles or nuts and bolts into one- or two-pound coffee tins.

Caution:
- *Be careful that small children can't get small, swallowable items out of their rattles.*

Family Gatherings

Family gatherings do not have to be limited to holidays. Some families hold an annual reunion—often in the form of a picnic. Here is one picnic recipe that your children can help with easily, and that seems to stand nicely for the essential wholeness of a family.

Consult relatives as to favorite sandwich ingredients and spreads. Buy a sufficient number of very long loaves of bread. Let your child arrange ingredients on different plates, and put out spreads in separate bowls. Split the loaves of bread lengthwise. When it's time to eat, the loaves are filled with your family's favorite sandwich ingredients, the top of the loaf is put back in place, and the whole thing is cut into sandwich-sized slices.

Family Tree

Help your child gradually understand his relatedness to various members of the family by making a simple family tree. Follow the pattern below by pasting snap-

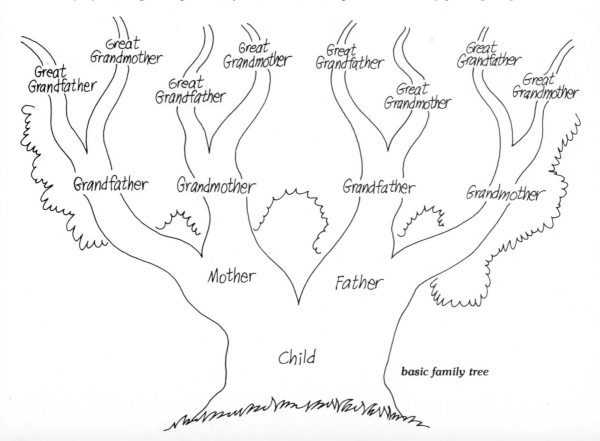

basic family tree

shots of relatives onto a large sheet of poster board (available at art supply departments or stores). Your child will be delighted (or perhaps amused or even incredulous) to discover that you have a mommy, too. He will be pleased to see himself so surrounded by those who are related to him.

What if your own part of the family is isolated from other relatives? What can you do to give your child a sense of being part of a larger family group? Telling stories about the others helps explain your own childhood relationships with parents and siblings, who are now your child's grandparents and aunts and uncles. Keeping snapshots on the wall or in an album, or "building" the family tree suggested above will also be reassuring. When you write letters or cards to relatives, read them aloud to your child.

BIRTHDAYS

We suggest here rather simple, rather matter-of-fact ideas for birthdays in this section: ways to help your child gauge his own growth, ways to "remember when" and record a child's life story in snapshot form.

For those who love a birthday party there are games for groups of children. The games are specially for preschool children. There are no winners or losers, and if there are prizes, everybody gets one. You'll find that at this age, noncompetition makes for calmer, happier parties! And for those who don't have birthday parties, there are many pleasurable alternatives you might like to try.

There are many things your child and you can do together to prepare for a birthday party, and it is advisable to share these preparations so that your child doesn't expect more than he is getting. If you make your own cupcakes, your child can smear on the icing with a dull knife. He can decorate plain paper plates with crayoning around the edges (it is safe to decorate the middle, too, but the flavor of wax may be noticeable). If he can write letters of the alphabet, he can mark pieces of paper with the guests' initials, or do the same with paper napkins. He can help to count out candles, gumdrops, balloons, and favors—if you have them. He can help to set the party table.

Party Games

There are very few games for groups of really young children that are successful at parties. Some, such as pin-the-tail-on-the-donkey and blindman's-buff, require a blindfold, which is disorienting and scary to many youngsters. Others, such as tag and hide-and-seek, include chasing and catching, which can be scary, too. Here are a few suggestions that seem to avoid worry and subsequent wildness:

1. *Hit the Hippo*. Draw a hippopotamus (or any other animal you can manage) on a large piece of paper. Cut out the figure and attach it to the floor

with tape. Have the children stand at a certain distance (four or five feet for three-year-olds, more for older children). Taking turns, each child tosses a beanbag at the hippo.

2. *Favor Fish.* Cut out a few dozen paper fish. You can color them if you like (so a child can fish for "bluefish" and "redfish") or decorate them with patterns, stripes, shapes, numbers, or letters. Tape a small favor (it must be light like a balloon or a charm) on each fish. Put a paperclip over each fish's mouth. Tie a magnet to a string, the string to a stick, and let children take turns fishing for a favor fish.

3. *Spider Web.* Make or buy a small party favor for each child, and wrap it. Tie the end of a ball of string to one present, hide the present, then unravel the string here and there, under a table, behind the couch, around a chair. Tie the end of that string with a piece of paper labeled with a child's name. Repeat for every child who will be at the party. To play the game, each child follows his own string to find his favor.

Caution:
• *Supervise small children carefully if small, swallowable items are used.*

4. *Make a Clown.* On a large sheet of paper, draw the outline of a clown face. It need be only a circle or an oval. Tape it onto the wall. Using colored paper, cut out a big circle for a nose, a smiling mouth, rosy cheeks, eyes, ears, and hair or a triangular hat. Each child can reach in turn into a bag or box to pull out one of these pieces. Then each child gets to put his piece on the oval (you tape each piece as the child decides where it goes) until the clown is all finished.

What if the children at the party won't play the games, or can't manage them? What if they fight over the presents your child has received, or cry to go home, or get wild? You can't expect everything to go well, but the less ambitious and the less rigid your plans are, the more likely you can adjust to the actual event. For instance, plan to make the party no more than an hour and a half for three-year-olds and no more than two hours for older preschoolers. Warn the other children's parents that you may call them (and you hope they'll be home) if there is reason to pick up their child earlier than planned. And by having alternatives in mind, you can nip wildness in the bud—by either offering food, sending everyone outside to run and jump for a few minutes, or capturing interest with a new game. Above all, keep the group small, and invite children you know well.

No-Party Parties

For those who can't face birthday parties at all, here are some alternatives:
For warm-weather birthdays, choose a nice spot in the park or in a nearby country spot, and just have a picnic. The kids will think of their own games. Or

take a small (no more than three, so you can watch them) group of children to the beach or a pool. Or take a few children to the zoo or a nature center. In cold weather, try a museum party, a sledding party, or a pizza parlor dinner. After any of these outings, you can stop home for the birthday or cupcake ritual before the children are picked up.

There are some children who are not comfortable with the idea of any sort of party that includes a group of other children. An alternative might be to take one good friend with your child on a nice outing as a birthday treat—a movie, for instance, or bowling, or to a roller-skating rink. Another alternative is to have a "family only" party, with siblings, parents, and perhaps favorite aunts, uncles, cousins or grandparents.

What if a good friend refuses to come to your child's party, or doesn't invite your child to his party? Or what if your child won't go to a party to which he has been invited? These are unavoidable trials of everyday life. Often the reason is simply anxiety. Very many children find it too difficult to visit without their parents. You might want to invite parents as well as children, or to accompany your own child at least for the beginning or cake-eating part of another's birthday party. On the other hand, if the refusal stems from real dislike of another child, there's nothing you can do but be polite. "I'm terribly sorry, Paul won't be able to come to your daughter's party." Or, "Paul, I'm sorry but Nancy can't come to your birthday party."

"Grown Up" Presents

Naively—but understandably—children may expect to wake up not only a year older, but several inches taller on the morning of their birthday. They may think that now, at the grand age of five, they will suddenly be able to cross the street alone, stay up late, ride a two-wheeler. We expect such developments, too, but we can visualize the changes taking place slowly over the year to come, while a child may expect the changes magically overnight. It may be helpful in avoiding some disappointment to give a child a present that symbolically marks his new age. Inexpensive suggestions include: a three-ring notebook with lots of paper for scribbling, a set of marking pens, a flashlight, perfumed soaps or powder, costume jewelry, a baseball cap, a screwdriver, or sunglasses.

True Life Story

One way to help a child appreciate his own growth and development is to put together a special True Life Story about your child. See if you can put together a collection of snapshots that begin with your child as a newborn infant, and proceed through recognizable steps in his development—such as crawling, walking, riding a trike, playing with a friend, going to school. Under each picture write a short sentence such as: *Then David learned to ride a trike. He could make it go very fast.* Read the book together, and as a birthday approaches, wonder aloud what new things your child will learn to do in the year to come.

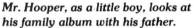
Mr. Hooper, as a little boy, looks at his family album with his father.

Without going to the trouble of making an album, you can simply remember to talk with your child about his past and about his immediate future: *I remember when you couldn't even zip your jacket. Do you remember that? I bet this year you will learn to do buttons by yourself.* By the way, keep your predictions modest; it's not only discouraging but also sad to predict that pretty soon he won't need your help at all.

Growth Charts

For many years, almost certainly until after six, a child equates "older" with "bigger." It strikes smallish children as not only unfair, but also incomprehensible that a child of fewer years may be bigger than he is. There is no use struggling

endlessly to explain concepts a child cannot yet grasp. State the truth as you know it, and wait out the confusion while your child's mind matures.

In the meantime, you can help your child become more aware of his own rate of growth by keeping a growth chart. Here are several ways to make growth charts for children:

1. The old-fashioned way is to mark a child's height each year (on his birthday or on some important family holiday) right on the wall. It seems easier for a child to compare the height of the marks if they progress step-wise, rather than one mark directly above the other. Label each mark with his name and age or date. A variation on this, which might have a greater sense of immediacy to a child, is to mark his reach rather than his height. Children are more often aware of their own growth when they stand on tiptoe and discover they can reach higher thay they used to.

2. Glue a tape measure directly onto the wall. To avoid hurting the paint, smear the area where the tape will be glued with rubber cement. Smear rubber cement on the back of the tape, too. When both are dry, stick the tape onto the wall from the bottom up. Wipe the extra glue off by rubbing it with your fingers. Mark heights and dates on the wall next to the tape.

Note:
- If you must repaint the wall where your child's growth is recorded, note the information written there on a piece of paper. Paint, and redraw the marks and data when the paint has dried.

3. Each time you measure your child, hang a ribbon as long as he is high up on the wall. This is probably the easiest comparison of all, and the date and measurement can be inked with a laundry pen on the ribbon itself rather than on the wall.

Oscar and his pet worm, Slimey.

FIRST PET

Kids and animals go together—at least in most children's minds. In fact, children don't see as great a distinction between themselves and animals as adults do. They may think a pet will understand what they say and feel, keep them company in times of distress, love them no matter how they behave. Whether this is true or not, children don't disillusion easily; pets do frequently give them the enjoyment they anticipated.

From the adult's point of view, pets can be important to a child's development because of the sense of responsibility that will grow from the care they require. But teaching responsibility for another living creature is a tricky thing. If the work is too hard, recriminations too severe, children may lose faith in the idea that they, like their parents, can nurture a living creature. They may feel guilty at their failure, without having learned responsibility.

Don't make up your mind ahead of time what aspects of pet care will be your child's responsibility. Say that since this is to be his own pet, there will be work he must do to take care of it. But wait a while until you settle on exactly what work, and how often. Perhaps changing a cage is too heavy a job, or too messy for him to do himself. His job may then be to hold the bag for you, to carry it to the garbage, or to dry the cage when it is washed. Perhaps he can't remember to check the water bottle, but maybe he can remember to feed the pet when he has his own breakfast. Children don't learn responsibility by failing to do what is expected of them. They learn by succeeding—even if your expectations are minimal.

Many pets aren't really gratifying to a young child. Fish are difficult for a preschool child to keep in good health and are not companionable. Mice are nervous and quite smelly. Most caged birds do not become tame. Guinea pigs require very frequent cage cleaning.

A dog is probably the most responsive, devoted and intelligent pet there is. But dogs are a great deal of work. In the city, they must be taken out at least three times a day. They all require some grooming, months of housetraining and simple obedience training, and an enormous amount of affection and attention. Because of these demands, which no preschooler can possibly meet, a dog does not make a good "own" pet for a young child. Of course, you may wish to have a dog anyway, but be sure everyone understands it is a *family* pet.

For a child's "own" pet, we discuss only three animals in this section: a parakeet, a gerbil, and a cat. All become reasonably tame and companionable, and are relatively easy to care for.

To make care of a caged pet easier for a child, keep the cage in some part of the house where you are often together. That way, you can notice the need for changing, feeding or watering, and also help with the job. Keep bedding or flooring materials nearby, as well as the food and a wastebasket. Routines will be helpful. For instance, choose a particular day and time when your child is not usually involved in anything special for the two of you to clean the cage. Make feeding time for any pet coincide with some clearly defined daily event—a bedtime ritual, or breakfast time.

One word of caution that applies to almost any kind of pet: Animals scratch and bite. No pet, not even the faithful family dog, shares the child's point of view that they are "pals" under all circumstances. Parakeets, gerbils, and cats will defend themselves when startled, frightened, cornered, or abused. Try to explain this to a child when he first gets a pet.

Parakeets

If a parakeet is to be your child's pet, buy only one parakeet; two become attached to each other rather than to their owner. Have the bird's wings clipped by the dealer before you take it home.

Choose a cage that seems easy to clean and easy to take the bird in and out of. The cage should come with food and water cups and two perches. You'll also need parakeet seed mix, a small bag of medium-grit sand, and liquid bird vitamins.

Care: Throw out old seed daily and refill the cup. Clean the water cup and refill with fresh water, adding a drop of bird vitamins.

Offer fresh fruits or greens such as raw spinach and lettuce several times a week to supplement the parakeet's seed diet. Keep sand sprinkled on the paper at the bottom of the cage, as birds need grit in their gizzards to grind up the hard seeds. Newspaper is perfectly good for lining the cage floor. Change it once or twice a week.

Taming: Offer the parakeet treats like peanuts in the shell, bits of apple or lettuce from your fingers in the cage. Let your child hand-feed the bird, too. Over the weeks the parakeet will begin to remain calm when you reach into the cage. At this point, begin putting your index finger close to its body, just above its legs. As the bird calms enough to stay put (and not attempt to bite), push your finger against its tummy lightly. It will soon react by stepping onto your finger.

From here on, the taming procedure is simply to repeat the maneuver often until you can take the parakeet from its cage on your finger, sit on the floor with it (so it doesn't hurt itself attempting to fly) and get used to handling it. When the bird is reliable with you, teach your child to get it onto his own finger the same way. As time goes by, the parakeet will prefer shoulders or the tops of heads, from which pleasant perch it will lovingly groom your hair by gently pulling at the strands.

Gerbils

Get a gerbil that has just been weaned (about one month old). Before you bring the gerbil home, make a cage or buy a small aquarium with a wire-mesh top or a commercial cage. It should be equipped with a water bottle. Brackets to hold the bottle inside an aquarium are available in pet stores, as are wire brackets that hold the bottle outside other types of cages. Use torn-up newspapers, or buy pine shavings as bedding. Plain garden dirt is good bedding in an aquarium cage. Buy gerbil seed and pellet mixture, and liquid gerbil vitamins.

Care: Feed the gerbil a tablespoon of food every day. The food can just be dropped into a corner of the cage. Offer snacks of a variety of cereals such as unsugared breakfast cereals, unsalted popcorn, and so on, as the spirit moves you. Very small amounts of raw vegetables like carrots and spinach may be appreciated, but too much causes diarrhea. Refill the water bottle with fresh water once

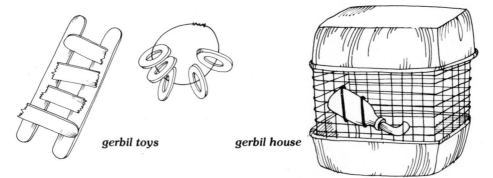

gerbil toys   gerbil house

a week, adding vitamins as directed on the label. (Gerbils are desert animals and drink very little.) Set up the cage with whatever bedding you have chosen. If you use shavings or dirt, supply soft paper such as a paper towel or facial tissue for nest-building. Change the bedding only once a month. Gerbils urinate only a few drops a day, and have little odor.

Taming: Handle the gerbil often, at least several times a day. Pick it up by scooping with both hands. Let your child sit out in the middle of the floor with the gerbil. The gerbil will be reluctant to run away over all that open space, and will prefer to explore your child, his shirt sleeves and pockets. A gerbil will become tame more quickly than a parakeet.

Kittens and Cats

To assure that your kitten will have a healthy personality, try to adopt one about eight weeks old that has been raised in a pleasant home, preferably with children. During this time kittens become socialized by their own mothers and litter mates, and by being fondly handled by humans.

Healthy kittens are sleek, heavily furred, bright-eyed, curious, and playful. They should retract their claws and seem calm when picked up and sometimes follow you when you walk in front of them. There should be no discharge from eyes or nose, and they should not be smelly. And the kitten should have a checkup by a veterinarian and receive all necessary shots during the first week you have it.

Care: Feed kittens three or four times a day. Use either canned cat food or, both for health reasons and because it is neater, dry cat food. Milk is appreciated, but fresh water available all the time is a must. Grown cats can have two meals a day, breakfast and dinner.

If your cat is to remain indoors, you will need a litter box. Various plastic containers are sold in pet stores, and so are various brands of cat litter that effectively reduce the odor. Remove feces from the box daily, and flush down the toilet. Change the litter every week, or as soon as the odor becomes noticeable.

Training: Housetraining is not necessary with kittens. Take the kitten to the litter box or an area of sand or soil outdoors after each meal the first few days. Scratch its front paws into the material. The kitten will get the idea of what to do next quite naturally. When a cat messes in the house, it is either because you have not changed the box (cats are fussy this way) or it is an expression of anger. The anger may be because you have not been affectionate enough with your cat, or you have left it alone too much. The only known cure is to lavish attention on it.

A kitten who is picked up often, petted a lot, and played with frequently will grow up to be far more responsive and affectionate than a kitten who is left to its own devices. This doesn't mean your child should be free to abuse the cat by dragging it by its tail, slapping it, or dropping it; but it does mean that attempts to wheel it about in the doll carriage or to carry it everywhere are perfectly all right.

If the kitten strongly objects, it knows how to say so with claws and teeth. Show your child how to jiggle a toy or roll a ball to encourage the kitten to play. Try the toys suggested below.

You might also get a kick out of watching a cat's antics over catnip. Catnip toys are sold in petshops, but catnip seeds are often available where seeds are sold in springtime. They can be planted according to package directions, either in a pot indoors or in a corner of the yard. Both the live plant and the dried leaves have a smell that seems to give ecstatic pleasure to the cat, and therefore to the giver.

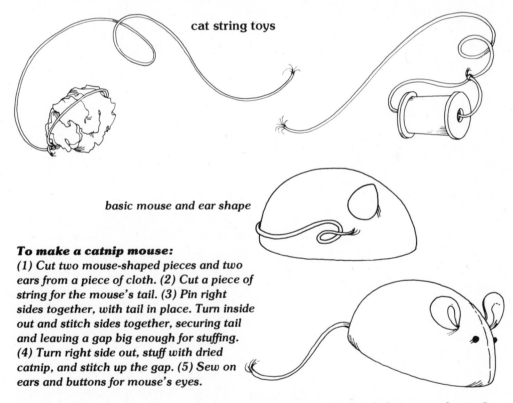

cat string toys

basic mouse and ear shape

To make a catnip mouse:
(1) Cut two mouse-shaped pieces and two ears from a piece of cloth. (2) Cut a piece of string for the mouse's tail. (3) Pin right sides together, with tail in place. Turn inside out and stitch sides together, securing tail and leaving a gap big enough for stuffing. (4) Turn right side out, stuff with dried catnip, and stitch up the gap. (5) Sew on ears and buttons for mouse's eyes.

What if your child, who so desperately begged for a pet, fails to care for it? In all fairness, a gerbil does not remain fascinating forever, and neither does a parakeet unless it is well-tamed and affectionate. It may happen that the reality of having a pet does not live up to the wonderful fantasies that preceded it. The only practical thing to do is ask for no more than a cooperative effort from your child (*Hand me the food, Wash the water dish, please*); but at the same time, show by your own behavior that once having taken on the responsibility for any living thing, you must continue to care for it. In the extreme event that no one in the family, including yourself, wishes to care for the pet, discuss the alternative of finding another home for it. If a friend or a petshop can take the pet in, it may be a relief to everybody.

Any family that keeps pets will eventually be faced with the death of a pet. Gerbils live about four years, parakeets, cats, and dogs average ten years. Many die sooner through accident or illness. To very many children, the event is their first experience of death.

What do you do about it? Realize that the way you handle even so small a death as a gerbil's will say something to a child about how humans feel about the value of all life, and how they grieve at death. The body should not be flushed down a toilet or thrown in the garbage. It should be treated kindly—wrapped in something soft, snuggled into a box. You may wish to have a funeral, and, if possible, a burial. As at any funeral, you can say things that were good about the pet. He was cuddly, or he could whistle, or he purred when he was petted. And as at any burial, his grave should be marked with a stick or a stone or flowers or leaves as a sign that he will not be forgotten. Granted, this is terribly difficult to do in the city; perhaps impossible. If so, then explain to your child what you would wish to do were you able.

LITTLE CELEBRATIONS

Celebrations—little ones—are to honor any member of the family for any achievement. Perhaps you have lost weight, gotten a job, given up cigarettes, or enrolled in an adult education course. Time to celebrate! Perhaps your child has given up the bottle, helped you with your work, learned to tie shoelaces, or successfully shared blocks or toys for the first time. Cause enough for celebration.

Celebrate the good fortune of others outside the family, too. It's fine to celebrate when your candidate wins an election, or when your team wins a game.

Sometimes we overlook a child's achievement because we underestimate how difficult it has been. Giving up the bottle involves as much will power, and probably as much anxiety, as giving up cigarettes or sticking with a diet. Getting through the first day of nursery school is as strange and uncomfortable as getting through the first day at a new job. And learning to tie a shoelace takes all the perseverance and concentration of learning to sew a garment or change the brake shoes on a car.

Sometimes we celebrate—or make a fuss—too early. New achievements, both for adults and children, may require an interval of consolidation before we make much of them. For example, you wouldn't celebrate giving up cigarettes right away. If you did, and started to smoke again the next day, you would be disappointed. So would the child who gave up the bottle for a day, and then wanted it back. Better to be sure an achievement is solid before celebrating it.

Fancy Meals

You can make the most ordinary meal into an impromptu party by just dressing it up. Hamburgers with sprigs of parsley stuck into their tops may look silly to you, but pretty fancy to a kid. Ice cream served with multicolored sprinkles is another idea. Or try carrot curls instead of carrot sticks, tuna-fish salad in hollowed-out tomatoes, macaroni and cheese baked in individual dishes, slices of sausage or hot dog broiled on skewers, or sandwich spreads served on toast rounds instead of plain bread slices.

Little Decorations

If there is countryside nearby, pick wildflowers, grasses or even bare twigs to decorate the table. The merest handful of daisies or buttercups looks lively in an empty bottle, and grasses with handsome seed heads can look festive if you put them in an empty can with a colorful label. In winter, small branches can be decorated with cotton balls (glued in place with white glue) or hung with cut-out, colored paper ornaments. If the outdoor materials are not available, a roll of crepe-paper streamer goes a long way toward making a room look festive.

Dinner by Candlelight

Especially for little celebrations in honor of an adult, consider a formal dress-up dinner. By candlelight, of course. The food needn't be expensive, but it should be something out of the ordinary—something you don't eat often. Everyone should dress up in his very best. And dress the table, too—with gay paper plates, or your best table linens, or with flowers or greenery gathered from outdoors. Don't forget soft music to go with the candlelight.

Breakfast in Bed

In honor of anyone, adult or child, who dislikes getting up in the morning, breakfast in bed may be a wonderful way to celebrate. Choose a breakfast that person particularly enjoys. Arrange it on a tray or on a breadboard made to look party-like with a colored paper napkin spread on it for a placemat. Let the person sleep late; then present the surprise breakfast when he or she awakens.

Indoor Picnic

There are certain meals that lend themselves to an impromptu indoor picnic. Let's say you are having bowls of chili or a rice dish for dinner. Set up a corner of the living room with all the pillows you can find—bed pillows, chair and couch cushions, decorative pillows. (Cover them with pillow cases if you want to be sure of keeping them clean.) Serve the children's portions in bowls, and with spoons (less easy to spill). Let everyone eat lounging on pillows. It's a relaxing change, and a good way to end a long, hard week.

Favors

You can acknowledge an achievement by the simple act of doing a favor. If an older brother has gotten his first job, the family can celebrate by doing his particular household chore for him. If Daddy has lost ten pounds, celebrate by letting him choose the TV shows all day Sunday. If John has played with his friend without squabbling, celebrate by picking up his toys for him.

Family Scrapbook

You can keep a scrapbook specifically for your small achievements, or you can use your family snapshot album for the same purpose. Note in the scrapbook any event you would ordinarily boast a bit about to friends and relatives. Of course, mark the date and, if possible, include a snapshot of the person taken at about the same time or that shows something about the event. In the future, the scrapbook will be a lovely record of little celebrations—and of the history of your own family during your children's childhood.

Index

NOTE: Entries that appear in *italics* refer to Sesame Street Curriculum concepts discussed but not always named in the text.

NOTE: Entries that appear in *italics* refer to Sesame Street Curriculum concepts discussed but not always named in the text.

NOTE: Entries that appear in *italics* refer to Sesame Street Curriculum concepts discussed but not always named in the text.

NOTE: Entries that appear in *italics* refer to Sesame Street Curriculum concepts discussed but not always named in the text.

NOTE: Entries that appear in *italics* refer to Sesame Street Curriculum concepts discussed but not always named in the text.

NOTE: Entries that appear in *italics* refer to Sesame Street Curriculum concepts discussed but not always named in the text.

NOTE: Entries that appear in *italics* refer to Sesame Street Curriculum concepts discussed but not always named in the text.

NOTE: Entries that appear in *italics* refer to Sesame Street Curriculum concepts discussed but not always named in the text.

NOTE: Entries that appear in *italics* refer to Sesame Street Curriculum concepts discussed but not always named in the text.